# THE PRACTICE OF PIETY

THE HISTORICAL SERIES OF THE REFORMED CHURCH IN AMERICA
NO. 64

# THE PRACTICE OF PIETY

The Theology of the Midwestern
Reformed Church in America,
1866-1966

**Eugene P. Heideman**

*[handwritten inscription:] With much appreciation for your friendship*

*[signature] Geo. Heideman*

*Mar 31, 2010*

WILLIAM B. EERDMANS PUBLISHING COMPANY
Grand Rapids, Michigan / Cambridge, U.K.

Wm. B. Eerdmans Publishing Co.
2140 Oak Industrial Drive S.E., Grand Rapids, Michigan 49503 /
P.O. Box 163, Cambridge CB3 9PU U.K.
www.eerdmans.com

Printed in the United States of America

Print Management by
HeuleGordon, Inc.
Grand Rapids, MI

**Library of Congress Cataloging-in-Publication Data**

Heideman, Eugene P. (Eugene Paul), 1929-
  The practice of piety : the midwestern Reformed Church in America, 1866-
1966 / Eugene Heideman.
      p. cm. -- (The historical series of the Reformed Church in America ; no.
64)
  Includes index.
  ISBN 978-0-8028-6551-9 (cloth : alk. paper)  1. Reformed Church in
America--History.  I. Title.
  BX9515.H45 2009
  285.7'3209034--dc22
                          2009040145

Dedicated to

# Richard C. Oudersluys

Biblical Theologian

Distinguished Seminary Professor

Dedicated Servant of the Church

Esteemed Mentor and Friend

Faithful Disciple of Jesus Christ

**The Historical Series of the Reformed Church in America**

The series was inaugurated in 1968 by the General Synod of the Reformed Church in America acting through the Commission on History to communicate the church's heritage and collective memory and to reflect on our identity and mission, encouraging historical scholarship which informs both church and academy.

General Editor
Rev. Donald J. Bruggink, Ph.D., D.D.
Western Theological Seminary
Van Raalte Institute, Hope College

Associate Editor
George Brown, Jr., Ph.D.
Western Theological Seminary

Copy Editor
Laurie Baron

Production Editor
Russell L. Gasero

Commission on History
Douglas Carlson, Ph.D., Northwestern College, Orange City, Iowa
Mary L. Kansfield, M.A., East Stroudsburg, Pennsylvania
Hartmut Kramer-Mills, M.Div., Ph.D., New Brunswick, New Jersey
Jeffery Tyler, Ph.D., Hope College, Holland, Michigan
Audrey Vermilyea, Bloomington, Minnesota
Lori Witt, Ph.D., Central College, Pella, Iowa

# Contents

# Illustrations

# Preface

From the earliest days of the church of Jesus Christ, the ark has been a symbol of its presence in the world. As in the days of Noah, God has gathered into the church all those who are being saved from the floods of destruction threatening a corrupt and wicked humanity. The World Council of Churches has adopted the symbol of the ark, portrayed as a single-hulled sailing ship, as a reminder of its mission in the present age.

Reformed and Lutheran denominations in America sail more as twin-hulled catamarans than as single-hulled arks. They have maintained their distinctive roles in American Christianity by resting on their confessional statements on the one side and their ethnicity on the other. The Reformed Church in America claims to be one of the oldest ethnic-confessional denominations in the New World. It has maintained a continuous existence in Manhattan since 1628. It became an ethnic denomination under the Classis of Amsterdam in the Netherlands following the English capture of Manhattan in 1664. Its Dutch ethnicity was officially recognized in May 1696, when William the Third of England granted a charter to the Netherlands Reformed

Congregation in New York under the English title, "Reformed Protestant Dutch Church."[1] The name of the denomination underwent several changes over time. Since 1867, its name has been "Reformed Church in America." That designation is used throughout this book, including the time before 1867.

Throughout its history in America, the Reformed Church in America has accepted the three Reformed confessions adopted by the Dutch National Synod of Dort in 1618-1619: the Heidelberg Catechism, the Belgic Confession, and the Canons of Dort. Its church order has been based on the one adopted at that synod, with modifications to suit American conditions. The Dutch language was used in worship in some congregations even after the Revolutionary War.

By 1847, when a new wave of Dutch immigrants was arriving in the United States, the Reformed Church in America was accepted as one American denomination among others that made up American Protestantism. It cooperated with Presbyterian, Congregational, German Reformed, and other Protestant denominations in the great adventure of building and evangelizing a Christian America. Almost all of its congregations were located in the eastern states of New York, New Jersey, and Pennsylvania. A few new congregations were being organized in Michigan, Ohio, and Illinois, in what was then known as the "West." Their membership was composed of Dutch descendents who migrated primarily from New York and New Jersey to take advantage of new land that was being made available by the federal government.

The new wave of Dutch immigration to the midwestern United States began in the 1840s as a result of widespread poverty in the Netherlands. Most of those who settled in colonies in the Midwest were part of a pietist movement that had spread across Europe and Great Britain in the seventeenth and eighteenth centuries. The pietism of the Dutch who came to America was characterized by a consciousness of human sin and depravity, the call to live a holy life through participation in Sunday worship, a personal experience of salvation, and living to the glory of God in daily practice.

In 1847, Dutch Reformed congregations had come together to form the Classis of Holland, which had its center in Holland, Michigan. In 1850, under the leading of the Reverend Albertus C. Van Raalte, the classis united with the Reformed Church in America, and thereby it reinforced the old ethnic base of the denomination. The decision to unite with an American denomination was greeted with suspicion by

[1]  *Appendix to the Acts and Proceedings of the General Synod of the Reformed Church in America,* 1867, 8-9.

some in the Midwest who feared that the old loyalty to the confessions and the church order had eroded in the American climate in the eastern United States. However, the majority of congregations approved of the action of the classis and became loyal participants in the life of the Reformed Church in America. They also came to know the tensions that arise in an ethnic-confessional denomination when its people face decisions about the extent to which they should cooperate with or isolate themselves from the surrounding culture.

The title and subtitle of this book point up its purposes. The title, *The Practice of Piety*, reflects the concern of Dutch pietists to live a holy life. Attention is given to the nature of the piety that the immigrant members of the midwestern Reformed Church in America practiced *after* arriving in America. It will be seen that the leaders in the Dutch enclaves were aware of the danger that their piety could slip over into an unhealthy "pietism" that is associated with narrow-minded bigotry, prudery, censoriousness, and ignorance. It will contend that James D. Bratt classified the mentality of the leaders of the midwestern Reformed Church correctly as "outgoing optimistic pietists."[2]

As practiced by the midwestern Reformed Church people, their piety must be distinguished from today's popular concept of "spirituality." "Spirituality" is often described as the "relationship of human beings with the divine and the shape which that relationship gives to human life."[3] One can be "spiritual" without having any clear concept of God or even whether God exists, but Reformed piety has its focus on God rather than on the development of one's self. Modern discussions of spirituality tend to interpret spirituality in individualistic terms, while the practice of piety by the Dutch Reformed immigrants had a strong emphasis upon the church gathered for worship on Sunday and upon the corporate devotional life of the family centered on Bible reading and prayer. Their understanding of Christian piety was part of a long tradition that looked back to John Calvin, who wrote,

> I call "piety" that reverence joined with love of God which the
> knowledge of his benefits induces. For until men recognize that

[2]  James D. Bratt, *Dutch Calvinism in Modern America* (Grand Rapids: Eerdmans, 1984), 47. Bratt applies the classification for that mentality specifically to the twentieth century, but the seeds of that attitude can be found in the immigrant leaders' view of "Christian" America almost from the time of their arrival in America.

[3]  Elsie Mc Kee, *John Calvin: Writings on Pastoral Piety* (Mahwah, N.J.: Paulist Press, 2001), 2.

they owe everything to God, that they are nourished by his fatherly care, that he is the Author of their every good, that they should seek nothing beyond him—they will never yield him willing service. Nay, unless they establish their complete happiness in him, they will never give themselves truly and sincerely to him.[4]

I. John Hesselink has pointed out the important role played by "piety" in Calvin's *Catechism*. Piety is

"reverence joined with love"; it is sometimes equated with the true worship of God; it is "a sincere feeling which loves God as Father" and "fears and reverences him as Lord"; it is the origin of and gives birth to true religion and the right knowledge of God.[5]

In Calvin, piety entails the duties of carrying out God's command. "Godliness is the beginning, middle and end of Christian living, and where it is complete, there is nothing lacking."[6]

The practice of piety among the Dutch Reformed was as concerned for theological integrity as for personal devotion to God. For that reason, this book will set forth a history of theological thought in the midwestern Reformed Church in America during the century from 1866 to 1966. That history provides insight into the ways in which the leaders of the midwestern Reformed Church sought to remain faithful to their theological and ethnic heritage while adjusting to the new demands of modernity and American culture. Special attention is paid to the writings of the leading pastors and theological professors who taught at Western Theological Seminary in Holland, Michigan. The goal is to enable members of the Reformed Church in America and people in other denominations to have access to the course of theological discussion that took place during the period when Dutch immigrants in the Reformed Church in America were coming to terms with their calling to live a life to the glory of God in the New World.

My writing of the history could not be separated from reflection on my own personal journey of faith. It has led me to a greater appreciation of what midwestern leaders accomplished in articulating in America the Dutch Reformed piety and theology that they had brought with them to America. They were pastors and teachers who

---

[4]    John Calvin, trans. Ford Lewis Battles, *Institutes of the Christian Religion* (Philadelphia: Westminster, 1973), I, 2, 1.

[5]    I. John Hesselink, *Calvin's First Catechism* (Louisville: Westminster John Knox, 1997), 46.

[6]    *Commentary on Acts, 10:2,* quoted in Hesselink, *Calvin's First Catechism,* 47.

knew that they were called to nurture the faith of those who had to adjust to the customs, enticements, and philosophical underpinnings of democracy in America. They did their work well and thereby enabled the Dutch Reformed immigrant communities in which they served to enjoy peace and prosperity while sustaining their faith as the people of God. Because what they wrote has been neglected to such a great extent—even their names have been forgotten—in this book I have tried to present the history more from their perspective than my own and have avoided the temptation to carry out a rigorous criticism of their efforts.

The intersection of my personal history with Reformed Church history results in the fact that in this book provincial ethnic history intersects with ecumenical history. It begins with concern about issues of personal faith, worship, and church order, and ends with the challenge to live in a pluralistic world with confidence and hope in God, who remains sovereign in that world.

This book is by no means a complete history of midwestern Reformed Church in America theology. Very little space is given to what was happening theologically in the eastern region of the denomination. The theological history of the East Fresian German language Reformed Church congregations in the Midwest is not covered at all. The theological dialogue with the Christian Reformed Church is but briefly discussed. It is my hope that this book will inspire others to deal in greater depth with what is covered here and that those areas not given space will be filled in by further research and publications.

I want to thank Donald J. Bruggink and Elton J. Bruins not only for encouraging me to write this book but also for the expert assistance and deep knowledge of the Reformed Church that they have constantly made available to me. Earl Wm. and Cornelia B. Kennedy have helped me understand Dutch vocabulary and idioms and checked Dutch spelling. They have provided as yet unpublished information about the individuals who led the churches and served in the Classis of Holland during the two decades from 1847-1866. I am indebted to those who work in the A.C. Van Raalte Institute for the way they welcomed me to join in their morning coffee times and for sharing with me their great knowledge of the life and theology of the Dutch in America since 1847. I am grateful for the help of others, including I. John Hesselink, Eugene Vander Well, Dennis Voskuil, Christopher Kaiser, and the members of the Reformed Church's Commission on History, who have read and made valuable suggestions for all or parts of early drafts. Lynn Japinga's comments have been especially detailed and helpful. The staff of the

Beardslee Library at Western Theological Seminary has always been ready to help locate materials and books. Jeffrey Reynolds and Lori Trethewey have faithfully provided materials from the collections in the Joint Archives of Holland and assisted in making copies whenever requested. Karen Schakel has provided assistance in working through the intricacies of putting footnotes and bibliographical references in proper form. Laurie Baron deserves special thanks for doing the final editing of the book.

Finally, the talented and long-suffering Russell Gasero deserves especial thanks for formatting the book, including typesetting, layout, and page formatting, and for taking extra care to make the numerous long photo captions both attractive and readable.

No one has worked harder in the process than my wife, Mary. She has read every page aloud to herself in order to discover the typing and other errors in the manuscript. She has insisted on eliminating the professorial passive voice and theological jargon.

I have been admonished not to write convoluted sentences that contain up to one hundred words. Although she would not claim to be a theologian, I have learned to listen to her when she raises theological issues. I am grateful to her not only for her help in writing this book, but especially for the fifty-seven years of her life that she has shared with me.

Eugene P. Heideman

CHAPTER 1

# The Midwestern Reformed Church and Its Leaders

In 1846, many pious Christians in the northern and eastern provinces of the Netherlands were facing a bleak economic future. Beginning already in the 1830s, those who were farmers suffered from low prices for the grain they sold on the market. One result was that they hired fewer day laborers, resulting in much unemployment in the rural areas. The whole country was affected by a decline in international trade. By 1841, 13 percent of the people were on welfare; by 1845, the ratio was 27 percent on welfare. Their misery increased manifold when the potato famine due to blight hit the country in 1845.[1]

Those Reformed believers who had seceded from the old church of the land, the *Nederlandse Hervormde Kerk* (Netherlands Reformed Church),[2] in the Secession of 1834 were even more concerned for their

---

[1]   Jacob Van Hinte, *Netherlanders in America: A Study of Emigration and Settlement in the Nineteenth and Twentieth Centuries in the United States of America*, ed. Robert P. Swierenga, trans. Adriaan De Wit (Grand Rapids: Historical Committee of the Christian Reformed Church, 2003), 77-85.
[2]   The Nederlandse Hervormde Kerk dated its history from the time of the Synod of Dort, held in 1618-1619. It was the official church of the land and

1

future than the rest of the population. They had suffered much during the years when the secession had gathered momentum. Their ministers had been placed under discipline and put out of their parsonages by the authorities of the Nederlandse Hervormde Kerk. They had been fined heavily for preaching in violation of the government's laws of assembly. At times they were imprisoned for weeks or months. Mobs ridiculed and threw stones at them or hit them with sticks. Heavy fines were levied on believers who allowed their houses and barns to be used for preaching services.

Although the persecution had come to an end in the 1840s, the memory of the imprisonments, fines, and other harassments had not faded away by 1846, when many became attracted by reports about America as the land of prosperity and freedom. The small number of Dutch who had emigrated in the 1830s sent back reports about their purchase of land and religious freedom. Those who had given up hope of owning land in the Netherlands read in the letters that it was possible to buy a large number of acres in America at a very low price.

Two ministers of the Secession, the Reverend Albertus C. Van Raalte and his brother-in-law, the Reverend Anthony Brummelkamp, recognized that many of the impoverished seceders in their congregations were contemplating emigration to America. They feared that the pressures and temptations of life in America could lead many of them to stray from the faith and that they would be exploited by unscrupulous American employers. They were convinced that for the sake of their spiritual welfare as well as their economic prospects, it would be far better for emigrants to settle in America as colonies rather than simply as individuals or families. Therefore, they organized a Christian emigration society that would enable emigrants to go as a colony accompanied by an orthodox pastor. Article 7 of the society's constitution read:

> The first mission is to create a Colony that is Christian. Therefore, it is recommended to the Committee taking care of the acceptance, help, and sending of emigrants, to find such "salting" elements for the colony as are necessary to insure a Christian majority. Therefore it will not accept any persons for colonization other than those who will be expected to submit to the Lord's

therefore often known as the *Grote Kerk* (Great Church). In order to avoid confusion with other churches in the Netherlands and the United States, it will be referred to by the name, *Nederlandse Hervormde Kerk*, even though it did not bear that name during much of its history.

Word, so that in that way not only a Christian consistory but also a Christian government will be present in order to uphold the law of God which is the foundation of every state.[3]

The plan of Van Raalte and Brummelkamp soon led to the settlement of pious colonies of Dutch immigrants in western Michigan. While Brummelkamp remained in the Netherlands, Van Raalte led a group to establish a colony in Holland in 1847. Van Raalte's initiative can be understood to mark the beginning of the history of the Reformed Church in America in the Midwest.[4]

Other groups of Dutch Reformed immigrants arrived. One group, under the leadership of the Reverend Hendrik P. Scholte, settled in Pella, Iowa, in the same year that Van Raalte and his followers settled in Holland. Following them, the Reverend Cornelius Van der Meulen, with his group of impoverished people from the province of Zeeland, founded the village of Zeeland six miles east of Holland. The Reverend Seine Bolks led many members of his congregation to settle Overisel five miles from Holland. By 1857, other Dutch immigrant colonies were founded in South Holland, Illinois; Sheboygan County, Wisconsin; and in the area around Alto, Wisconsin.[5] A number of the immigrants settled down in the area around Rochester, New York, rather than proceed all the way to Michigan.[6]

In 1849, just two years after the first settlement in Holland, the Reverend Isaac N. Wyckoff, pastor of the Second Reformed Church in Albany, New York, was sent by the Reformed Church in America's Board of Domestic Missions to visit the newly founded Dutch settlements in Michigan and Wisconsin. He reported that there were already seven Dutch immigrant congregations with a total of 922 communicant members in western Michigan. Their loyalty to the Reformed faith was deep and the level of devotion was impressive. He wrote:

Of all these communicants in these churches it may be said that

---

[3]  Quoted in Van Hinte, *Netherlanders in America*, 124.
[4]  There was a small number of Reformed Church in America congregations present in the Midwest prior to the arrival of the Dutch immigrants in 1847. They were organized by Reformed Church members who had moved from New York, New Jersey, and Pennsylvania. Most of those congregations were founded in small towns and disbanded after several decades. Several continue to exist to the present. The oldest surviving Reformed Church congregation in the Midwest is in Fairview, Illinois, organized in 1837.
[5]  For a detailed account of Dutch immigration between 1840 and 1895, see Van Hinte, *Netherlanders in America*, 120-50, 215-315.
[6]  Ibid., 148-49, 153, 159.

they are praying and hopefully converted persons. Their religious habits are very strict and devout. They do all things with prayer and praise. They sing and pray in the morning, after their dinner and before their supper. They pray when they meet for business. At a bee (or meeting for common work) they pray. The common council of the city opens its sittings with prayer. The appearances and tone of piety is purer and higher than anything I have ever seen and seemed like the primitive Christians and most beautiful.[7]

Wyckoff also reported that Christian education for their children was a high priority in the colony.

The colony is paying as much attention as possible to schools and Christian education. They have a Dutch school and English school in the city. At Zeeland, there is a Dutch school and they will soon have an English one and all the rest will follow. The teachers "must" be godly persons, who besides teaching reading and writing, must see that the children are prepared on the Catechism, and that they are taught to sing the Psalms. The ministers catechise (sic) all the children once a week, and if they are hindered, the elders take their place.[8]

After arriving in America, the pastor-leaders in the Holland, Michigan, area were diligent in encouraging newly arrived Reformed Dutch immigrants to settle near each other and be joined together in Reformed congregations in each place. More than one hundred Reformed enclaves existed by 1900. "It is estimated that between 1846 and 1900 three quarters of all Dutch emigrants settled in Reformed enclaves."[9] Robert Swierenga has referred to those enclaves as "cocoons" centered around their Reformed churches. The cocoons "marked the Dutch as a people of faith" who took their Reformed heritage seriously.[10]

---

[7]   Isaac N. Wyckoff, "Report of a Visit to the Holland Colonies," in Henry S. Lucas, *Dutch Immigrant Memoirs and Related Writings* (Grand Rapids: Eerdmans, 1997), vol. I, 453-54.

[8]   Wyckoff's comments about their enthusiasm for schools and Christian education probably reflected Van Raalte's and other pastors' perspectives more than it did the rank and file of the colonists. The pages of *De Hope* include repeated complaints that there was a lack of financial support for the schools; see also Van Hinte, *Netherlanders in America*, 256.

[9]   Wyckoff in Lucas, *Dutch Immigrant Memoirs*, 453.

[10]  Robert P. Swierenga, *Dutch Chicago* (Grand Rapids: Eerdmans, 2002), 2,

The Rev. John H. Karsten D.D.
(1833-1914)

*Courtesy Joint Archives of Holland*

John Karsten wrote the Sunday school lesson expositions in *De Hope* for twenty-nine years without interruption. "As a preacher, Dr. Karsten was a careful and lucid expounder of the Word, a man thoroughly acquainted with his Bible. His sermons were rich in thought and thoroughly evangelical. As a pastor he was sympathetic, friendly and faithful. In the larger circle of ministerial activity he was a leader. A man who inspired confidence; a loyal son of the Reformed Church having its varied interests at heart. A man with broad views and free from all narrowness of conception regarding the interests of the Kingdom, there was not a single activity of the church which he did not gladly support with word and deed."— *Acts and Proceedings of the General Synod of the Reformed Church in America* (hereinafter, *Acts and Proceedings*), 1914, 248.

The Dutch immigrants entering the Wisconsin and the Chicago areas did not arrive in organized groups; they began to cluster in their new locations after arriving in America as individuals or families. They drifted into Chicago. Some of them had intended to go on beyond Chicago but had settled there when they found jobs available. Others went to Chicago because they already had friends or relatives there.[11] The Reverend John H. Karsten, who served as pastor of churches in Alto and Oostburg, Wisconsin, wrote that the pioneers there "had no leaders. Individualism characterized the movement. There were no concerted plans or organized efforts. Places for settlement were not selected with any definite object in view—industrial, educational, or religious. Many places were settled by the merest chance."[12]

In spite of the haphazard nature of the movements of Dutch immigrants into the states of Indiana, Illinois, and Wisconsin, the spirit that led to the formation of the Dutch colonies in Michigan also

[11]  Ibid., *2*, 13.
[12]  John H. Karsten, "Settlement in Wisconsin, 1847-1897," in Lucas, *Dutch Immigrant Memoirs*, vol. II, 130.

encouraged the development of similar Dutch Reformed communities in those states as well as in Iowa. On the fiftieth anniversary of the founding of the first colonies, Karsten pointed out that it was the good counsel of ministers including Van Raalte, CorneliusVan Der Meulen of Zeeland, and other pastors that led to the organization of Reformed congregations in each of the communities. The congregations were in turn brought together into classes that could supervise them and their pastors.[13]

The Dutch Reformed people who settled in Indiana, Illinois, Wisconsin, and Iowa between 1847 and 1850 felt a common bond with each other because approximately two-thirds of all the Dutch who immigrated to America during those decades shared the piety of the Secession of 1834.[14] They had come out of a common experience of religious oppression by the authorities in the Netherlands. In addition to the Seceders, there were also members of the Netherlands Reformed Church who had not seceded but were sympathetic to the theology and religious outlook of the Seceders.

In 1869 Van Raalte was promoting the establishment of a new colony in Virginia.[15] He took the opportunity to state once again the reason it was so important for the Reformed Dutch immigrants to settle in colonies. He pointed out that in the building up of America, things do not stand still. People plant their principles in the land and those principles permeate the culture. Is it not important then, he asked, that we not simply allow the Reformed Dutch immigrants to be scattered in the land where they are likely to lose their spiritual inheritance? It is crucial to gather them into congregations so that they can be centers of nurture and Christian work. He called attention to the new colony being established in Orange City, Iowa, by people from Pella under the leadership of Henry Hospers and others. By keeping them together, their communities can become instruments of Christian

---

[13]   Ibid., 131-34. The Reformed Church in America's *Book of Church Order* provides that each congregation will be governed by a consistory that includes elected elders and deacons. The classis consists of the ordained ministers within their bounds and elder representatives from each of the congregations. The classes in turn meet together under regional synods. The General Synod, with representatives from each of the classes, meets annually during the month of June.

[14]   Robert P. Swierenga, *Faith and Family: Dutch Immigration and Settlement in the United States, 1820-1920* (New York: Holmes & Meier, 2000), 174-77.

[15]   Elton J. Bruins, Karen G. Schakel, Sara Frederickson Simmons, and Marie N. Zingle, *Albertus and Christina* (Grand Rapids: Eerdmans, 2004), 29; see also Van Hinte, *Netherlanders in America*, 523-34.

influence both for furtherance of the faith in America and for mission in other countries. He suggested that consideration could be given to new efforts in Texas, Mexico, South America, and elsewhere.[16]

Matthew Kolyn, a professor at Western Theological Seminary, gave several reasons for the success of colonization in an article in 1903. He wrote, first, that the Dutch people worked hard, were thrifty, and did not give up on a task that they had begun. Second, they had good leaders who made wise decisions. Third, the people had spiritual enthusiasm. Although most of the immigrants had come for economic reasons, they did not forget to praise the Lord for their blessings and for the freedom to practice their faith. They had a feeling of unity, of joy in Sabbath worship, and of being together in prayer. Above all, they had been supported by the blessing of God in their lives. He concluded, "To God alone be the glory!"[17]

The Dutch immigrants took Kolyn's concluding exclamation seriously. Living to the glory of God was at the heart of their faith. Central to such faith was the need to attend the public worship of the church twice or at least once each Sunday, to attend to the reading of the scriptures, to listen to the Word of God preached, to sing in praise of God, and to engage in prayer. During the week, it was their practice as families to honor God by reading the scriptures and engaging in family prayers at meals and at other times.

[16]   Albertus C. Van Raalte, "Kolonizatie en Opvoeding," *De Hope*, October 13, 1869, 1. *De Hope* reported regularly about what was happening in the various colonies, including new efforts in the states of Kansas, Missouri, Nebraska, the Dakotas, Montana, Texas, and Washington. At times Dutch land speculators managed to get their promotional ideas printed in *De Hope*; for an example of such competition, see A. Wormser of Cedar Grove, Wisconsin's notice about the good land available in Minnesota, in *De Hope*, September 29, 1885. It was followed by further information in *De Hope*, October 6, 1885, by Mr. Prins and Mr. Zwanenberg, land agents located in Chicago who give information about the possible location of a church. (Ultimately Prinsburg and Clara City, named after Zwanenberg's wife, were incorporated there.) In the November 17, 1885, issue, 3, a Mr. Stegeman asked why *De Hope* had given publicity to the Minnesota area when the Harrison, South Dakota, area had clear advantages. Stegeman's information was then disputed by yet another letter, December 22, 1885, 2-3. See also Robert Schoone-Jongen, "Clapboard Chapels on the Prairie: The Founding of Dutch and Ostfrisian Congregations in Central Minnesota: 1886-1905" in Paul Fessler, et. al., eds., *Dutch Immigrants on the Plains* (Sioux Center, Iowa: Association for the Advancement of Dutch-American Studies), 139-62.

[17]   Matthew Kolyn, "Middeloorzaken van het Welslagen onzer Nederzettingen," *De Hope*, August 12, 1903.

The Rev. Matthew Kolyn, D.D.
(1856-1918)

*Courtesy of Western Theological Seminary.*

Matthew Kolyn was a faithful pastor and teacher of youth. He wrote the youth page in *De Hope* for a number of years and was known for his catechetical and Sunday school teaching ability. He served as principal of Northwestern Academy in Orange City, Iowa, 1901-1910, prior to being called to serve as professor of historical theology at Western Theological Seminary in 1910.

## Sustaining the Hope that Led Them to America

The Dutch immigrants soon found it essential to face issues raised by their decision to settle as colonies in America. In the European colonial era, a colony was understood to be a company of people that settled in a new land while remaining loyal to its mother country. By its nature, a colony lives in relative isolation from its surrounding culture and is responsible for developing its own rules of governance that may be at variance with the rules of surrounding neighbors. However, if the vision for the colony is to be fulfilled, the leaders must develop appropriate institutional structures and maintain educational faithfulness that nurtures the vision in following generations. They must be vigilant against outside threats and be ready to re-examine the vision critically in the face of new circumstances.

During the first two decades in America, the leaders made three vital decisions: (1) the Classis of Holland united with the Reformed Church in America, which was located primarily in New York, New Jersey, and Pennsylvania; (2) they founded Hope College and its theological department that eventually became Western Theological Seminary in Holland, Michigan; and (3) they began to publish the

The Hope College Printing Office

weekly religious paper, *De Hope*, which became their primary means of theological conversation.

Although Van Raalte and Vander Meulen had been members of the separatist movement in the Secession of 1834 and led their followers to establish colonies in Holland and Zeeland, Michigan, they were neither separatists nor isolationists by nature. They intended to live as American citizens rather than remain primarily loyal to the Netherlands. When they led the Classis of Holland into union with the historic Reformed Church in America that dated its origin in Manhattan to 1628, the Reformed congregations in the Holland Classis were united into the mainstream of American Protestantism. In spite of the relative geographical isolation of their colonies in western Michigan, they welcomed the help and presence of Americans in enabling their communities to develop economically.[18]

In contrast to their leaders' moves in favor of integration into American society and evangelical American Protestantism, there were individuals and groups within the colonies that preferred to remain in

---

[18] See Van Hinte, *Netherlanders in America,* 231-43, for an account of commercial and governance relationships between the Dutch settlers and the Americans in the first decade of the colonies in Holland and Zeeland.

isolation, believing that their strength as a colony and as a church was to be found in their relative isolation from the mainstream of society. The fact that their colony had been founded as "Christian" implied that their children should be educated in Christian schools rather than religiously "neutral" public schools. Their Calvinistic theology had to be protected from the "Arminian" tendencies so powerful in American Protestantism.

During the first two decades of their life in America, it became increasingly evident that if the immigrants' hopes for living as Reformed Christians in America were to be fulfilled it was essential that means be found for continuing to nurture their people in the Reformed faith and life. Albertus Van Raalte favored policies that ensured a Christian education for children and youth in the colonies, whether through the establishment of separate Christian schools or through cooperation with public schools that maintained a Christian character.[19]

Van Raalte was particularly concerned that a school committed to Christian higher education be founded. He believed that the future of the Reformed Church in America in the Midwest depended on creating a school dedicated to the education of both lay and ministerial leaders. He saw the establishment of Hope College in Holland, Michigan, as his "anchor of hope." As his biographer, Henry E. Dosker, wrote, "It cannot be emphasized enough that Van Raalte's whole conception of the school crystallized around these last two things. For him, higher education did exist for the benefit of society; but *above everything else,* for the Kingdom of God. Without the ultimate aim of preaching the Word, this School had little meaning for him."[20] Van Raalte's vision was decisive for the ability of the colony to retain its identity in the context of American culture. Within two decades after the founding of the colony, Hope College in 1866 graduated its first class of which seven out of eight members became ordained ministers.[21]

The Dutch language weekly religious paper, *De Hope,* under the sponsorship of Hope College, began to be published in 1866.[22] It

---

[19]   See Elton Bruins, "The Educational Endeavors of the Reformed Dutch Church, 1628-1866," *Reformed Review,* 59/3 (2005-2006), 176-83. Van Raalte favored Christian schools but was also ready to accept a policy of cooperation with the public schools.

[20]   Quoted in James C. Kennedy and Caroline Simon, *Can Hope Endure? A Historical Case Study in Christian Higher Education,* Historical Series of the Reformed Church in America, no. 47 (Grand Rapids: Eerdmans, 2005), 31-32.

[21]   Wynand Wichers, *A Century of Hope, 1866-1966* (Grand Rapids: Eerdmans, 1968), 69-71.

[22]   Ibid., 78-79.

First page of *De Hope*, vol. 1/1

played a crucial role as a means of communication among the scattered colonies and enclaves of Dutch immigrants in the Midwest. The paper made it possible for the leading ministers and theological professors to remind members of the Reformed churches of the essentials of the

Reformed faith and defend the Reformed faith against other theologies and secular movements in America. From 1866 through its final issue in 1933, its writers constantly defended the orthodox theology of the Reformed faith. They evaluated the relation of Reformed theology to the theology of the American revival movements in other Protestant churches and promoted by evangelists such as Dwight L. Moody and Billy Sunday. They monitored theological developments in other denominations, particularly in the Presbyterian and Congregational churches. They warned against the encroachments of American liberal Protestantism. Each week, there were columns of news and commentary on events within America and in foreign lands, often including columns especially calling attention to political and religious events in the Netherlands.

*De Hope*'s masthead motto throughout its entire existence was *Voor de Kerk, de School, en de Maatschappij* ("For the Church, the School, and Society"). Its first editor, the Reverend Pieter J. Oggel,[23] stated the purpose for producing *De Hope* as a weekly paper. Succeeding editors called attention to his statement of purpose annually. Because his statement provides insight into the nature of the Reformed faith and life, it is important to consider it carefully. Oggel wrote that the call of the Christian press is to discuss the events of the day in relation to the coming of the kingdom of God:

> not so much to arouse curiosity according to the way of Athens, but to give an overview of what is happening in the world in which we live. How can one be alert to the signs of the time if one is not acquainted with his time? We hope to speak about the important events on earth. We hope to communicate what important Christian papers say concerning these matters (which

[23]    Pieter Oggel was born in the Netherlands. He was pastor of the Reformed Church in Grand Haven, Michigan, 1856-1859, and the First Reformed Church in Pella, Iowa, 1860-1863. He was the son-in-law of Albertus C. Van Raalte. In the first issue of *De Hope*, Oggel reported that he would be joined as coeditor by the Rev. A.B. Veenhuizen, who had been appointed to teach modern languages at Hope College. Veenhuizen had studied theology in Geneva, Switzerland, under Merle d'Aubigne, the renowned Reformed historian. Veenhuizen had been an associate of Van Raalte in the training of pastors in the Netherlands, first in Ommen and again at the theological school in Arnhem. However, Veenhuizen did not come to Holland but remained in Pultneyville, New York, where he served as pastor of the Reformed church there from 1862-1870.

cannot profit many Dutch folk, because they do not understand English). In contemplating the world we hope especially to pay attention to that which must be most essential for everyone: the development of the Kingdom of God.[24]

*De Hope* was produced in order to promote godly living in the home, promote the work of the schools, and enhance the knowledge of the scriptures.

We hope to promote that which is related to it [the kingdom of God] such as the knowledge of the Holy Scriptures, mutual love, the application of God's Word, education, in family as well as elementary and higher education. We especially do not wish to place the last in the background.[25]

*De Hope*'s purpose included education in church unity and Christian citizenship in America.

We wish to defend all good topics and enterprises in church and civic affairs. As far as parties are concerned, we will stay completely removed from politics. It is not our aim to speak for any party. If, however, our conscience dictates that we speak for biblical principles in civic matters, especially because of obedience to, and reverence for, the rulers (*Magten*), we will not avoid doing so, no matter what party. If we feel that we have to point to faults within or without our church, we hope to do so with faithfulness and gentleness. The columns of this paper are not open for vile correspondence or personal insults.[26]

In 1906 the English language journal, the *Leader,* took its place alongside *De Hope*, also with Hope College as its publisher, The two papers were merged October 3, 1934, with the eastern Reformed Church paper, the *Christian Intelligencer,* which had been published since 1831. The purpose for publishing the *Leader* was similar to that of *De Hope*. The editorial in the first issue stated that the religious press must be distinctly and emphatically Christian.

The great doctrines of the Scriptures...must nevertheless be the substance of its teaching. God as the creator of heaven and earth,

---

[24]   *De Hope*, December 12, 1865, 1. (Translation of Oggel's editorial by Cornelia B. Kennedy.)

[25]   Ibid.

[26]   Ibid.

Christ as the redeemer of men, the Holy Spirit as the applier of the mercy of God, the Scriptures as the only rule of faith and practice, rewards and punishments in this life and the next; these are the facts and principles that must be the atmosphere in which the religious weekly lives and moves and has its being.[27]

A religious weekly cannot confine itself exclusively to religious articles. "It stands related to a great organization, the Kingdom of God."[28] In the organized church, the journal must do more than simply report about the church's conferences and decisions. "It must have a high standard for denominational life, educational institutions and world-wide service; and, in the lowly spirit of the Master, labor incessantly for the attainment of specific ends."[29]

As a religious journal, the *Leader* had to be a guardian of the home. "The purity and integrity of the family are of fundamental importance both to the church and the nation."[30] It had to be patriotic as well as religious.

> Next to the love of God is the love of country. Christ appreciated the man of whom it was said, "He loveth our nation." And while the religious paper can not be a party paper in the narrow, ward-politician's sense, nevertheless, it must be a watchman on the walls and must fearlessly announce the dangers that threaten national life."[31]

The *Leader* had to deal with the whole person.

> Moreover, it must never be forgotten that man has a physical, intellectual and aesthetic as well as a moral and religious nature. When piety smothers intellectuality or when intellectuality uproots piety, neither the one nor the other is doing God's service. The whole man must be brought as a living sacrifice unto God. No part of him must remain untouched.[32]

The "Golden Text" that appeared on the masthead of the *Leader* every week beginning with the first issue was, "Behold I have given him for a witness to the people, a leader and commander of the people" (Isa.

---

[27]  Evert J. Blekkink, "The Religious Press," *Leader,* September 13, 1906, 1.
[28]  Ibid.
[29]  Ibid.
[30]  Ibid.
[31]  Ibid.
[32]  Ibid.

55:4). The text is clear evidence that the publisher and editors of the *Leader* and also of *De Hope* believed that they had a calling from God as well as a leadership role in guiding their readers in living the faith in America. Moreover, the midwestern members of the Reformed Church in America remained appreciative of that leadership throughout the whole time the papers were published, 1866-1933. At no point in those decades did any major opposition to their leadership arise.[33] Several other papers came into being to serve more regional or language communities, such as the Dutch language *De Volksvriend*, published in Orange City, Iowa, 1874-1951, and the German language *Der Mitarbeiter*, published in German Valley, Illinois. Those papers could not, however, provide the breadth of theological discussion and church and political news that was available though *De Hope* and the *Leader*.

In this study of the history of theology in the midwestern Reformed Church in America, it is also important to consult academic course materials and other writings collected from professors at Western Theological Seminary and from a number of leading pastors in the Midwest.[34] They published many articles in the church press. Only a few of their letters survive and very few essays have been written about them.

Our research to date does not help us discover our spiritual mothers. Recently a journal kept by Geesje Van Der Haar Visscher has come to light. Her pious faith and her interaction with friends, relatives, and pastors shed important light on the nature of piety of both men and women. Her journal at present is virtually unique in its category.[35]

---

[33] In asserting that no major opposition arose, it is not claimed that there was no opposition. There always were individuals who did not wish to follow the leaders, and at times the majority of Reformed Church members did not share enthusiasm for the plans of the leaders. But such differences did not lead to widespread controversy or theological debate, in contrast to the situation in the Christian Reformed Church, where competing journals were established in the twentieth century.

[34] These materials are now housed in the Western Theological Seminary Collection in the Joint Archives of Holland, Hope College, Holland, Michigan (hereinafter WTS/JAH).

[35] A copy of her journal is included in the personal papers of Elton Bruins and is located in the Albertus C. Van Raalte Institute in Holland, Michigan. Mary Kansfield has recently written an important book about women in mission for the Historical Series of the Reformed Church in America, *Letters to Hazel: Ministry within the Woman's Board of Foreign Missions of the Reformed Church in America* (Grand Rapids: Eerdmans, 2004). Firth Haring Fabend, *Zion on the Hudson: Dutch in New Jersey in the Age of Revivals* (New

Reformed Church women in the nineteenth century and first half of the twentieth century were not encouraged to write articles for the religious papers, were not accepted as theological students, and were not permitted to serve as ministers, elders, and deacons in the church. The male leaders must not be excused by saying that they were after all simply acting according to the standards of their own times. They were often behind even their own times when they were cautious about permitting women to gain the right to vote in civil elections, not to mention the church elections. Research into what the women thought necessarily involves a diligent search for letters, diaries, and devotional materials that may have been developed by women. A number of Reformed Church women became missionaries and wrote letters home about their work.[36]

As one reads *De Hope* and the *Leader* along with the other materials available, several characteristics of the leaders emerge that were constant from 1866 until approximately the beginning of World War II. While new perspectives began to emerge in the 1930s, articles written after World War II often have a different point of view from what had gone before. Therefore, while this book finds its focus largely in the period 1866-1945, the post-World War II perspective will be considered in the final chapter. The characteristics that are recognized in the leaders are particularly true for those who gave leadership prior to World War II but also persist even into the later decades.

The first characteristic is that most of the leaders prior to World War II were primarily Reformed Church pastors and preachers

---

Brunswick: Rutgers Univ. Press, 2000) contains a wealth of information about women in the eastern region of the Reformed Church in America. A number of letters written by women immigrants to Iowa are contained in Johan Stellingwerff, *Iowa Letters: Dutch Immigrants on the American Frontier*, ed. Robert P. Swierenga, trans. Walter Lagerwey, Historical Series of the Reformed Church in America, no. 47 (Grand Rapids: Eerdmans, 2004).

36   Renee S. House and John W. Coakley, *Patterns and Portraits: Women in the History of the Reformed Church in America*, Historical Series of the Reformed Church in America, no. 31 (Grand Rapids: Eerdmans, n.d.) contains eleven excellent chapters on women in the history of the denomination. Most of the chapters focus on women in the eastern region. The chapter by Karsten T. Ruhmohr-Voskuil and Elton Bruins, "Is a 'Joyful Death' an Oxymoron? The Christina de Moen Van Raalte Story" (87-94), provides insight into her faith. The chapter by Johan van de Bank, "The Dealings of the Lord's Love with Dina van den Bergh," (33-51) is an excellent example of the practice of piety during the Second Reformation in the Netherlands and in pious Reformed Church families on the American eastern seaboard in the eighteenth century.

rather than academic theologians. They had received their theological training at New Brunswick Theological Seminary, Western Theological Seminary, or seminaries of other denominations under the direct control of a church. The two Reformed Church seminaries, as agents of the Reformed Church General Synod, gave a "professorial certificate" that permitted a classis to examine a candidate for ordination following graduation from the seminary.[37] As late as 1937, the Reverend Dr. Albertus Pieters wrote that Western Theological Seminary existed for *one* purpose only. That purpose was to train Reformed Church men to serve as pastors in Reformed churches.[38] Students who wished to earn the academic degree of bachelor of divinity received it by meeting the requirements of Hope College beginning in 1917. The seminary itself gave no academic degree until the early 1940s. The lack of concern about academic degrees meant that theological studies at Western Theological Seminary always had a pastoral purpose. Theology should serve to build up the life of the congregation and strengthen the moral fabric of the whole community in order that God would be glorified.

Lack of concern for academic degrees did not mean that theological learning was minimized. The Dutch-speaking immigrant congregations had elders and other members who knew their Reformed theology and were alert to deviations from Reformed orthodoxy. Sermons were expected to have solid theological and biblical content. Humor in the pulpit was discouraged because it indicated that the preacher was not wholly serious about his task. Ministers were required to cover the points of doctrine in the Heidelberg Catechism at least once every four years, although congregations sometimes complained about the heavy content of the doctrinal preaching.

A second characteristic is that these spiritual and theological leaders operated on the principle that they already *were* Americans rather than simply *becoming* Americans. Although a good number of members of their congregations may have had nostalgia for things Dutch, the Reformed Church leaders in the colonies had no

[37]   The General Synod required that those teachers at New Brunswick and Western Theological seminaries who had been installed by the General Synod in the office of professor of theology had responsibility to issue a "Professorial Certificate" to those candidates for ministry who were judged fit by the professors at one of the two seminaries. A classis was not allowed to ordain a candidate who had not received the certificate. The requirement was intended to uphold the spiritual and academic quality of the ordained ministry in the denomination.

[38]   Albertus Pieters, "What Western Theological Seminary Seeks To Do," *Intelligencer-Leader*, May 25, 1937, 17.

hesitation about affirming that they were Americans. The process of Americanization that was going on in the congregations and the colonies was a movement within and among those who were already Americans.

Van Raalte, as leader of the Holland colony, and Scholte, as leader in Pella, intended to be Americans from the day they set foot on American soil. The Pella immigrants gained their American citizenship in record time, as was the case in the Holland colony. After arriving in Pella in August 1847, Scholte managed to persuade the state official in Pella to receive their petition for American citizenship. On September 17, 1847, the first of the Pella immigrants, about two hundred men, raised their arms swearing allegiance to America and relinquishing all allegiance to foreign powers.[39]

Henry Dosker recalled that Van Raalte had no intention to establish a "little Holland" in Michigan. Holland, Michigan, must be an American town. From the moment he landed in America, he considered himself an American citizen, with all a citizen's rights and privileges. Dosker wrote:

> The Hollander who comes to America and becomes a citizen *(burger)* in a new land makes America his fatherland. We have no false ideals about the possibility of living here in America "among ourselves" and establishing a small Netherlands in America, a sort of political pietism equivalent to "ecclesiola in ecclesia" a little church within the church....Whether we will it or not, we must go forward.[40]

There was opposition in the colony to Van Raalte's position. The Reverend Gerhard De Jonge, writing sixty years after the settling of Holland, recalled that there was a minority who continued to want to live as Netherlanders in America. They wanted to hold on to the Dutch language and have schools where their children could study in the Dutch

---

[39]   Van Hinte, *Netherlanders in America*, 281. Scholte was also critical of America and held to a clear separation of church and state. He believed that "Babel" is also present in America. He wrote, "We are fully justified in calling Rome the heart and center as well as the oldest part of Babylon, but at the same time we must recognize that in the course of the centuries various Protestant districts have been added and that this [outward] expansion still has not come to a halt. The United States of America do not stand outside this development...every impartial observer must admit that the Spirit of Babylon also reigns there" (Stellingwerff, *Iowa Letters*, 473-74).

[40]   H. Dosker, "Wekelijksch Budget," *De Hope*, November 20, 1901. The "Wekelijksch Budget" column was written each week by one of editors

language.[41] Eugene Osterhaven wrote in 1957, the centennial year of the secession of the Christian Reformed congregations, that Professor Nettinga had said that the fundamental issue in the secession of 1857 was that of Americanization. "Should the early Dutch immigrants in Michigan reproduce a little Holland on this side of the sea, or should they identify themselves with American ideals and customs and language and all that belongs to true Americanism?"[42] The Classis of Holland was in agreement with Van Raalte. In April 1854, it declared that since the number of English-speaking American children was growing in Holland, the classis must encourage the public school to shift gradually from instruction in the Dutch language to instruction in English. Furthermore, it declared that it anticipated the time when English-speaking Reformed Church ministers would be called to serve as pastors of Reformed congregations in the colony.[43]

A major reason that the majority of immigrants so quickly affirmed that they were Americans was that in their judgment America was a Christian nation, in contrast to what the Netherlands had become after the French Revolution, with its increasingly neutral and sometimes even antagonistic stance toward religion. They were impressed with the Protestant character of the public schools, the laws that encouraged observance of Sunday as a day of rest, and the American president's annual proclamation of an official Thanksgiving Day, as well as the high regard for the morality of the Ten Commandments. The editors of De Hope and the Leader never failed to include the text of the president's proclamation.

> We have become so accustomed to [the annual Thanksgiving proclamation—eph] that we scarcely recognize the significance, but there is no occurrence in the year that so distinctively places us before the world as a Christian nation as this annual proclamation by its chief executive. The name of God is not found in the Constitution, and some years ago there existed a society

---

("redactors"). It included reports about what was being written in other periodicals and comments about church life, political events and personalities, theological issues, and whatever else the writer deemed important. Some of the writers confined themselves to about two long columns; others filled three or more columns or even a whole page.

[41]  G. De Jonge, "De Kolonisten en de Amerikanisatie," De Hope, July 23, 1907.
[42]  Eugene Osterhaven, "Quia Semper Reformanda Est," Reformed Review, 1957, 11/1 (1957), 8.
[43]  Classis of Holland Minutes, 1848-1858, 154-55.

which had for its expressed purpose the insertion of the name in the fundamental law of the land, but our annual Thanksgiving Day is a better guarantee for the continued faith of the nation in the vital principle of Christianity than the mere name in the Constitution could be.[44]

The Reverend Evert J. Blekkink included patriotism as a virtue in his "political creed." After stating his belief that the scriptures are to be our guide for thought and deed (Art. 1) and that the church with the Bible as authority is the teacher of the state (Art. 2), he stated, "I believe that in the good pleasure of God I was born an American under the stars and stripes, that I am a citizen of a great nation, and I have no desire to change for another." [45]

The Reverend Gerrit H. Dubbink included patriotism as one of the duties of Christian ethics. Patriotism includes the duty to secure the enactment of wholesome laws, to oppose political corruption, to oppose the liquor traffic, to uphold civic respect and honor, and the obligation to pay taxes.[46]

A third characteristic of the theology of the midwestern Reformed Church leaders was that they all readily subscribed to Reformed theology as it was stated in the Belgic Confession, the Heidelberg Catechism, and the Canons of Dort. The Synod of Dort (1618-1619) had adopted the three confessional statements that came to be known as the "Standards of Unity." All ministers were required to sign a form stating that they fully agreed with the theology of the statements and that, in the case there were any doubts about them, they must first communicate the doubt to the classis before the minister would preach or write publicly against them. In its Explanatory Articles, adopted when it became independent from the church in the Netherlands in 1792, the Reformed Church in America had maintained this requirement for all ministers in the denomination.

The midwestern leaders held firmly to doctrinal conformity because during the seventeenth and eighteenth centuries the increasing liberalism of the Reformed Church in the Netherlands had allowed this requirement to be very freely interpreted. When King William I

[44]  Evert Blekkink, *Leader*, November 21, 1906, 50. In several of the following chapters it will be important to take note of the doubts about whether America is still a Christian nation as the Protestant faith became less dominant in America.
[45]  Blekkink, *Leader*, June 29, 1932, 1.
[46]  Gerrit Dubbink, "Outline of Christian Ethics," WTS/JAH, 18.

in 1816 promulgated the revised church order, an attempt was made to compromise between the liberal and conservative positions by requiring ministers to sign that they accepted the doctrines as stated in the confessions as in accord with the scripture. The phrase in the Latin could be interpreted either to mean *"because* they are in accord with scripture" or *"insofar as* they are in accord with scripture." Those who believed it necessary to hold to Dort's orthodox position firmly objected that "insofar as" allowed ministers to adopt a wide variety of heretical positions.

All of the first generation of ministers who immigrated to the Midwest during the first two decades after 1847 were part of the seceder movement that in 1834 had broken with the Netherlands Reformed Church. The subscription requirement of Dort had been one of the central issues in the Secession of 1834.[47] Against that historical background, the midwestern ministers believed strongly in the importance of the subscription requirement for the sake of theological unity in the Reformed Church in America. No minister or professor had ambitions to be a creative or innovative theologian. It was crucial to hold to the Christian faith as it had been expounded in the ancient creeds and Reformed confessions. They knew that the word "heresy" was a translation of "opinion" and that a heretic was one who held to his own opinion against the orthodox teachings of the church.

Professor Charles Hodge of Princeton Theological Seminary has often been ridiculed for giving thanks at the semicentennial celebration of the seminary that no new idea had ever originated at Princeton. His full statement was

> They were not given to new methods or new theories. They were content with the faith once delivered to the saints. I am not afraid to say that a new idea never originated in this seminary. Their theological method was very simple. The Bible is the Word of God. That is to be assumed or proved. If granted: then it follows, that what the Bible says, God says. That ends the matter.[48]

The Western Theological Seminary professors would have agreed with him. They understood themselves to be called to nurture the

---

[47]  Gerrit J. Ten Zythoff, *Sources of Secession,* Historical Series of the Reformed Church in America, no. 17 (Grand Rapids: Eerdmans, 1987), 43-45.

[48]  Channing Renwick Jeschke, *The Briggs Case: The Focus of a Study in Nineteenth Century Presbyterian History,* diss. (Chicago: Divinity School of the Univ. of Chicago, 1966), 57.

church in that faith that had always been present since the days of the apostles. As the world around them changed, they could give new perspectives on old truths but not introduce new ideas that ignored or contradicted the old truths. The Standards of Unity served to keep the church on a steady course without being deflected by every wind of doctrine. The Reverend Henry Dosker was typical of all of them when he wrote on the twenty-fifth anniversary of his ordination,

> [I chose] "to know nothing among you other than Christ and him crucified." And then, in all my endeavors, to hold high the banner of Reformed truth under which the fathers fought, and which is the inheritance of thankful children, or at least they must be thankful.[49]

The three Reformed confessions played a much larger role in the midwestern leaders' theological orientation than did the writings of John Calvin. In their study and teaching of systematic theology, they referred far more often to the "scholastic"[50] Reformed theologians of the seventeenth and eighteenth centuries than they did to Calvin. They accepted the Federal Theology with its emphasis on the covenant of works with Adam, as set forth in the Westminster Confession.[51] They held to the Anselmic tradition of the doctrine of the atonement, as it had been modified in the Heidelberg Catechism.[52] They referred to themselves constantly as "Reformed" and were hesitant to call

---

[49]  Dosker, "Aan Een Oud Studie-Makker te Holland," *De Hope*, May 4, 1904.

[50]  "Scholastic" is often a term of scorn used against theologians who carry out technical arguments, such as "how many angels can dance on the head of a pin." In this book "scholastic theologians" are held in respect even though their method is not used. The use of the scholastic method of teaching by Reformed theologians such as Gijsbertus Voetius in the seventeenth century does not in itself indicate that Voetius differed essentially from John Calvin, for example. "The term 'scholastic' indicated an academic style and method....a Reformed or Calvinist scholar who used the scholastic method in the classroom of a university would not use it in preaching or in catechizing the young," Richard A. Muller, "John Calvin and Later Calvinism: The Identity of the Reformed Tradition," in David Bagchi and David C. Steinmetz, eds., *Reformation Theology* (Cambridge, U.K.: Cambridge Univ. Press, 2004), 141.

[51]  Albertus Pieters was the first Western Theology Seminary professor to criticize the Federal Theology teaching of the covenant of works ("Objections to Federal Theology," lecture given to Western Theological Seminary Adelphi Society, October 16, 1951, Pieters Box 1 WTS/JAH).

[52]  Q. 12-18.

themselves "Calvinists." On the whole they did not favor using the name of John Calvin for congregations, programs, or institutions, although there were some exceptions.

In 1891, when Abraham Kuyper was advocating his worldview that came to be known as "neo-Calvinism,"[53] The Reverend Nicholas Steffens, Reformed Church pastor and professor, sought to define the "Calvinistic perspective" for the midwestern Reformed communities. He stated that Calvinism is a perspective on life and the world rather than a unique set of doctrines. The Calvinistic world view is based on the holy scriptures; its central principle is the glory and honor of God. It emphasizes that God is creator of all things and that God will fulfill the divine purposes through his activity in the world. God is the Alpha and the Omega; human beings are not the center or goal of creation. God's glory is to be reflected not only in human beings as the image of God, but also in the church, family, society, and culture, including the state. The earth must be filled with the glory of God.[54]

However much they accepted the work of John Calvin as one of the fountainheads of their Reformed traditions, midwestern theologians were careful to make a distinction between "Calvinist" and "Reformed" in preference to the latter. Henry Dosker in 1901 pointed out that according to the Dutch theologian Herman Bavinck, Calvin himself did not teach any unique Calvinistic truth. Calvin intended to preach nothing else than the pure truth of God and the unadulterated gospel of Jesus Christ. Dosker agreed with Bavinck that the word "Calvinism" may never be used to draw lines of division between churches, because Reformed churches can never allow themselves to become sectarian. Dosker complained at the end of his article that unfortunately there are

---

[53]  Kuyper's Stone Lectures at Princeton in 1898 introduced his neo-Calvinism to Americans in *Lectures on Calvinism*, a book that is still in print (Eerdmans, 2007) and remains influential among many American evangelicals. See John Bolt, "From Princeton to Wheaton: The Course of Neo-Calvinism in North America," in George Harrinck and Dirk van Keulen, eds., *Vicissitudes of Reformed Theology in the Twentieth Century*, 163-84. Abraham Kuyper was the leader of the "Doleantie" believers who seceded from the Nederlandse Hervormde Kerk and ultimately joined with the seceders of 1834 to form the *Gereformeerde Kerken in Nederland* in 1892. Kuyper was a brilliant theologian, educator, newspaper man, and statesman who for several years served as prime minister of the Netherlands.

[54]  Steffens, "De Calvinistische Wereldbeschouwing," *De Hope*, March 11, 1891. Steffens probably stood closer to Kuyper's neo-Calvinism than did any of the other nineteenth-century leaders, but he did not seek to implement Kuyper's political or social programs in the American context.

those among us in the Reformed Church who ignore Bavinck's warning against using "Calvinism" as a divisive term.[55]

Although they agreed with Hodge that no new ideas should be introduced throughout the time of their ministries, they had to use all the theological power at their disposal to reaffirm the old truths in the constantly changing context of American life and Protestant Christianity. In the rapidly changing American culture of the nineteenth and twentieth centuries, there were not only theological, sociological, and scientific threats on the horizon, but the nature of their individual and communal piety was shifting and new denominational patterns were emerging in the decades between 1866-1966.

---

[55]  Henry Dosker, *De Hope*, November 20, 1901. Herman Bavinck was a colleague of Kuyper in defining the movement that has come to be known as "neo-Calvinism."

CHAPTER 2

# The Practice of Piety: Worshiping God in a New Land

## Declaring the Glory of God

The glory of God is the central principle of Reformed piety and worship, according to the midwestern pastors who led their people in the Dutch colonies in the Midwest.[1] The ministers who came after Van Raalte taught that worship must be God-centered rather than human-centered.[2] Professor Gerrit Dubbink at Western Theological Seminary was firm in teaching that the two must not be played off against each other. He taught that "the supreme end is the declarative glory of his name; the subordinate end, the happiness of his creatures. We insist on both."[3]

In carrying out the ministry of Word and sacrament, the doctrine that all of life must be lived to the glory of God cannot be overestimated.

[1] Gerrit Dubbink, "Preface, Chapter I," *Systematic Theology,* 1. Unpublished course lectures located in WTS/JAH.
[2] Nicholas Steffens, "Het Goddelijke in de Godsdienst," *De Hope,* April 20, 1887.
[3] Dubbink, "Preface, Chapter I," *Systematic Theology,* 13.

25

Nicholas Steffens, one of the first two full-time theological professors at Western Theological Seminary, represented the consensus in the community that neither the doctrine of predestination nor the doctrine of total depravity is the central Reformed principle, in spite of the popular stereotype of Calvinism. The central principle is the glory of God. This principle is even more central than the atonement of Christ, since Jesus in his highly priestly prayer on his last night clearly spoke of the glory of God as the purpose for which he had been sent into the world (John 17:1-26).[4]

When it gathered for worship on the Sabbath Day, the church celebrated not only the redemptive activity of God in Christ, but it also glorified God for the divine activity of creation and providence. The whole world as a creation of God was intended to be a hymn of praise to God. It was made to be a dwelling place of God, a temple with heaven as a throne and the earth as God's footstool. On the morning of the first Sabbath Day, the world was at rest with potential to attain its glorious goal.[5] God made human beings "as a final and crowning feature of that creation, which was to show forth his glory."[6] Because the activity of God relates to everything and everyone in creation, Reformed preachers insisted that they had to preach the "whole counsel" of God as set forth in the scriptures rather than confine themselves to a narrower focus on the conversion of sinners and spiritual experience of believers. Preachers may not constantly focus on one or another favorite theme, such as the love of God, the total depravity of the human race, or one or another theological issue.[7]

## Attending to the Preaching of the Word

Regular attendance at services on both Sunday morning and afternoon was characteristic of the piety of the Reformed colonies in the Midwest. The tradition of two services on Sunday dated back to the sixteenth-century practice in the palatinate where the Heidelberg Catechism was written. There the morning service included the celebration of Holy Communion. The afternoon service was intended

[4]   Nicholas Steffens, "The Principle of Reformed Protestantism and Foreign Missions," *Presbyterian and Reformed Review*, 5/18 (April, 1884), 244-45.

[5]   Nicholas Steffens, "Schepping en Wedergeboorte," *De Hope*, September 1, 1886.

[6]   John W. Beardslee, *Notes on Messianic Prophecy* (Holland, Mich.: Privately printed, 1908, located in Western Theological Seminary special collections), 5.

[7]   Nicholas Steffens, "Niets dan Liefde?" *De Hope*, August 25, 1897.

to be the time when the Heidelberg Catechism was taught, especially for the youth. In the Netherlands, the morning service became known as the *Eeredienst* (service of worship) and the afternoon service as the *Leerdienst* (teaching service).

Nothing was more essential to Reformed piety than hearing the Word of God preached. The Synod of Dort emphasized that when it wrote:

> And that men may be brought to faith, God mercifully sends, to whom and when he will, messengers of this most joyful message, by whose ministry men are called to repentance and faith in Christ the crucified. *And how are they to believe in him of whom they have not heard? And how are they to hear without a preacher? And how can men preach unless they are sent?* (Rom. 10: 4, 15).[8]

The reformers believed that church attendance and hearing sermons is crucial because the Holy Spirit comes with and through the Word preached. Hearing sermons is quite different from hearing lectures on theology or morality. Such lectures call for an intellectual response rather than conversion of hearts. Moreover, the Holy Spirit does not normally work mystically apart from the Word of God by some sort of "inner light." Instead, while the Word of God is being preached, the Holy Spirit is working in the hearts and minds of those who hear. The Canons of Dort are emphatic on this point and worthy of being quoted at length:

> But when God carries out his good pleasure in the elect and works in them true repentance, he sees to it that the Gospel is externally preached to them and that their minds are effectually enlightened by the Holy Spirit, so that they may rightly understand and discern the things of the Spirit of God. He also instills the mighty working of the same life-giving Spirit into the inmost recesses of the heart; opens the heart that is closed; softens the heart that is hard; purifies the heart that is impure. He infuses new qualities into the will and makes the dead will alive; the wicked will, good; the unwilling, willing; the rebellious, obedient; and so moves and strengthens the will that, like a good tree, it can bring forth fruits of good works.[9]

---

[8]    Canons of Dort, I/3.

[9]    Ibid., III/IV, 11. We will come back to this article of Dort in chapter 4 when we consider the doctrine of election and the *ordo salutis* (the "way of salvation").

In accord with the articles of the Canons of Dort, midwestern Reformed ministers taught that the preaching of the gospel is made effective by the Holy Spirit. The action of the Holy Spirit rather than the rhetorical art of the preacher is decisive. The parable of the sower in Mark 4:1-20 was a favorite passage for preachers for explaining why people responded in differing ways when they heard the Word of God. The Reverend E.C. Oggel explained in his sermon on sowing and reaping that the response comes as people are moved by the Holy Spirit who requires a response, whether it be positive or negative, from those who hear.[10]

It was essential to preach and hear the Word of God from week to week because the Holy Spirit does not normally work apart from the Word. The Reverend Dr. John R. Mulder, professor of theology at Western Theological Seminary, summed up the theology of his predecessors when he taught the distinction between the "external call" and the "internal call" exercised by the Holy Spirit. The external call reaches all who hear the gospel, but it is resisted by many. The internal call is irresistible and efficacious and leads to faith and perseverance in obedience to Christ.[11] In making the distinction between the two types of call, however, it is crucial not to separate them. A mysticism that emphasizes an inner light or spiritual illumination apart from the external Word must be resisted.

The style of a sermon had to be consistent with the fact that its content had to expound the meaning of the scriptures and to call those who heard to faith and obedience. The Reverend Peter Moerdyk wrote a series of articles on preaching in the Netherlands in the sixteenth and seventeenth centuries. His clear intent was to provide advice for his own colleagues. He pointed out that the preacher should speak in a plain style, avoiding the use of Hebrew, Greek, and other foreign words. The style should have a measure of dignity and include vocabulary

---

[10]  E. Christian Oggel, "Zaaien en Maaien," *De Hope*, September 9, 1868. Engelbert Christian Oggel (1841-1910) was born in the Netherlands and graduated from New Brunswick Theological Seminary in 1866. He served pastorates in Michigan, Illinois, and New York. He was editor of *De Hope*, 1869-1871.

[11]  John R. Mulder, unpub. course notes on Christology and Soteriology, located in WTS/JAH, 23-24. See also Egbert Winter, "Soteriology," unpub. course notes on theology, chapter II, located in WTS/JAH, 19-24. Regarding the call of the gospel, Winter wrote that this comes "and speaks to all alike, and unconditionally....This means that God is in earnest about the matter. His love and grace are presented, and the call is attended with the strongest motives," ibid., 19-20.

Peter Moerdyk was the youngest member of the pioneer 1866 graduating class at Hope College and its last survivor. Alongside his pastoral and teaching responsibilities, he served the Particular Synod of Chicago as its stated clerk from 1885 until the day of his death. "Dr. Moerdyke was friendly, a good conversationalist, well versed on various subjects; but withal a man of very decided convictions, and did not hesitate on occasion to defend his views. He could indeed be very sharp in stating his views. He was a fearless man, aggressive in debate, but having stated his position, he also knew how to respect the opinions of others."—*Acts and Proceedings*, 1924, 675.

*Fiftieth Anniversary Catalog of Hope College*, 1916, 44.

Rev. Peter Moerdyke, A. M.
Assistant Professor 1871-1873

The Rev. Peter
Moerdyk D.D.
(1845-1923)

appropriate to the congregation. He advised against speaking in slang or colloquial language that could demean urgency of the message. A sermon should be positive in the sense that it did not spend too much energy in arguments against opponents and old heresies. It should not seek to impress the congregation by expounding hidden allegorical, typological, and prophetic ideas that supposedly underlay the text.[12] Moerdyke's advice is a good representation of the nature of preaching in the midwestern Reformed Church in America during the century from 1866-1966.

## Preaching the Word in Accordance with the Heidelberg Catechism

The Synod of Dort sought to insure that the full counsel of God would be preached by including Article 76, which stipulated,

> Every minister shall in the ordinary afternoon service on the Lord's Day, briefly explain the system of Christian doctrine comprehended in the Catechism, adopted by the Reformed churches; so that if practicable, the explanation may be annually

[12]  Peter Moerdyke, "De Nederduitsche Predikaties in Vroegere Eeuwen, II," *De Hope*, November 8, 1905. Peter Moerdyke (1845-1923) was born in the Netherlands and was a member of the first class to graduate from Hope College in 1866 and Western Theological Seminary in 1869. He served Reformed churches in Michigan, Illinois, and Indiana. For information about his very significant ministry at the English language Trinity American Reformed Church in Chicago, 1892-1907, see Robert Swierenga, *Dutch Chicago*, 141-48, and consult the many other references listed in the index.

completed, according to the sections made for that purpose in said Catechism.[13]

The stipulation in the church order that ministers must use the Heidelberg Catechism as a guide to the subject matter and doctrines to be covered annually in their sermons served to ensure that preachers would lay before their congregations the great teachings of the Christian faith. The catechism is effective both as an instrument to instruct members of the church on the basic theological doctrines of the church and as a pastoral guide for believers on the path of spiritual maturation. On matters of theology, it teaches the absolute necessity of the atoning work of Jesus Christ, who is the Mediator of salvation. It provides an exposition of the Apostles' Creed, the doctrines of faith and the sacraments, the Ten Commandments, and the Lord's Prayer. In dealing with matters of theology and biblical exposition, it never loses its focus on the salvation of the one who is being taught and questioned. It teaches that there are three things we must know in order to have comfort or assurance in matters of life and death:

> First, the greatness of my sin and wretchedness. Second, how I am freed from all my sins and their wretched consequences. Third, what gratitude I owe to God for such redemption.[14]

The Heidelberg Catechism opens with a question about what gives us assurance of our salvation. Martin Luther's answer to that question was that our assurance lies in the fact that justification before God comes by faith through grace alone, apart from any good works of

[13]   Daniel J. Meeter, *Meeting Each Other in Doctrine, Liturgy & Government*, Historical Series of the Reformed Church in America, no. 24 (Grand Rapids: Eerdmans, 1993), 87. The Heidelberg Catechism includes 129 questions and answers, apportioned in fifty-two Sundays. In 1833 the Reformed Church amended its constitution to allow for the exposition of the catechism to be covered during a period of four years. See Edward T. Corwin, *A Digest of Constitutional and Synodical Legislation of the Reformed Church in America* (New York: Board of Publication of the Reformed Church in America, 1906), 315. The relaxation of this rule was one of the objections made by some churches in western Michigan that seceded from the Reformed Church in America in 1850 to form what became the Christian Reformed Church. The 1857 controversy has been covered by a number of writers; a convenient summary can be found in Elton J. Bruins and Robert P. Swierenga, *Family Quarrels in the Dutch Reformed Churches of the 19th Century*, Historical Series of the Reformed Church in America, no. 32 (Grand Rapids: Eerdmans, 1999), 60-103.

[14]   Q. 2.

devotion or benevolence that we do. Although the catechism includes Luther's doctrine in Questions 59-62, it opens by asking the believer for a personal confession of assurance of salvation. The answer called for does not require any introspection about the quality of one's faith or spiritual maturity. The answer is grounded in the fact that the believer belongs to God, the Father, Son, and Holy Spirit.

> Question 1: *What is your only comfort, in life and in death?*
>
> Answer: That I belong—body and soul, in life and in death—not to myself but to my faithful Savior, Jesus Christ, who at the cost of his own blood has fully paid for all my sins and has completely freed me from the dominion of the devil; that he protects me so well that without the will of my Father in heaven not a hair can fall from my head; indeed, that everything must fit his purpose for my salvation. Therefore, by his Holy Spirit, he also assures me of eternal life, and makes me wholeheartedly willing and ready from now on to live for him.

Given the warm personal tone of the Heidelberg Catechism, one would expect that sermons related to its questions and answers would also be very pastoral and personal in nature. Unfortunately, that was not always the case. Catechism sermons became "doctrinal sermons." People complained about sermons that were more like theological lectures than sermons intended for their spiritual edification. Ministers and people alike became reluctant to deal with the catechism every week. The result was that in many areas the custom of catechetical preaching eroded.[15]

Complaints about too much "doctrinal preaching" at times were related to a deeper issue. The extreme pietists wanted "experiential preaching" rather than an emphasis on the doctrines taught in the catechism. Nicholas Steffens wrote that the issue was whether one must preach Christ or whether one must preach the Christian experience.[16] Steffens taught that we must not seek to choose between the two. The scriptures teach us that Christ must be preached, but whenever Christ

---

[15]   The Reformed Church in America *Book of Church Order* today requires that the "points of doctrine" rather than the questions and answers themselves must be handled at least once in four years. In the emphasis on "points of doctrine," the warm personal tone of the questions and answers can be lost (*Book of Church Order,* 1,I,2, Sec. 11, f.)

[16]   Steffens, "De Harmonie Tusschen het Voorwerpelijke en het Onderwerpelijke in den Godsdienst," *De Hope,* April 2, 1890; and "Voorwerpelijk of Onderwerpelijk?" *De Hope,* April 4, 1900.

is preached, then Christians are born, nurtured, and strengthened. True preaching is both objective and subjective.[17]

The catechism encouraged preachers to sustain an appropriate balance between the objective and subjective elements in sermons. For example, in its exposition of Questions 33 and 34, the catechism reads,

> Q. 33: *Why is he called "God's only-begotten Son," since we also are called God's children?*
>
> Because Christ alone is God's own eternal Son, whereas we are accepted for his sake as children of God by grace.

> Q. 34: *Why do we call him "Our Lord"?*
>
> Because not with gold or silver but at the cost of his blood, he has redeemed us body and soul from sin and all the dominion of the devil, and has bought us for his very own.

The Heidelberg Catechism was especially influential through the requirement that the Ten Commandments (Q. 92-115) be handled in sermons every year, or at least once in every four years. Sermonic exposition of the Ten Commandments was to take place in the context of the third section of the catechism, which deals with thankfulness to God for salvation, rather than in the first section, which deals with sin and depravity. John Hesselink defined the role of the Ten Commandments in the catechism when he wrote:

> God revealed his will through his law and bound them to himself, not to subject them to a new bondage, but to guarantee their freedom. For only in the obedience and service of their true Lord could they enjoy any enduring freedom. The Decalog, therefore, was a "document of freedom which Jehovah gave to his people whom he had redeemed from Egypt."[18]

---

[17] Ibid. The midwestern leaders in the nineteenth century constantly developed their thought in terms of "objective truth" (especially of science) and "subjective truth," that in theology they related to Schleiermaker's "feeling of absolute dependence." They did not have available to them the concept of "truth as encounter" (intersubjectivity) of later twentieth century theologians. See John E. Kuizenga, "Truth as Encounter," *Western Theological Seminary Bulletin*, II/2 (1948), 4-9. In their doctrine of the Holy Spirit as active both in the inspiration of the Bible and in giving of faith to the believer, they remained open to the language of truth as encounter as well as a source of doctrine.

[18] I. John Hesselink, "The Law of God," in Donald J. Bruggink, ed., *Guilt, Grace, and Gratitude: A Commentary on the Heidelberg Catechism Commemorating*

Midwestern leaders were aware that emphasis on the Ten Commandments could tend toward legalism. They consistently warned against any idea that one could gain any merit by works and that believers must be on guard against legalism. This issue will be discussed further in chapter 5 on the practice of piety in a godly community.

## The Word in the Liturgy

Between 1866 and World War II, midwestern leaders maintained that nothing should get in the way of the plain preaching of the Word. Henry Dosker wrote that the pulpit must occupy the central place in Reformed church liturgy and architecture. Everything else, organ and music, Lord's Table and baptismal font, must remain subordinate to the preaching of the Word.[19] In almost every church, the pulpit stood in the center of a raised platform, while the Lord's Table was on the floor below in front of the pulpit.[20] The use of liturgical candles, crosses, or other sacred vessels encountered great resistance. Not only were such items opposed because there was resistance to anything that resembled Roman Catholicism, but also because it was firmly held that anything that is added to the Word or sacraments actually serves to distract from their true focus.

---

*its 400th Anniversary* (New York: Half Moon Press, 1963), 198. The clause within the quotation marks is from J. J. Stamm, *Der Dekalog im Lichte der neueren Forschung* (Bern: Verlag Paul Haupt, 1958), 55.

[19]   Henry Dosker, "Wekelijksch Budget," *De Hope*, July 21, 1897. The Dutch immigrants were accustomed to the use of organs in worship in the Netherlands, although objections to the way the organist played did arise. "Mr. Th." in 1875 wrote that he favored the use of an organ, but objected to allowing the organist to play in interlude between each stanza ("Iets over een Kerkgezang," *De Hope*, May 19, 1875). In the same issue, C. Doesburg responded by defending the use of interludes to give time for the members of the congregation to take a breath. He also advocated the use of four-part harmony. He wrote that the psalms were being sung too slowly and suggested that singing societies be organized to improve the singing and teach harmony. Doesburg was a member of the faculty of Hope College and for many years the business manager for *De Hope*.

[20]   Its placement was more likely due to the fact that the vast majority of American Protestant churches in the Congregational, Presbyterian, Methodist, and Baptist traditions did it that way. The small size and placement of the Table where it was inconspicuous served to emphasis the primary place of the preaching of the Word. See Donald J. Bruggink, and Carl Droppers, *Christ and Architecture* (Grand Rapids: Eerdmans, 1965), 220-21.

During the decades at the turn of the nineteenth century, there was a general interest in liturgical reform in American Protestant worship. The Reformed Church in America was also engaged in a process of revising its liturgy, but midwestern leaders showed little enthusiasm for the process. In most of the congregations the liturgy was limited to the bare essentials, consisting of the

> Call to worship
> Invocation
> Salutation: "Grace and peace..."
> Opening psalm or hymn
> Reading of the Ten Commandments and the Two Great Laws
> Reading of scripture
> Pastoral prayer (popularly known as the "Long Prayer")
> Psalm or hymn (offering received during singing)
> Sermon
> Prayer after the sermon
> Closing psalm or hymn
> Benediction.

By the turn of the twentieth century, some congregations were beginning to add an anthem by the choir. The singing of the psalms and hymns by the congregation was still considered to be very important. Henry Dosker opposed allowing a choir to replace the congregation for the singing of any of the hymns. He knew that it was true that in many congregations the quality of singing left much to be desired, but he believed it was better to encourage the congregation in its singing than to shift the responsibility to a choir. When there was a choir, it must remain clearly subordinate in the worship service.[21]

By 1911, Steffens was lamenting the fact that the liturgy was taking more and more time away from the sermon. Previously it had been customary for people to regard everything prior to the sermon as introduction leading up to the sermon. After the sermon, the service could be brought quickly to an end. The simple Reformed liturgy had properly replaced the Roman Catholic Mass with all its complexity and pageantry, and it was believed that the Mass had left the people without knowledge, and that they had sunk ever deeper into ignorance. Steffens bemoaned the new situation, in which the music with organ and choir became a "concert" and the sermon, lasting only fifteen minutes, becomes a "talk." Steffens included a prayer in his short essay, "O Lord,

---

[21]   Dosker, "Wekelijksch Budget," *De Hope,* July 21, 1897.

give us longer sermons; we do not mean terribly long sermons, but give real sermons that are not just little 'talks!'"[22]

Midwestern Reformed Church ministers did not follow a church lectionary from Sunday to Sunday. They and their congregations believed that it was important for a pastor to know the spiritual needs of the congregation and be free to choose scripture texts for edifying sermons. Series of sermons based on continual reading through a book of the Bible, as well as series preached on a topic of special interest, were often appreciated by congregations. The provision in the Palatinate church order that the afternoon service was the time to preach using the Heidelberg Catechism was often modified so that catechism preaching would take place in the morning service.[23]

Little change took place in the liturgical structure of midwestern Sunday morning worship until the revised Reformed Church Liturgy was adopted in 1966 and published in 1968.[24] The order for Sunday morning worship in the revised liturgy was somewhat more complex than that in general use in midwestern congregations. It included a prayer of confession of sin, words of assurance, and the summary of the Law, the singing of a psalm or the Gloria Patri, and a prayer for illumination before the reading of scripture. One innovation for many congregations was the placing of the offering and general prayers after the sermon. The shift undermined the idea that the sermon is the climax of the service around which all the other elements revolve.[25] On the whole, the new order was well received and adopted for use in many congregations.

## The Sacramental Presence of Christ at the Lord's Table[26]

It is difficult for Protestants today to appreciate the bewilderment that came over multitudes of members of the church in the sixteenth

[22]    Steffens, "Liturgiek en Homiletiek," *De Hope*, September 26, 1911.
[23]    The Palatinate church order was given to the church in the Heidelberg area along with the Heidelberg Catechism.
[24]    Gerrit T. Vander Lugt, ed., *The Liturgy of the Reformed Church in America together with the Psalter* (New York: Board of Education, 1968).
[25]    Ibid., 7-17. Aldrich Sonnega, a Reformed Church member in Muskegon, Michigan, wrote to complain: "At one time the pulpit was called 'the throne of Protestantism' but it has lost its unique place in the world and now also in the Church. Formalism has been a plague throughout church history. There is evidence that liturgical worship does not charge people to think," "Letters to the Editor," *Church Herald*, April 3, 1964, 16.
[26]    Consideration of the sacrament of baptism is postponed to chapter 3, on church order.

century when town councils and the nobility in northern Europe replaced the Mass with Protestant worship.[27] Before Martin Luther entered the scene, people knew that when they went to church, Jesus Christ was *right there* in his body and blood on the altar. Every time the Mass was celebrated, a great miracle took place when the consecrated bread and wine actually became the body and blood of Christ. So holy was the transubstantiated bread and wine that special care had to be taken that none of it be spilled. The laity could receive the bread, but to avoid sacrilege the wine was not offered to the laity. Although the faithful could attend the Mass often and be in the presence of Christ on the altar, they did not have to commune every time they came; in fact many communed only once a year and then only received the bread. It was enough that they were present, even though they understood few of the Latin words of the Mass.

The rejection of the medieval doctrine of transubstantiation took the heart right out of Roman Catholic piety. If the bread and wine are not literally the body and blood of Christ, then how is Christ present with us? Martin Luther answered that Christ is present "in, with, and under" the bread and the wine and that although Christ is ascended into heaven, that his human body is so united with Christ's divinity that it is everywhere present where the Lord's Supper is celebrated.[28]

[27]   Protestant historians usually have highlighted the corruption, theological deficiencies, and popular resentment against the hierarchy at the time of Reformation while ignoring the strong hold that the Roman Catholic sacramental system had on the common people. For a description of the strength of late medieval Roman Catholic practice of piety and its persistence into the Protestant era, see J. William Black, *Reformation Pastors: Richard Baxter and the Ideal of the Reformed Pastor* (Waynesboro: Paternoster Press, 2004), 20-24. Richard Baxter's seventeenth-century book, *The Reformed Pastor*, was influential in shaping pastoral practice in Puritan England and America as well as in the Netherlands. Albertus Van Raalte had a copy of Baxter's book, *A Call to the Unconverted*, in his library. Earl Wm. Kennedy has shown recently that suspicion of Baxter's orthodoxy played a role in the decision on the part of several ministers and congregations to secede from the Classis of Holland in 1857; see Earl Wm. Kennedy, "Richard Baxter: An English Fox in a Dutch Chicken Coop?" in *A Goodly Heritage*, 121-61.

[28]   The midwestern Reformed Church leaders, following the Heidelberg Catechism, all rejected the Lutheran position; see Heidelberg Catechism (Q & A 48); Egbert Winter's comment on the "ubiquity" of Christ's body is typical: "The ubiquity of our Lord's body is absurd. That body can be present only in one place at the same time. And herewith the basis for the whole theory vanishes from under it." *Dogmatic Theology* (course notes, WTS/JAH, 159).

Ulrich Zwingli in Zurich suspected that Luther's teaching only opened the door once again to what in Zwingli's mind was Roman Catholic superstition and magic. He tried to turn the focus away from the question of just how Christ is present. He taught that the Lord's Supper *recalls* the once-for-all sacrifice of Christ on the cross for our salvation.[29] The different understandings of how Christ is present and the extent to which he is present in the Lord's Supper led to (or grew out of) quite different expressions of Christian devotion.

Our concern here is to understand the theology and practice of the midwestern Reformed Church with regard to the Lord's Supper, without further regard for other Christian traditions. In his long series of articles in *De Hope* in 1894, Egbert Winter pointed out that Reformed piety takes account of not only the presence of Christ but also the absence of his body. Thus it lives with the experience of the absence as well as the presence of Christ. The experience of the absence of Christ's body is essential because it means that we have confidence that Christ's once-for-all atonement on the cross is a completed event. It is not to be completed in the daily offer of the Mass.[30] Having completed his work of redemption, Jesus ascended to the right hand of God to our continuing benefit, because,

> First, that he is our Advocate in the presence of his Father in heaven. Second, that we have our flesh in heaven as a sure pledge that he, as the Head, will also take us, his members, up to himself. Third, that he sends us his Spirit as a counterpledge by whose power we seek what is above, where Christ is, sitting at the right hand of God, and not things that are on earth.[31]

Experience of the absence of Christ from the earth in the present age has made Reformed believers more conscious of the redemptive and

---

[29]  Zwingli has often been misinterpreted to mean that the Lord's Supper is simply a memorial feast that brings to mind what Christ accomplished in his atonement. The re-calling of the once-for-all sacrifice of Christ involves the present reality of the relation of Christ to the believer; it is far more than simply re-telling the story of the formation of the American Declaration of Independence, for example. Winter taught that we accept Zwingli's teaching but move beyond it ("Het H. Avondmaal," *De Hope*, October 24, 1894). For a careful exposition of Zwingli's theology of the sacraments, see W. Peter Stephens, "The Theology of Zwingli," in David Bagschi and David C. Steinmetz, eds., *The Cambridge Companion to Reformation Theology* (Cambridge, U.K.: Cambridge Univ. Press, 2004), esp. 84-91, 96-98.

[30]  Winter, "Het H. Avondmaal," *De Hope*, October 24, 1894.

[31]  Heidelberg Catechism, 49.

providential activity of the Holy Spirit through human history than is the case for other Christian traditions. Not only is there a strong consciousness of the completed nature of Christ's task on earth, but there remains a strong expectation and longing for his return at the end of the age when "he will take us up...to himself" in "heavenly joy and glory."[32]

Winter went on to ask how we can hold communion with Christ who is absent in the body. At this point he stood firmly within the Reformed tradition when he said that Christ is really *sacramentally* present and united with us in faith with the bread and wine when we partake of the Holy Communion.[33] If one asks why it is necessary to participate in the celebration of the Lord's Supper, the answer is that

> God has ordained for the support of bodily and earthly life earthly and common bread that serves this purpose and is common for all men, as is life itself. But for the support of the spiritual and heavenly life, which believers have, he has sent a living bread which came down from heaven, namely, Jesus Christ, who nourishes and supports the spiritual life of believers, as he is eaten, that is, appropriated and received by faith, in the Spirit.[34]

Christ has promised to be with us in the Holy Communion and we take him at his word. Winter's comments reflect the Reformed faith as expressed in the Belgic Confession:

> This supper is a spiritual table at which Christ communicates himself to us with all his benefits and gives us to enjoy himself as well as the merits of his suffering and death: nourishing, strengthening, and comforting our poor comfortless souls by the eating of his flesh, and refreshing and gladdening them by the drinking of his blood.[35]

The Lord's Supper was truly a *Holy Communion* of the believers with Christ, with whom they were *sacramentally united* in the eating of his body and drinking of his blood. Therefore special measures had to be taken lest one partake of the sacrament in "an unworthy manner" (1 Cor. 11:27). Although John Calvin had called for a weekly celebration of the sacrament, almost all midwestern Reformed churches celebrated

[32]   Ibid., 52.
[33]   Winter, "Het H. Avondmaal."
[34]   Belgic Confession, 35.
[35]   Ibid.

it once every three months. They expressed fear that the Lord's Supper would become a mere formality or a superstitious rite if celebrated too frequently. Their reluctance to observe the sacrament frequently was closely related to the fear of eating and drinking unworthily and to the linkage of participation in the sacrament to the exercise of personal and ecclesiastical discipline.

The Reformed Church *Liturgy* called upon those intending to participate in the Supper to examine themselves beforehand. This usually meant that an announcement was made in worship that on the following Sunday the sacrament would be observed. On the Sunday before Communion, the liturgical form of preparation would call upon members of the congregation to examine themselves individually on three points: first, that they consider their sins and then humble themselves before God, recognizing the great wrath of God against sin; second, that they examine their own hearts, whether they believe the faithful promise of God that all their sins are forgiven through the passion and death of Jesus Christ; and third, whether they purpose henceforth to show thankfulness to God in all things and intend to put aside all that is evil while walking in love and peace with their neighbors.[36] The self-examination prior to receiving the Lord's Supper was a powerful encouragement for living a pure, honest, disciplined life in the family and community. It encouraged people to restore broken relationships and to avoid activities that were frivolous or harmful to themselves and others.

The call to self-examination was paralleled by the provision in the church order that the board of elders had responsibility prior to every celebration of the Lord's Supper to ask whether there were any members in the congregation who were in need of special admonition or discipline prior to partaking of the sacrament.[37] Because God's covenant was with the church as well as with the individuals in the church, the disciplined life of the individual had its counterpart in the disciplined life of the congregation. The discipline exercised in relation to the Lord's Table had three purposes: to promote the purity of the

---

[36]   *The Liturgy of the Reformed Church in America,* 61-62.

[37]   This provision remained in force in the *Book of Church Order* of the Reformed Church in America throughout the whole century of our study, 1866-1966. The responsibility is no longer specifically related to participation in the sacrament. The present provision is that the board of elders, at each regular meeting, must determine "whether any members are: a. in need of special care regarding their spiritual condition...." (*Book of Church Order,* 1/1,5, 3.a).

church, to benefit the offender, and to vindicate the honor of the Lord
Jesus Christ.[38] With those purposes in mind, elders felt responsible
to admonish those who neglected attendance at Sunday worship, to
warn those who were in danger of going astray, and to place under
ecclesiastical discipline those who were notorious sinners. Elders
and pastors also encouraged believers to examine whether their sins
included spiritual pride, censoriousness of others, lack of humility,
and lack of the spirit of obedience. The result of the personal self-
examination combined with the oversight of the board of elders was
the establishment of a well disciplined community with a low crime
rate, stable families, and a good educational system. Unfortunately,
the supervisory role and rules of elders also could result in legalism, a
measure of hypocrisy, and covert resentment against authority on the
part of members.[39]

Until 1966, "The Office for the Administration of the Lord's
Supper" used in the Reformed Church remained close to that from the
time of the Synod of Dort and the first Reformed Church Communion
service held in 1628. The revision previous to 1966, that of 1906, still
remained firmly in the tradition of Dort. [40] The revised liturgy adopted

[38]   The Reformed Church in America's *Liturgy* in 1882 placed the order
for "Church Discipline" immediately following the order for "The
Administration of the Lord's Supper" (*The Liturgy of the Reformed Church in
America*, 1882), 85. The 1907 edition placed it on pages 92-95. The "Order
for the Administration of the Lord's Supper" was included on pages 29-
47, thus placing the exercise of discipline at a greater distance from the
Holy Communion. The 1968 edition of the *Liturgy* followed the 1907
arrangement, placing "The Order for the Sacrament of the Lord's Supper"
on pages 63-70 and "The Orders for Church Discipline" on pages 194-95,
*The Liturgy of the Reformed Church in America*.

[39]   Henry Dosker in 1881 reflected on a question asked of a theological student
at his examination for licensure, "Does the church order permit an elder to
preside at the celebration of the Lord's Supper?" The student responded
that it is not permitted. Since the student had answered correctly, the
examiner moved on to the next question. Dosker would like to see the
classis reflect further on the question. He believed that the real task of elder
is oversight of the congregation rather than preaching or leading at the
time of the Lord's Supper, but he was also aware that in order to meet the
needs of congregations in the early days of the Afscheiding, some elders
did preside ("De Bedienaars der Sacramenten," *De Hope*, 7, December 14,
1881).

[40]   In developing the revision of 1966, the Committee on Liturgy reached back
to the Reformation era liturgies that had come into place in Strasbourg
under the leadership of Martin Bucer and in Geneva under the influence of
John Calvin while retaining much of the strength of the liturgy traditionally

in 1966 reflected a shift in the practice of piety throughout the Reformed Church between 1906 and 1966. The tone of the 1966 order was joyful in contrast to the somber tone of the 1906 order, which placed heavy emphasis upon the depth of our sin and the sacrifice and atonement of Christ on the cross. The 1906 liturgy was heavily didactic in nature. It required the reading of a long exposition of the meaning of the Lord's Supper. It was followed by the admonition to "humble ourselves before God and with true faith implore His grace." The admonition was followed by the prayer that by the power of the Holy Ghost, we may be "fed and comforted with His [Christ's] true body and blood."[41]

## Singing Psalms to the Glory of God

The piety of the Reformed Dutch immigrants to the United States in the nineteenth century was to a large extent shaped by the singing of Dutch psalms in their homes as well as in church. The recently translated diary of Geesje Van Der Haar Visscher provides a record of the role played by the psalms in the nineteenth century.[42] It gives rich evidence of the midwestern faith that was sustained by singing psalms to glorify God and to express gratitude for God's providential faithfulness to them. There was a verse of a psalm for every family event, community anniversary, personal emotion, and disaster in the community.

She recorded the use of Psalm 134 on several different occasions, including the fiftieth anniversary of the founding of Holland.[43] Psalm 68:2 was sung at the funeral of her husband, Jan Visscher,[44] as well as at that of the Reverend Albertus Van Raalte.[45] Psalm 68:10 was sung at her son Arend's birthday and the birthday of her grandson.[46]

Psalms were also sung in churches and public meetings to give comfort after great disasters. On the Sunday after most of the city of

---

used in the Reformed Church in America. For a detailed account of the history of the doctrine of the Lord's Supper in the Liturgy of the Reformed Church in America, see Christopher Dorn, *The Lord's Supper in the Reformed Church in America* (New York,: Peter Lang, 2007).

[41] *The Liturgy of the Reformed Church in America* (New York: Board of Publication, 1951), 34-35. Discussion of the revision of the *Liturgy* is taken up again in the final chapter of this book.

[42] Geesje Van der Haar Visscher, C.L. Jalving, trans. *Diary* (located in files of Elton J. Bruins, Van Raalte Institute, Holland, Michigan), 1.

[43] Ibid., 158.

[44] Ibid., 145.

[45] Ibid., 54.

[46] Ibid., 128, 97.

Holland was destroyed by the great fire of October 8-9, 1871, Psalm 119:38 was sung:

> I know, Oh Lord, that your judgments
> Are righteous. You allowed oppression only
> Because you are true. O may your favor come
> To pull me from fear and dire grief!
> Comfort me, your servant, in fearful pining now,
> Since you promised that for times of trouble.[47]

It is possible that the singing of the psalms more than anything else sustained the piety of the Second Reformation[48] from the seventeenth through the nineteenth century. The psalms gave them biblical language of the majesty of God that kept them free from an eighteenth-century deism that taught that after creating the world God let the world run its own course as a watchmaker sets the watch free from further interference. For those who sang the psalms, the songs of lament never ceased to ask God why the evil kings are not put down and why the wicked prosper and the righteous suffer. They always waited expectantly for an answer to the question, "How long, O Lord, how long?"

On the other hand, they never gave way to the nineteenth-century romanticists who tended to identify God so closely with the realm of nature that the distinction between the Creator and the creation disappeared. As long as the people sang the psalms they knew that they could not stay away from church on Sunday morning to go out and find God in nature.

The psalms enabled them to live in confidence that they could trust in the providence of God, even though they could not understand God's ways when their children died, when the city of Holland burned to the ground, or when the grasshoppers ate their crops in the fields of the Dakotas. Their doctrine of the providence of God led them neither to a stoic, unquestioning acceptance of whatever happened to them nor to a bitterness that gave up the struggle of faith. In the psalms they found language to express their anger and their doubts, to wrestle with God in hope for an answer while also learning from the psalmist that God does not finally forsake those who call upon God's name.[49]

[47]    Translation by Cornelia B. Kennedy.
[48]    The "Second Reformation" is a translation of the Dutch *Nadere Reformatie,* which refers to the pietistic movement in the Netherlands in the seventeenth and eighteenth centuries. Those who were part of the Secession of 1834 were heavily indebted to the "Old Writers" of the Second Reformation.
[49]    One of the major objections against the Classis of Holland's decision to unite with the Reformed Church in America was that hymns alongside

Their loyalty to the psalms made their pietism different from that of the German pietists who lived within the context of the Lutheran tradition. Luther had taught the Germans to sing hymns. The German pietists Zinzendorf and the Moravians made the suffering and obedience of Jesus Christ the central theme of their music. Those who sang were encouraged to consider how much it had cost Jesus to come to redeem them from their sins and save their souls. The psalms do not allow such a narrow focus on Christ's redemption from personal sin. They deal with far more than one's personal relationship with Christ as savior. When the psalms are sung, all of creation, including the sun, moon, and stars, is called upon to join in the hymn of praise. The rise and fall of nations as well as one's personal restlessness and thirst for the living God come into play. One simply cannot understand the nineteenth-century midwestern Reformed Church in America without becoming immersed in the psalms.[50]

The use of English-language hymns and songs entered the church's worship by the avenues of revival meetings, the Sunday school, and young people's societies. We first find references on the pages of *De Hope* to the use of English hymns in the year 1877. The February 7 issue reports that the hymns, "Jesus Lover of My Soul" and "Rock

---

psalms were used in Sunday worship. It became one of the reasons that a number of congregations left in 1857 to form what ultimately became the Christian Reformed Church. For a history of the use of psalms and hymns in the Reformed Church in America and the Christian Reformed Church, see Harry Boonstra, "Singing God's Songs in a New Land: Congregational Song in the RCA and CRC," in *A Goodly Heritage,* Jacob E. Nyenhuis, ed., Historical Series of the Reformed Church in America, no. 56 (Grand Rapids: Eerdmans, 2007), 1-30; and Harry Boonstra, "Singing Hymns? We've Never Done That Before: The CRC's First *Psalter Hymnal*," *Calvin Theological Journal,* 42/1 (April 2007): 110-31.

[50] The Rev. Dr. Albertus Pieters, who was a missionary in Japan for thirty-two years and then taught at Western Theological Seminary from 1926-1939, is best known for his writings on matters of current controversies in the church, including the controversy of the Reformed Church in America with the Christian Reformed Church, the theory of evolution, pacifism, premillenialism and dispensationalism, the doctrine of inspiration and biblical criticism, the observance of the Sabbath, and infant baptism. Yet the real gem of all his writings may be his *Psalms in Human Experience* (New York: Board of Publications, Reformed Church in America, 1942). In 1923 the Pieterses had to leave Japan because of the illness of their daughters and the death of one of their daughters. It is in the reading of his exposition of the psalms that one gains insight into what sustained him when they left Japan as well as amid all the other trials of his life.

of Ages," were sung at the funeral of a Mr. Wormser in Pella, Iowa. In the February 28 issue we read that Sankey's song book was used at the Christian Youth Rally in Milwaukee. Among the hymns that were sung were "Jesus, the Light of the World," "Watching and Waiting," "Roll on O Billows of Fire," and "Sunset." The December 5 issue reports that "Pass me not O Gentle Savior" was sung.

The Reverend Jacob Van Der Meulen, Sr., in 1887 took note of the fact that *Gospel Hymns* of Sankey was being used as a hymnbook in many places. However, a recent Dutch hymnbook, *Lofzangen en Liederen*, was much to be preferred.[51] Three months later a Dutch translation of the gospel hymn, "Ninety and Nine," was published on page 1 of *De Hope*.[52] An advertisement appeared in the March 9, 1904, issue for *The Sunday School Hymnbook*. It reported that this hymnbook was "Safe, Singable, Durable—approved by General Synod—edited by members of the Reformed Church."

Henry Dosker contributed a long series of articles to *De Hope* in 1895 that provided a detailed history of the practice of psalm and hymn singing in the history of the church with special reference to the tradition in the Netherlands. He contended that hymns are necessary because the psalms do not express enough about salvation in Christ.[53] For that reason it is necessary for the church to sing hymns as well as psalms. Dosker favored using the hymns of Luther and Calvin and gave approval to the hymns of Watts, Mason, Wesley, and others. He commented that only a few midwestern churches were still holding out against hymns in 1895. To oppose the singing of hymns, he wrote, is narrow minded.[54]

It may be true that much of the opposition to the singing of hymns was narrow-minded, but there was also good reason for concern. Introduction of hymns in English meant that a shift in focus

---

[51] Jacob Van Der Meulen, Sr., "Een Lofwaardig Boek," *De Hope*, March 16, 1887.

[52] June 1, 1887.

[53] Dosker, "De Christelijke Kerk en Haar Lied," *De Hope*, August 14, 1895.

[54] Ibid., August 28, 1895. Those who emigrated from the Netherlands to the Midwest had opposed strenuously the requirement of the Netherlands Reformed Church that hymns as well as psalms be sung in Sunday morning worship. Those who separated from the Reformed Church in America in 1857 to form what became the Christian Reformed Church gave the Reformed Church's use of hymns as one of the reasons for their action. Dosker's articles on the history of the use of the psalms and hymns in the history of the church were written in support of the Reformed Church's use of hymns as well as psalms.

The Rev. Henry E. Dosker, D.D.
(1855-1926)

*Courtesy of Western Theological Seminary*

"In him qualities of mind and heart which are not usually found in happy combination were strikingly blended. He was deeply emotional without being shallow; intellectually strong with all absence of intellectual aloofness; tenderhearted without sacrificing saneness of judgment; so vigorous in thought as to be free from any tendency to mental stagnation while at the same time so healthfully progressive as to avoid all fevers of that kind of liberalism that is such only in name."—Evert J. Blekkink, "Dr. Henry J. Dosker," *Leader,* January 5, 1927, 2.

was taking place in the faith of the congregation. The psalms as rhymed by Peter Dathenus and others found their focus in God's providence and salvation. Without explicitly mentioning Jesus Christ, their use of words such as "Lord" and "salvation" (*heil*) could be understood by Christians in a fully trinitarian sense beyond a literal understanding of the psalms in their Old Testament setting. Although Dutch Pietists loved the psalms, the psalms they sang could not be sung in a narrow pietistic sense that limited their meaning to personal salvation without reference to the wider community or to God's governance of creation. The English hymns of Isaac Watts also had the same broad context of faith. However, many of what came to be the most loved English hymns came from the revival and gospel song tradition and had a more narrow focus on an individual believer's relationship to Jesus Christ, as in "Rock of Ages, Cleft for Me," and "Blessed Assurance, Jesus is Mine." The narrow focus of the gospel hymns added a new dimension and joy to midwestern congregational worship and as such they played a valuable role in sustaining the faith. However, when they replaced the older piety of the psalms, much was lost. The gospel hymn tradition promotes a legitimate but different kind of piety than do the lyrical psalms.[55]

As more and more congregations changed from Dutch to English in their Sunday worship, psalm-singing faded into the background. For example, the 1955 *Service Hymnal* used by perhaps the majority of midwestern Reformed Church congregations lists in its index only 17 psalms out of a total of 501 hymns, psalms, and responses.[56] The major issue after 1920 in the Reformed Church in America was no longer that of the singing of psalms. It was about the extent to which "evangelical" or "gospel" hymns that find their focus in the spiritual experience of the believer should be prominent in the hymnbook. When the Reformed Church in America cooperated with Presbyterian churches in producing *The Hymnbook* in 1955, it was pointed out that 74 metrical psalms were included among 597 offerings.[57] The Reverend Bastian Kruithof recommended use of *The Hymnbook*. He wrote that it was the answer to a need in the church. "Our concern should be for the highest and the richest. God's direction in His Word should...inspire us. The trivial and...the cheap, answering to most primitive rhythms, are not for us."[58]

In spite of the recommendation of a number of leading ministers and musicians, many congregations continued to use *The Service*

---

[55]  The Reformed Church in America has not resolved the tension that exists between the two types of piety. Although there are several reasons that its latest attempt to develop a hymnbook, *Rejoice in the Lord*, ed. Eric Routley (Grand Rapids: Eerdmans, 1985) did not gain wide acceptance, its failure to include more than a very few gospel hymns was an invitation to rejection because it ignored the nature of a midwestern Reformed Church piety that had been nurtured by gospel hymns since those congregations had begun to sing in English. The contemporary form of the old psalm piety vs. hymn piety comes to the surface very quickly when a congregation decides to choose a new hymnbook.

[56]  It did include portions of 21 psalms for responsive reading; *The Service Hymnal* (Chicago: Hope Publishing Company, 1955). The index listing is on page 473. The Christian Reformed Church continues to include all 150 psalms in its *Psalter Hymnal*.

[57]  Bernard J. Mulder, "A Singing Book for a Singing Church," *Church Herald*, October 22, 1954, 13.

[58]  Bastian Kruithof, "The Hymnbook—An Achievement," *Church Herald*, January 20, 1956, 4. Kruithof was widely respected in the midwestern church, especially because he wrote the weekly editorial in the *Sunday School Guide* that was used in the great majority of midwestern Reformed Church congregations. See also Benes, "The New Hymnbook," *Church Herald*, January 20, 1956, 6-7, 22.

*Hymnal* and similar hymnals because they missed the presence of many of their favorite old gospel hymns.[59] At the end of the century, 1866-1966, the midwestern Reformed congregations lived with at least two major traditions of hymnody and two forms of piety in its worship.

## The Practice of Piety in Families

Midwestern Reformed Church ministers and theologians taught that the family is the basis of human society. It is society in miniature.[60] They all agreed that the father is the head of the family but that fathers and mothers must be held in equal honor by their children.[61] Parents are responsible for the spiritual nurture of their children according to the promises they make at the time of baptism. Mothers have a special responsibility to speak words of spiritual nurture while children are still young and ready to listen to their parents. Parents must pray for their erring children and trust in God for their salvation.[62]

---

[59]  *The Hymnbook* that was published cooperatively by the Presbyterian Church in the United States, the United Presbyterian Church in the USA, and the Reformed Church in America in 1955 included twenty hymns by Watts, fifteen by Charles Wesley, three by John Wesley, five by Fanny Crosby, and four by Frances Ridley Havergal. It did not include any hymns or songs written by Ira Sankey (1840-1908), the song writer associate of Dwight L. Moody, or Homer Rodeheaver (1880-1955), the associate of Billy Sunday. Its index lists fifty-five psalms included from the Presbyterian 1915 psalter. *The Hymnbook* was used by a minority of the midwestern Reformed churches. Hymnbooks published by the Hope Publishing Company were far more widely used. (The Hope Publishing Company was not related to the Reformed Church in America). The undated edition of the *Service Hymnal* used during and after World War II did not provide a list of psalms in its index. It included fifteen hymns by Watts, ten by Charles Wesley, two by John Wesley, twenty-two by Fanny Crosby, and nine by Havergal. It included seven by Ira Sankey. The indices of the two hymnals provide a clear indication of the shift in the forms of piety in the midwestern Reformed Church as it moved from use of the Dutch language to English. For a helpful discussion of the social background and theology of the gospel hymns, see Sandra S. Sizer, *Gospel Hymns and Social Religion: The Rhetoric of Nineteenth-Century Revivalism* (Philadelphia: Temple Univ. Press, 1978), 111-37.

[60]  John H. Karsten, "De Sabbathschool: De Tien Geboden:" *De Hope*, June 15, 1887; Cornelius Vander Schoor, "Gij zult niet Echtbreken," *De Hope*, December 30, 1930.

[61]  Blekkink, *Lectures on Theology* (located in John R. Mulder, Box 1, WTS/JAH, n.p., under heading, "Parents of Children").

[62]  Adrian Zwemer, "Huiselijke Woorden," *De Hope*, February 7, 1877.

It is not correct to speak of the family at worship as if it is the church in the home or a "conventicle" of believers.[63] On the contrary, the family gathered together to read the Bible, pray, and sing psalms can better be understood as a "first fruit" of the Spirit at work setting right God's creation. It is a sign of the presence of the kingdom of God among the community of humankind. As a human institution the family is closer to the school and the state than it is to the church.

The practice of piety in the family was one of the hallmarks of the Dutch community in America in the nineteenth century. Not only did they go to church together on Sunday, but during the week it was standard practice to ask a blessing on the food prior to eating and a prayer of thanksgiving at the end. Reading a portion of the Bible at one or more of the meals during the day was also standard practice. When urban life became more complicated in the twentieth century, H.P. Witman reminded readers that the family altar is a necessity and that a convenient time of at least ten minutes must be found morning, noon, or evening for the practice, in spite of the busy schedules of members of the family.[64]

The practice of prayer and Bible reading at meal time continues in many midwestern homes to this day. However, not all have been so faithful to the tradition. Already in 1908, the Reverend Peter Moerdyk in Chicago bemoaned what was happening. He wrote that a new generation was growing up without adequate training in the Christian faith and suggested that Christian schools should be promoted to fill in the gap.[65]

> Family worship and the use of the Bible at home are, according to quite general testimony, out of date even in most so-called Christian families. The benighted condition of a generation growing up without the knowledge of God and His revelation is the average defect that we meet and feel everywhere. The public

[63] Jean Labadie (1610-1674) had led a reform movement within the Netherlands Reformed Church in which he encouraged his followers to gather in small circles or "conventicles" that met alongside and sometimes in conflict with the church at worship. In those small gatherings of believers, spiritual practices could be exercised and a more experimental form of belief could be shared; Karel Blei, *The Netherlands Reformed Church, 1571-2005,* trans. Allan J. Janssen, Historical Series of the Reformed Church in America, no. 53 (Grand Rapids: Eerdmans, 2006), 45-46.
[64] H.P. Wittman, "Het Huis Altaar: Kan de Huiselijke Godsdienst nog Onderhouden worden?" *De Hope,* May 14, 1918.
[65] See chapter 3 for a discussion of the relation of family nurture to catechetical instruction and Sunday school.

education in only rare instances enlightens youth as to heaven's truth; parochial and Christian schools emphasize this study and...have...a unique opportunity and field during the present dearth.[66]

Peter Moerdyk's pessimism about what was happening indicates that family nurture in the Christian faith was not as effectively carried out as people today recall that it was. Throughout the entire period that *De Hope* was published in the nineteenth and twentieth centuries, there were reports about what was happening with the youth. Pastors complained that although much was good among the youth, the young people wanted to engage in amusements such as dancing, rolling skating in roller rinks, drinking alcoholic beverages, cursing, and breaking the Sabbath.[67]

## The Practice of Piety in Society

The midwestern practice of piety in society will be discussed more fully in later chapters. At this point consideration is given only to (1) the way in which the midwestern Reformed Church leaders taught that the family is the basic unit of society, and (2) how the editors of *De Hope* included society within their purview.

As already noted, midwestern ministers and professors agreed that the family is the basic unit of society and that society is a "body" linked together by family, friendship, and other activities. [68] Society (*Maatschappij*) constituted the broad network of human activities including government, economic activity, social organizations, culture, and innumerable other forms of social organization.

The fact that the family is the basic unit of society and that the father is the head of the family means that theologically speaking society also is patriarchal in nature.[69] The Heidelberg Catechism taught that we can rest in the providence of God to meet our needs and care for us. The providence of God is

---

[66] Peter Moerdyk, "A Plea for Bible Study," *Leader*, January 8, 1908, 162.

[67] See for example, Gerhard De Jonge, "Het Godsdienstig Samenleving der Baanbrekers," *De Hope*, August 20, 1907.

[68] See for example, Peter De Pree, "Wekelijksch Budget," *De Hope*, March 22, 1905.

[69] Their belief that family and society are patriarchal in nature became a major point of controversy in America and in the Reformed Church in America in the nineteenth and twentieth centuries. More attention will be given to the issue in chapter 5 on the practice of piety in a Godly community.

the almighty and ever-present power of God whereby he still upholds, as it were by his own hand, heaven and earth together with all creatures, and rules in such a way that leaves and grass, rain and drought, fruitful and unfruitful years, food and drink, health and sickness, riches and poverty, and everything else, come to us not be chance but by *his fatherly hand.* [70]

In society and political life we are called upon to honor all those in authority with the same respect that we are to honor our parents in family life. The Heidelberg Catechism makes this very clear in its exposition of the fifth commandment. The fifth commandment requires

> that I show honor, love, and faithfulness to my father and mother and to all who are set in authority over me; that I submit myself with respectful obedience to all their careful instruction and discipline; and that I also bear patiently their failures, since it is God's will to govern us by their hand.[71]

None of the midwestern Reformed Church in America leaders attempted to set forth a clear set of guidelines about the nature of Christian participation in society. However, in 1908 the Reverend Dr. Herman Bavinck, professor at the Free University in the Netherlands, published his book, *Het Christelijk Huisgezin (The Christian Family).*[72] In that book he set forth the implications that flow from the proposition that the family is the basic unit of society. He began with Genesis 1-2, where we learn that human beings were created male and female. Bavinck taught that men and women were not first of all individuals whose relationships evolved into families over the course of millenia. Rather, the first human pair and their offspring were family. Human beings in marriage are a "bi-unity" who with their children form a "tri-unity," with fully formed familial responsibilities of mutual love, parental care, and childhood obedience.[73] The history of the human race did not begin as a loose group of individuals but organically in marriage and family.[74]

[70]  Heidelberg Catechism, Q. 27.
[71]  Ibid., 104.
[72]  (Kampen, Netherlands: J.H. Kok, 1908). Herman Bavinck's father was a pastor in the Christian Separated Church and a professor in its theological school in Kampen. He was one of Nicholas Steffens's teachers. The midwestern Reformed Church leaders held Herman Bavinck in high regard and placed his books in the Western Theological Seminary library.
[73]  Ibid., 6-10.
[74]  Ibid., 142.

As human culture develops out of the interaction of the family unit and relationships with other kin,[75] language increases its range, work must be done, and tools are invented. Goods are produced and shared; art and literature come into being. The whole process has been seriously distorted by the fall into sin and the corruption of the race; the social network may have become mutilated but it is not destroyed. Other spheres of activity come to stand alongside the family, including the state, labor, education, and the church. But it must not be forgotten that the family is the only one that has been there from the beginning, before the fall. The others do not arise directly out of the family. The state and the church and the other forms of society are brought into being after the fall, each with its own sphere of activity and each ultimately accountable to God.[76]

Bavinck's understanding of the nature of Christian participation in society was appreciated by the midwestern Reformed Church leaders. In chapter 5 further consideration is given to how they understood the role of the Christian faith in society.

---

[75] The Dutch language has two words for family: *gezin* refers to the nuclear family, while *familie* includes the members of the extended family. For our purposes it is not necessary to distinguish sharply between the two.

[76] Ibid., 150.

CHAPTER 3

# The Practice of Piety: All Things Decently and in Order

Under the leadership of the Reverend Albertus C. Van Raalte, the Dutch immigrant Reformed congregations organized themselves into the Classis of Holland in 1848. Two years later, in 1850, the Classis of Holland entered into union with the Reformed Church in America.[1] The Reformed Church in America dated its history from 1628, when the first congregation was organized and the sacrament of Holy Communion was celebrated on Manhatten Island.[2] Between 1628 and 1772 the Dutch Reformed congregations in America were organized by and accountable to the Classis of Amsterdam in the Netherlands. Only

[1]   For an account of the events leading up to the union and an evaluation of the significance of the union, see Elton J. Bruins and Robert P. Swierenga, *Family Quarrels*, 36-60. During the course of its history in the United States, the denomination went through several changes of name. In this book the official name of the church since 1867, "Reformed Church in America," will be used for its entire history in America.

[2]   Arie R. Brouwer, *Reformed Church Roots* (New York: Reformed Church Press, 1977), 33-34. See also Donald J. Bruggink and Kim N. Baker, *By Grace Alone: Stories of the Reformed Church in America*, Historical Series of the Reformed Church in America, no.44 (Grand Rapids: Eerdmans, 2004), 21-25.

when it received ecclesiastical independence from its mother Reformed church in the Netherlands in 1772 did it become a separate American denomination.[3]

## The Union of 1850 with the Reformed Church in America

In 1792, the Reformed Church in America adopted for itself the Church Order of Dort as modified by a set of "Explanatory Articles" designed to adapt the Church Order to American conditions.[4] In 1850, when the Classis of Holland entered into union with the Reformed Church in America, it became obligated to function according to the Church Order of Dort as it had been amended from time to time by the Reformed Church in America.[5] It also agreed that the articulation of the faith was that which was set forth in the Standards of Unity, namely, the Heidelberg Catechism, the Belgic Confession, and the Canons of Dort. Each ordained minister, upon being enrolled in the membership of a classis, was required to sign his agreement with the teachings of the Standards of Unity and to agree that if he had any doubt about any of their provisions, he would report his concerns to the classis and be subject to its judgment. The nineteenth-century Dutch Reformed immigrants were in accord with the constitution and confessional standards of the Reformed Church in America. As members of the *Christelijke Gereformeerde Kerk*[6] that had come into being following the Secession of 1834, they had adopted the Church Order of Dort and the Standards of Unity as the basic documents for their church. They believed that the new church

[3]  Gerald F. De Jong, *The Dutch Reformed Church in the American Colonies*, Historical Series of the Reformed Church in America, no. 5 (Grand Rapids: Eerdmans, 1978), 1, 236.

[4]  The text of the 1792 *Constitution of the Reformed Church in America* is available in Edward Tanjore Corwin, *A Digest of Constitutional and Synodical Legislation of the Reformed Church in America* (New York: Board of Publication of the Reformed Church in America, 1906), v-lxxxvii, and in Daniel J. Meeter, *Meeting Each Other, In Doctrine, Liturgy, and Government*, Historical Series of the Reformed Church in America, no. 24 (Grand Rapids: Eerdmans, 1993), 56-144. When a revision of the *Constitution* was adopted in 1967, the *Book of Church Order* became the designation of a part of the denomination's *Constitution*, together with its *Liturgy* and the Standards of Unity. In this book the designation, *Book of Church Order* will be used to refer to that part of the *Constitution* as above.

[5]  The text of the 1833 revision that was in force in 1850 is included in Corwin, *Digest.*

[6]  *Christelijke Gereformeerde Kerk* translated into English becomes "Christian Reformed Church." For the sake of clarity, the name of the Dutch denomination is left untranslated in this book in order to avoid confusion with the North American denomination, the Christian Reformed Church.

order that had been implemented by King Willem II in 1816 was in contradiction to the major provisions of the Church Order of Dort.[7] They also had very strong objections to the liberal theology that was being taught at the theological schools in Groningen and Leiden, especially by the Groninger professor, Petros Hofstede de Groot. They objected that the Netherlands Hervormde Kerk was not only failing to discipline those who departed from the doctrines taught in the Standards of Unity, but also that its leaders actually favored the liberals and persecuted those who taught according to the standards.[8] In light of what they had experienced prior to their departure from the Netherlands, the union of the Classis of Holland with the Reformed Church in America was like a homecoming to the old church and the old faith for the Dutch immigrants to America.

There were some in the Classis of Holland who opposed the union with the Reformed Church in America. Some of the opposition may have had to do with personal relationships and with suspicions that had been brought with them from the Netherlands.[9] Stated reasons given by those who seceded from the Classis of Holland to form what became the Christian Reformed Church included complaints that the Reformed Church did not enforce the weekly preaching of sermons related to the Heidelberg Catechism, that its congregations sang hymns as well as psalms, and that it did not exercise discipline carefully when inviting people to the Lord's Table.[10]

Opponents of the Union of 1850 suspected that the Reformed Church was lax in maintaining the doctrines of predestination and the atonement as set forth in the Canons of Dort. They found evidence for such suspicion in the procedures and final decision of the General Synods of 1819-1822, regarding the complaint against the Reverend Conrad Ten Eyck that he "did not believe that Christ had atoned for any man...but for sin."[11] The synod declared in 1822 that it was satisfied with Ten Eyck's orthodoxy, and it urged every minister to

[7]    See Ten Zythoff, *Sources of Secession*, 17-70.
[8]    Ibid., 99-136.
[9]    Janet Sjaarda Sheeres, *Son of Secession: Douwe J. Vander Werp* (Grand Rapids: Eerdmans, 2006), 110-19.
[10]   Bruins and Swierenga, *Family Quarrels*, 73-89; for a balanced Christian Reformed perspective, see John Kromminga, *The Christian Reformed Church: A Study in Orthodoxy* (Grand Rapids: Baker, 1949), 27-39. See also James A. De Jong, "Reassessing 1857: Overlooked Considerations Concerning the Birth of the Christian Reformed Church," (Lecture Series No. 3, Visiting Research Fellows Program, Van Raalte Institute, Hope College, Holland, Mich., 2006).
[11]   Conrad Ten Eyck (1756-1845) graduated from New Brunswick Theological

adhere strictly to the teachings of Dort. However, Ten Eyck's answers to the questions that had been posed to him by the synod were to some extent ambiguous. The result was that a small number of ministers and congregations left the Reformed Church to form "The True Christian Reformed Church."[12]

In spite of the fact that a small number of the immigrants refused to remain in the Reformed Church in America, the great majority agreed with the Union of 1850 made by Van Raalte and the Classis of Holland. Van Raalte was no separatist. He was a "reluctant seceder"[13] who held to the doctrine of the unity of the church as taught by the Belgic Confession:

> We believe and profess one unique catholic or universal Church, which is a holy gathering of true believers in Christ, expecting all their blessedness in him, being washed by his blood, sanctified and sealed by the Holy Spirit.[14]
>
> Rather, we believe that all men owe it to themselves to join and unite with it, maintaining the unity of the Church, submitting themselves to its teaching and discipline, bowing their necks under the yoke of Jesus Christ, and as mutual members of the same body, serving for the upbuilding of the brethren, according to the gifts God has given them.[15]

The Classis of Holland did not waver in its decision to unite with the Reformed Church in America because it believed that for the sake of the unity of the church there had to be a church order that recognized the offices of minister, elder, and deacon, "chosen by lawful election of the church, with prayer to God, and in the good order which the Word of God teaches."[16] It confessed that the church experienced its unity according to the "pure preaching of the Gospel" and "the pure administration of the Sacraments as instituted by Christ," as well as by the practice of discipline in relation to the sacraments.[17]

---

Seminary in 1799 and served Reformed churches in New York. Between 1812 and 1830 he was pastor of the Owasco, New York, Reformed Church.

[12]   Eugene Heideman, "Theology," in James W. Van Hoeven, *Piety and Patriotism*, Historical Series of the Reformed Church in America, no. 4 (Grand Rapids: Eerdmans, 1976), 99-100.

[13]   See chapter 12, "The Reluctant Seceder," in Bruggink and Baker, *By Grace Alone*, 125-34.

[14]   Belgic Confession, Art. 27.

[15]   Belgic Confession, Art. 28.

[16]   Belgic Confession, Art. 31.

[17]   Ibid., Art. 29.

Following the Union of 1850, the Reformed Church in America was a denomination located geographically in two regions, East and Midwest.[18] The Reformed Church in the eastern region had two hundred years of experience of living in America; the Reformed Church in the midwestern region existed in colonies or enclaves of Dutch immigrants whose language was still Dutch and whose memories of the Netherlands were still richer than their experience of America. Nevertheless, in spite of all the tensions that could arise, they remained resolute in their commitment to the unity of the denomination.

During the century, 1866-1966, historical developments forced the Reformed Church in America to deal with three major interrelated issues regarding its theology and church order as it sought to maintain its internal unity. These issues were (1) who may the elders admit to the Lord's Table and to membership in full communion; (2) what is the nature and authority of the General Synod in relation to the classes and to the consistory in the local church; and (3) the relation of the Reformed Church in America to other denominations, including the possibility of merging with another denomination. In the remainder of this chapter, each of the three issues will be discussed, with particular reference to the positions taken by leaders in the midwestern region of the denomination.

## Admission to Membership in Full Communion

According to the provisions of the Church Order of Dort and the Explanatory Articles, it was the responsibility of the minister with the elders in the congregation to admit baptized believers to be members in full communion with privileges to partake of the Lord's Supper.[19] In the 1870s a bitter controversy erupted over the issue of admitting members of the Freemason Society to be members in full communion. Many early American leaders, such as George Washington and Thomas Jefferson, had been Freemasons. Many members and some ministers of Reformed churches in the eastern region of the church belonged to that "secret society." However, the midwestern Dutch Reformed leaders believed firmly that membership in the Masonic Order was incompatible with loyalty to Jesus Christ. The controversy that went on for decades in the

---

[18]  This generalization is not totally accurate. There was a Classis of Michigan in existence whose members had migrated from New York, New Jersey, and Pennsylvania, and in many cases could trace their family history back to the colonial era. There were congregations in New York and New Jersey whose mindset more closely resembled that of the midwestern region.

[19]  Church Order of Dort, 61; Explanatory Articles 62.

Midwest poisoned relationships with the Christian Reformed Church, caused divisions within congregations, and brought to the fore serious issues about the authority of the elders in the consistory in relation to the authority of the General Synod. It also complicated efforts in the 1890s to effect a merger with the (German) Reformed Church in the United States.[20]

The controversy had spilled over from the Netherlands. The Freemason Society was a secret order, but enough was known about its official statements to conclude that its teachings were in contrast to the orthodox Reformed position. Many new immigrants entering the country from the Christelijke Gereformeerde Kerk objected to allowing Freemasons to be members of the church, as did the majority of the Midwesterners. The classes of Wisconsin and Holland sent overtures to the General Synod asking that Freemasonry be condemned and its members not accepted into membership in the church.[21]

The General Synod in June, 1880, adopted a recommendation that counseled Reformed Church members against membership in the Freemason Society but stopped short of ruling that the board of elders or consistory could not admit them to membership. The full statement reads:

> No communicant members, and no minister of the Reformed Church in America ought to unite with or to remain in any society or institution, whether secret or open, whose principles and practices are anti-Christian, or contrary to the faith and practice of the Church to which he belongs. This Synod solemnly believes and declares that any system of religion or morals whose tendency is to hide our Savior, or to supplant the religion of which He is the founder, should receive no countenance from his professed followers. That this Synod also advises Consistories and Classes of the Church to be very kind and forbearing, and strictly constitutional in their dealings with individuals on this

[20]   The membership of the Reformed Church in the United States was made up of immigrants from Germany and had enjoyed close relationship with the Reformed Church in America from the time of the American Revolution. In order to avoid confusion in this book, that church will often be referred to as the German Reformed Church in the United States, but it must be remembered that "German" was never part of the name of that denomination.

[21]   *De Hope*, May 20, 1874; April 21, 1880; May 19, 1880. These overtures followed after a number of other attempts in previous decades requesting that action be taken to ban Freemasons. For a careful account of the controversy, see Bruins and Swierenga, *Family Quarrels*, 108-35.

subject, and that they be and are hereby affectionately cautioned against setting up any new or unauthorized tests of communion in the Christian Church.[22]

There was great disappointment in the Midwest with this decision. It was believed that the General Synod had used a technicality of church order to avoid making a decision against permitting local consistories to admit lodge members. The Midwest wanted the synod to make a blanket rule against the admission of lodge members that would apply to every local consistory in the denomination. However, the decision of the General Synod remains the rule in the Reformed Church in America to this day. It is the judgment of the board of elders concerning the confession of faith of individuals, rather than any rule of a classis or the General Synod, that determines who shall be admitted to full communion and the invitation to partake of the Lord's Supper.

The classes of Wisconsin and Holland each met in the fall of 1880 to express their objections to the decision. They consulted about what further recourse there was for them. A few people urged that the Midwest be patient. The Reverend James F. Zwemer in Holland called upon the readers of De Hope to be patient, saying that the paper would consider the matter in due time, but wanted to avoid any hasty words.[23] The Reverend Derk Broek warned against leaving the Reformed Church over the issue, because to secede is to open the door to many other questions. He pointed out that there were many other serious differences as well.[24] The editors of De Hope reported on June 22, 1881, that the General Synod had affirmed again its decision of the previous year. They said that the Reformed Church had lived with the situation for thirty years and that having Freemasons in some classes and congregations had done it no harm. To divide the church over this issue would be to create greater harm.[25] The issue of church membership could not be separated from the issue of the unity of the church.

The conflict about the church membership of Freemasons had immense impact upon the future of ecumenical relationships of the Reformed Church. Its immediate impact was upon its relationship with the Christelijke Gereformeerde Kerk in the Netherlands. Prior to the controversy, that church had been suspicious of the secession movement in America of the Christian Reformed Church; therefore,

22   *Acts and Proceedings of the General Synod of the Reformed Church in America* (hereinafter, *Acts and Proceedings*), 1880, 536.
23   *De Hope*, August 25, 1880.
24   *De Hope*, August 24, 1881.
25   *De Hope*, June 22, 1881.

The Rev. James Frederick Zwemer,
D.D. (1850-1921)

*Courtesy of Western Theological Seminary*

James Zwemer served as managing editor for both *De Hope* and the *Leader.* "His great work was his long continued labor for the financial interest of the educational institutions in the West." "Dr. Zwemer was a tireless worker both as a pastor and as an Agent. In the various pastorates which he held he gave evidence of his ability and devotion. He was a ready speaker, a faithful pastor, a genial companion and a helpful friend. No one ever called on him in vain, wherever he could be useful he was willing to serve. If he had a weakness, it was this, that he sought to do too much; for the greater part of his ministry doing double service."— *Acts and Proceedings*, 1922, 962.

it had maintained a favorable attitude toward the Reformed Church in America. However, after the Reformed Church General Synod's decision in 1882 refusing by "new or unauthorized tests" to exclude Freemasons from membership, the Christelijke Gereformeerde Kerk in the Netherlands advised its members immigrating to America to become members of the Christian Reformed Church.[26] This advice led to a rapid growth in membership in the Christian Reformed Church

---

[26]  Steffens objected to an article published in the Christelijke Gereformeerde church paper, *De Bazuin,* by Anthony Brummelkamp, who advised those immigrating to America to join the Chistian Reformed Church because of the Reformed Church in America's permitting Freemasons to become members. He complained that Brummelkamp did not understand the situation in America, with the result that there was a devastating division in the Reformed Church congregation in Zeeland, Michigan, where Steffens was serving as pastor ("Wat is de Zaak?" *De Hope,* April 12, 1882). He also complained that the Amsterdam classis had given advice to the Reformed Church in America when it did not understand the American situation ("Aanteekeningen en Opmerkingen" *De Hope,* January 18, 1882),

while the growth from immigration in the midwestern Reformed Church in America slowed in comparison to the Christian Reformed Church. Competition for immigrants remained a source of irritation into the twentieth century.[27]

Late in the nineteenth century a movement began to explore whether the two churches in the Midwest could unite in some way. In 1888, the Christian Reformed Synod declared the desirability of fellowship with the immigrant members of the Reformed Church. Discussions with midwestern leaders began and reached a climax in 1894. A public meeting was scheduled to be held in Holland, Michigan, November 15, with each side being asked to present its conditions for closer relationships. Upon receiving the Christian Reformed paper that insisted upon rejection of lodge members, the Reformed delegates withdrew their support of the meeting. That ended the attempt to enter into any formal union or cooperation. It was generally agreed that the two denominations could best continue to exist side by side without formal agreements.[28]

The two denominations continued to live next to each other like twin sisters who could never ignore each other or cease to regret that the breach that had occurred. As late as 1947 a sharp exchange took place between Albertus Pieters and the Reverend Dr. Henry J. Kuiper, editor of the Christian Reformed magazine, the *Banner*. Kuiper had written an editorial objecting to Pieters's interpretation of the history of the secession of 1857. Pieters agreed with Kuiper that the seceding congregations had a "right" to secede. But he rejected the traditional Christian Reformed position that based that right on what Dr. Wyckoff

---

and that, without having a good knowledge of the actions of the Classis of Grand Rapids in its condemnation of the Rev. L.J. Hulst for going with his congregation, the Fourth Reformed Church, into the Christian Reformed Church, Brummelkamp had unjustly condemned the classis for its action ("Aoerman, sta even still" *De Hope*, February 1, 1882).

[27] Following World War II there was a new wave of Dutch immigration into Canada. In order to forestall unsavory competition, there were some formal contacts and more "gentlemen's agreements" among the two American denominations and the Dutch churches. In general, the Reformed Church in America would offer assistance in resettlement to members of the Nederlandse Hervormde Kerk, and the Christian Reformed Church would do the same for those from the Nederlandse Gereformeerde Kerken, the name of that denomination after 1892.

[28] J. Krominga, *Christian Reformed Church*, 104-106; James A. De Jong, "Accountability or Parity: Ecumenical Principles in Tension between the CRC and RCA, 1898-1904," *Calvin Theological Journal* 42 (April 2007), 50-64.

as the representative of the Reformed Church in America had said at a meeting with the Classis of Holland in 1849. Pieters disagreed with the seceders' 1857 action. But he went on to say that he did not think that the Christian Reformed Church "today" (1947) was in the same position as in 1857. Pieters spoke on the Secession of 1857 again at the meeting of the Particular Synod of Iowa May 3, 1950. In spite of his sharp criticism of the secession, he said that "we have no quarrel with the Christian Reformed Church today."[29] His comments reflected the general attitude in the Midwest after World War II and opened the door to the positive cooperation that exists between the two churches today.

The desire to strengthen relationships locally with Christian Reformed churches lies deep in the mentality of Reformed congregations in the Midwest, Florida, and even on the West Coast. On the other hand, most congregations in the eastern areas of the denomination have no regular contact with members of the Christian Reformed Church. The eastern Reformed congregations' primary historic relationships have been with congregations of other "mainline" protestant denominations, especially Presbyterians and the United Church of Christ, into which the successor denominations of the German language Reformed Church in the United States merged in 1960. This difference in primary relationships is not to be underestimated in sorting out the reasons that all attempts to merge with another denomination have failed.

## The Authority of the General Synod in Relation to Classes and Consistories

Deep issues of theology as well as church order were involved in the controversy about admission of Freemasons to full communion in the church. Several years after the General Synod had made its decision on the matter, Nicholas Steffens, professor of theology at Western Theological Seminary, wrote that he had come to the conclusion that the General Synod was theologically correct in its decision.

The heart of Steffens's position was that Jesus Christ is the only head of the church and that the church order must be so devised that final authority can rest nowhere else than in Christ. Therefore the church order must be horizontal rather than hierarchical. There may be no domination from above or below. He agreed with the Church Order of Dort that all congregations and classes must be equal in rank. The offices of minister and elder were also equal in rank and authority. No

---

[29]   Albertus Pieters, "The Union of 1850," Address given before the Particular Synod of Iowa, May 3, 1950. located in WTS/JAH.

The Rev. Nicholas M. Steffens,
D.D. (1839-1912)

*Courtesy Western Theological Seminary*

Nicholas Steffens was the leading theologian in the midwestern Reformed Church from the time of his arrival in America in 1872 until his death. He had read widely in Dutch, German, and French philosophy and theology. He knew German, Dutch, English, Spanish, Italian, and the biblical languages. "An eminent divine of the Presbyterian Church declares Dr. Steffens as one of the ablest defenders of Calvinism of the twentieth century....To preach the gospel from the pulpit was his delight....The result of his preaching always was exalted ideas of Christ as Prophet, Priest, and King, and the believing hearer as always drawn closer to his redeemer."— *Acts and Proceedings*, 1913, 890.

minister could enjoy a higher rank and authority than another.[30]
According to the Belgic Confession,

> the marks by which to know the true Church are these: if the Church practices the pure preaching of the Gospel, if it maintains the pure administration of the Sacraments as instituted by Christ, and if it exercises Church discipline for punishing sin; in short, if those in the Church set themselves to administer all things in the Church according to the pure Word of God...acknowledging Christ as the only head.[31]

[30]  Steffens, "De Kerk van Christus," *De Hope*, October 17, 1882, 1. *Church Order of Dort*, Art. 17, *Explanatory Articles*, XVIII, in Edward Tanjore Corwin, *A Digest of Constitutional and Synodical Legislation of the Reformed Church in America* (New York: Board of Publication, Reformed Church in America, 1906), xx.

[31]  Art. 29. It was the third mark of exercising discipline that was of special concern in the Christian Reformed Church in considering whether the

Since the three marks are present in the local congregation, nothing essential can be added to its being as church by the broader assemblies of classis, provincial synods, and General Synod. Each local church has all the attributes of a church. It is independent.[32]

> One must note that without the well ordered congregations there is no Presbyterian/Reformed church, for the synod does not give the right to exist to the congregations, but the congregations give it to the synod....The center of gravity of the church lies...in the local congregation for the Presbyterian/Reformed church.[33]

The congregations therefore live in a free association with each other, regulated by a church order.

With his emphasis upon the primacy of the local congregation, Steffens had to explain why he was not Congregationalist in theology and polity. In response, he took issue with the position of the Reverend Dr. Abraham Kuyper in the Netherlands, who insisted upon the autonomy of the local church. Kuyper maintained that the idea of a "Great Church" (*Groote Kerk)* in the Netherlands had originated with the liberals. The local consistory must be the highest ecclesiastical power, above classes and any synod. Therefore Kuyper refused to grant the name "church" to any of the broader assemblies of a denomination. The church of the Seceders of 1834 had distinguished between the "congregation" as the local body and gave the name "church" to the denomination, the Christelijke Gereformeerde (*Afgecheidene*) Kerk. They did not teach that the congregation by itself is autonomous or self-existent. It had, as it were, an element of its autonomy in its participation in the whole—the synod.[34] Thus, although the congregation with the

---

Reformed Church in America was adequately diligent in maintaining orthodox Reformed theology.

[32]  Steffens, "Wekelijksch Budget," *De Hope*, January 6, 1892.
[33]  Steffens, "Wekelijksch Budget," *De Hope*, October 17, 1882.
[34]  Steffens, "Gereformeerde," *De Hope*, February 9, 1887. The "Doleantie" movement led by Kuyper and the Christelijke Gereformeerde Kerk, descended from the Afscheiding of 1834, eventually entered into union with each other in 1892. One of the difficult points in the negotiation process was how to reconcile the view of the Doleantie with that of the Christelijke Gereformeerde Kerk. The name eventually adopted, "Gereformeerde Nederlandse Kerken"—with the plural "Kerken," indicates that the position of Kuyper prevailed, at least in the formulation of the name, if not always in practice. For a full account of the negotiation process, see Hendrik Bouma, *Secession, Doleantie, and Union: 1834-1892* (Pella, Iowa: Inheritance Publication, 1995).

Word and sacraments and the practice of Christian discipline is central to Reformed Church order, according to Steffens, it does not exist in isolation from all the other congregations.

Steffens wrote that the union of congregations into a classis and classes into a synod was more than an association voluntarily joined together by a common confession. The association of churches to sustain the unity of the church needed to have not only a common confession, but also a constitution or church order. Without the church order there is no union. Only by having a church order can the mutual encouragement, discipline, and order among the congregations be sustained. The church order must be so written as to indicate the particular responsibilities of the national, regional, and local assemblies in their relationships to each other.[35]

For example, the definition of the nature of the offices of elder, minister, and deacon in their relation to each other, the roles of the assemblies, and the liturgy is the responsibility of the General Synod. Decisions concerning the ordination of persons to the office of ministry, general supervision of consistories, and the incorporation or dismissal of congregations into the denomination are the responsibilities of the classes. Decisions concerning baptizing and admitting individuals into the membership of the church, as well as maintaining regular times for worship, are the responsibility of the local consistory.[36]

In accord with his understanding of the crucial role of the local congregation and consistory, Steffens observed in 1887 that the General Synod had made the right decision regarding admission of Freemasons to membership. Had the General Synod ruled that no Freemasons may be admitted, it would have been guilty of usurping the authority that rightly belongs to the board of elders or consistory. The General Synod, which has the responsibility of general superintendence over the life of the church, had exercised that responsibility when it advised strongly against membership in the Freemason Society. At the same time, it left the local office bearers free to exercise their judgment in the cases of individuals who came before them to make confession of their faith.[37]

---

[35]   Steffens, "Iets over Het Onderscheid tusschen Gereformeerde end Congregationalistische Kerkregeering," *De Hope*, April 5, 1893.

[36]   For a full discussion of the theology and history of how the basic principles of the Church Order of Dort and the Explanatory Articles are understood in the Reformed Church today, see Daniel J. Meeter, *Meeting Each Other in Doctrine, Liturgy & Government*, Historical Series of the Reformed Church in America, no. 24 (Grand Rapids: Eerdmans, 1993).

[37]   Article 30 in the Church Order of Dort reads, "In those assemblies,

Suspicion of the powers of the General Synod was characteristic of the leaders in the midwestern Reformed Church, who were opposed to any hierarchical principles in the church order. Steffens called attention to the danger inherent in a little noticed resolution of the General Synod in 1884 that made the synod a "continuing body."

According to the Church Order of Dort, the General Synod was not a permanent body; it existed only when it was actually in session. Article 50 provided that it would ordinarily meet once every three years. A local church would be charged with nominating the time and place for the next meeting of the General Synod. In practice Article 50 became a dead letter in the Netherlands. No General Synod was ever called until 1945. In 1816, a Directorate replaced the General Synod in the church order. In the United States, however, the General Synod of the Reformed Church in America met annually after 1800, but its existence was limited to the time it was in session.

The fact that the General Synod was not a continuing body meant that it did not have a legal existence under American law. It could relate to corporations such as a board of direction and boards of foreign and domestic missions and a board of publication that would function on its behalf, but the General Synod itself did not exist legally between sessions. In 1884, the General Synod passed a resolution that made it a continuing body. Few people noticed the change or thought it more than a mere technical matter.

Steffens objected to the General Synod as a continuing body in two articles in *De Hope* in 1892. He believed that a theological principle had been violated. He feared that the General Synod would grow in power in relation to the other assemblies of the church and the local congregation. This would undermine the principle of a horizontal church order in which it is constantly apparent that Christ is the only head of the church. He also warned that the move would open the way to a bureaucracy that could use its power against the congregations as well as on their behalf. Apparently few people were interested in pursuing what they saw as merely a technical change in organization; no one else commented on his reflections. Nevertheless he was correct in his opinion that the synod's action would have a long term effect on the life of the denomination.[38]

---

ecclesiastical matters only shall be transacted, and that in an ecclesiastical manner. A greater assembly shall take cognizance of those things alone which cannot be determined by a lesser, or that appertain to the churches or congregations in general, which compose such an assembly," Meeter, *Meeting Each Other*, 73.

[38] Steffens, "Open Brief aan N. N.," *De Hope*, February 3, 1892.

## The Relation of the Reformed Church in America to Other Denominations, Including the Possibility of Mergers

During the 1890s, when proposals were being formulated in favor of a merger with the (German) Reformed Church in the United States, in favor of a denominational Federal Union with other Presbyterian and Reformed churches, and in favor of a union of Reformed immigrant congregations in the Midwest with the Christian Reformed Church, Steffens set forth his thought about what constitutes a "denomination." He reminded his readers that when the Belgic Confession was written there was no sense of a "denomination" in the modern sense of the word. Upon their arrival in America, the Dutch immigrants entered into the world of American denominationalism. The word "denomination" originated in the early years of the evangelical revival in England and America.

> John Wesley said, "I...refuse to be distinguished from other men by any but the common principles of Christianity...I renounce and detest all other marks of distinction. But from real Christians, of whatever *denomination,* I earnestly desire not to be distinguished at all....Dost thou love and fear God? It is enough! I give thee the right hand of fellowship." [39]

The Synod of Dort also did not envision the development of denominations. It did not give the church of its land a name, but simply referred to it in its opening words, "For the maintenance of good order in the church of Christ...." (Art. I). Thus the whole matter of separately existing denominations and merger of denominations is a modern problem. In the course of time, wrote Steffens, the denomination "has succeeded in getting a real existence as a body, although the original importance of the local church has not been entirely lost...." [40]

Denominations were a new type of church. Previously, in Europe and Great Britain, churches were either the established church of the land or were known as "dissenters," "sects," or "seceders." The issues facing the leaders of the Secession of 1834 were typical of the contests that went on between established churches and dissenters. "Denominations" were different in that they neither anticipated being the established church nor sought to live more or less separated from the majority of other churches.

[39] Quoted in Winthrop Hudson, *American Protestantism* (Chicago: Univ. of Chicago Press, sixth impression, 1972), 33.

[40] Steffens, "The Proposed Plan of Federation of the Reformed Churches," *Presbyterian and Reformed Review*, 6/5 (October, 1894), 670.

The basic contention of denominational theory is that the true Church is not to be identified exclusively with any single ecclesiastical structure. No denomination claims that all other churches are false churches. Each denomination is regarded as constituting a different "mode" of expressing the outward forms of worship and organization in that larger life of the Church in which they all share.[41]

Steffens recognized that he was dealing with a new form of church life when issues of denominationalism were raised. On the one hand, denominations represented a new way for Christians to live in unity with each other by avoiding the dilemma of either civil establishment or sectarianism. On the other hand, the fact that modern denominations exist as separate bodies is a sign of the brokenness of the church in the modern era. Reformed Christians must always be seeking the unity of the church. "I venture to say, that the Reformed Church...has been, from the very beginning of its existence, favorably inclined towards union with sister churches."[42]

In an age when denominational theory served to minimize confessional differences, Steffens taught that union between two denominations must be on a confessional basis. If there is no unity of confessions, then the union is based on an illusion; it disunites rather than unites.[43] Confessions are the band by which churches are bound together; without a common confession, a church may be a collegial body, but it does not remain a living organism.[44] His objection to most of the schemes of Federal Union being proposed between 1880 and 1910 was that they were attempts to bring about union in church order while not dealing with confessional differences. He feared that in entering a Federal Union, the synods or assemblies of the denominations entering into the union could move later in confessionally opposed directions, without adequate processes in place in the church order to deal with the increasing confessional diversity.[45]

---

[41]   Hudson, *American Protestantism*, 34.
[42]   Steffens, "Proposed Plan of Federation...," 666. In the nineteenth century, the Episcopal churches did not seek to enter into union with Protestant denominations who did not accept the Historic Episcopate. The Reformed Church in America was not ready to accept bishops.
[43]   Ibid., 667.
[44]   Steffens, "Wekelijksch Budget," *De Hope*, June 28, 1893.
[45]   Steffens, "Proposed Plan of Federation," *Presbyterian and Reformed Review*, 20 (October, 1894) 670-71.

Many of the advocates of church union in Steffens's day charged that the continuing existence of separate denominations is a sin. He disagreed with such statements, but said it was important to explore when and under what conditions it is sinful to continue to live in separate denominations. It is not wrong, he said, for Protestants to maintain separate organizations. It is wrong to expect people simply to worship together week after week when there are serious differences on theological issues and liturgy, such as there are between Lutherans and Reformed, or Reformed and Baptists. They are, however, free to seek a variety of ways to exercise their faith together and to cooperate in carrying out deeds of mercy.

Steffens was all in favor of Reformed and Presbyterians continuing to seek ways to be united as denominations on the basis of the Reformed confessions. He did not believe it was sinful to remain separate while they were seeking to resolve their differences. On the other hand, he was troubled by the continuing separation of the Reformed Church in America and the Christian Reformed Church. The two have the same confessions and same Church Order of Dort. Their liturgies are for all practical purposes the same. Why then do they remain separated? Yet the two churches continue to seek to drown out each others' voices. Hatred and animosity continue to seek ways to gain some advantage. "Is such a situation not sinful?"[46]

Twenty years later, Gerhard De Jonge wrote in *De Hope* that on the whole there were good relationships among American denominations. He pointed out that there were three major sources of separation among them. The first was ethnic or national in background. Many of the denominations had come to America with one or another movement of immigrants from one of the countries of Europe. If they had remained in Europe they would have been embedded in the church of that land. Had England not taken over New Amsterdam, the Reformed Church rather than the Church of England would have been the established church.

The second source was historic theological differences between the Reformed/Presbyterian churches and the Methodists and Baptists. De Jonge said that these historic theological differences no longer were loaded with the fierce antagonism of previous generations. They did not accuse each other of being false churches. There was little debate between American Calvinists and American Methodists about

---

[46]    Steffens, "Wanneer is Het Zonde Indien Geloovigen niet samen wonen in Ger. Kerkverband?" *De Hope*, December 21, 1892.

predestination and related doctrines. These churches lived together in friendship and cooperation.

The third source was the separation between churches that have no essential differences, such as between the Reformed Church in America and the Christian Reformed Church. In such cases, one or both hold to their isolation and spirit of separatism. The more recent the separation is, the more clearly seen is the sectarian spirit. De Jonge did not press the point but clearly was indicating that it was time to seek reconciliation.[47] The articles written by Steffens and De Jonge for the readers of *De Hope* represent well the prevailing spirit of cooperation and favorable attitude toward unity with other Presbyterian and Reformed churches.

## Entering into Alliance and Merger with other Protestant churches

The editors of *De Hope* were strong supporters of the Presbyterian Alliance founded in 1846 by churches in Europe and North America. The Reverend Derk Broek attended the conference in 1873 and wrote a day-by-day report of its proceedings in a series of two articles. He listed the nine Reformed theological affirmations at the heart of the alliance as the basis on which it worked. The goal of the alliance was not to unite all of the churches into one international denomination or to interfere with the internal life of its members.

> Its goal is simply to advance cooperation among them and to further evangelical confessional truth in opposition to Rome and to unbelief. Moreover, it works for the obtaining of freedom of worship, especially in Roman Catholic lands, and finally, to consult with each other on ways to further the general interests of the Kingdom of God while searching for ways in which the enemies of the truth can best be combated.[48]

The Reverend Egbert Winter attended the 1881 conference of the Presbyterian Alliance in Philadelphia. He was impressed with the variety of perspectives represented there. In general, the American churches were more conservative than their continental mother churches, but the most conservative churches had the upper hand at the conference. Because of the objection some of the churches had to hymns and organ music, no such music was used in the public worship. Neither could the members of the alliance celebrate the Lord's Supper together. Nevertheless, Winter wrote enthusiastically about the conference in his

[47]   G. De Jonge, "De Denominatien in Amerika," *De Hope*, October 17, 1911.
[48]   D. Broek, "De Evangelische Alliantie," *De Hope*, October 22, 1873.

series of articles. He observed that the careful theological thinking of the Dutch, the firm character of the Scots, the elasticity of the French, and the American emphasis on practical action all melded together into a fruitful mix.[49]

In spite of this bias toward cooperating with other churches and looking for greater unity, the classes of the midwestern Reformed Church in America in 1893 defeated the proposal to merge with the German Reformed Church in the United States. It is important to examine the issues surrounding that plan of union.

The major issues came to the forefront between 1886 and 1894, when the synods of the Reformed Church in America and the German Reformed Church in the United States formally considered and voted upon the plan to unite the two denominations. The classes of the Reformed Church in America voted twice on the proposal. In 1892, two-thirds of the classes voting did favor union, but in view of three conditional affirmative votes it was decided to resubmit the question to the classes. During the following twelve months, opposition to the plan grew. More midwestern classes voted against it, resulting in its defeat in 1893 by a count of sixteen for, eighteen against.[50] For our purposes it is not necessary to review the history. This study confines itself to reviewing the theological and ecclesiastical issues as understood by the midwestern leaders.

The merger issues were debated in the pages of *De Hope*. Two highly respected midwestern ministers, John Karsten and Peter

---

[49]  Egbert Winter, *De Hope*, January 12, 1881.

[50]  For accounts of the plan and its controversy, see Reformed Church in America, *Acts and Proceedings,* 1892, 577-84; 1893, 816-19; see also Herman Harmelink, *Ecumenism and the Reformed Church in America,* Historical Series of the Reformed Church in America, no. 1 (Grand Rapids: Eerdmans, 1968), 38-52, and Eugene Heideman, "Reformed Ecumenicity, 1888-1893," in *Reformed Review,* vol. 18, (September, 1964), 16-25. The *Christian Intelligencer* and *De Hope* each devoted much space to keeping their readers fully informed of developments. In my 1964 article, I wrote, "Further, one does not read any objections being raised with regard to the creeds or polity of the respective churches. It would have been difficult to make any objection, for the creeds and structure were very similar," 21. Having read the articles in *De Hope,* I now believe that the objections were weightier than I previously thought, especially in light of what was happening in 1893 with regard to the New Theology being taught at Andover Theological Seminary, controversies about science and religion, and the issues revolving around the use of higher criticism in biblical studies. At the time I wrote the article in 1964, I believed that objections to the "Mercersburg Theology" of Schaff and Nevin played an important role in midwestern opposition to the merger. The articles in *De Hope* by Steffens and others

Moerdyk, and a leading elder, Isaac Cappon, were members of the committee that prepared the plan for union. [51] Karsten and Moerdyk wrote in support of the plan, as did Egbert Winter in January 1892.

By 1892 Steffens was strongly opposed to merger with the German Reformed Church in the United States. His attacks in the pages of *De Hope* against the plan played a crucial role in its ultimate defeat. He was not a separatist by nature, however. In the first years after his arrival in the United States in 1872, he wrote positively about movements toward organic union with the Presbyterian Church in the United States of America. In 1875, he wrote,

> Our church is no longer the old Dutch Reformed Church. The Presbyterian church has also lost her Scottish nature. Both have become American. They are like two shoots grafted on to the same stem. Their history encourages us to recognize that the time has arrived to unite what belongs together.[52]

He went on to accuse those who opposed efforts to bring about organic union of being separatists (*Afgescheiden*) who demanded stability rather than true conservatism.

> Is the conservative principle equal to that of stability? Then certainly there cannot be thought of uniting, and our Separatist brethren are correct when they refuse to give up their history. For, however Calvinistic our church may be, or however pure our Presbyterian church order may be, the *Christelijke Gereformeerde Kerk* in The Netherlands has a distinctly different history from ours. True conservatism does not have the same meaning as stability. True conservatism has an essential regard for the

opposed to the merger do not mention Mercersburg or Nevin specifically. There was continuing suspicion of Schaff, who by 1892 was teaching at the Presybterian Union Theological Seminary in New York and had sided with Briggs in regard to interpretation of scripture and the need for revision of confessions. By 1892, Mercersburg Theology was at most a side issue no longer needing to be mentioned in *De Hope.*

[51]   John Karsten was one of the ministers who had led the movement to ban Freemasons from membership in the denomination. In 1892 he was pastor of the Reformed Church in Alto, Wisconsin. Peter Moerdyk was a member of the first class to graduate from Hope College in 1866 and Western Theological Seminary in 1869. In 1892 he was pastor of the Trinity Reformed Church in Chicago, an English-speaking congregation. Cappon was one of the leading citizens of the city of Holland.

[52]   Steffens, "Bladen uit eene oude Potefouille," *De Hope,* January 6, 1875.

historical life-principle, but it however is also ready to give up something for sake of the continuity of its history in order to conserve what is valuable in itself. When this is understood, one is no longer ruled over by an instinctive fear of "organic union" nor carried along by the impetuous enthusiasm of the friends of this movement.[53]

Steffens's progression from a cautiously favorable stance toward organic union with other Calvinistic American denominations to strong opposition to union with the German Reformed Church can best be understood as theological rather than provincial or ethnic in nature. His caution grew between 1875 and 1892 in the light of theological developments taking place in other American denominations. Among those developments were proposals for calls for new confessional statements, increasing ambiguity in theological language under the influence of the "New Theology" being taught especially at Andover Theological Seminary, and the increasing influence of higher critical methods in the teaching of the Bible. Those developments will be discussed in subsequent chapters of this book.

By 1887, Steffens was displaying reluctance about a merger with the German Reformed Church in the United States, but he still recognized good reasons to move ahead in conversations about organic union.[54] Too much time, money, and effort were being spent by Protestants maintaining their separate denominations. Lutherans, Baptists, Remonstrants, and Calvinists could live together as good neighbors in America but would experience great tension if they had to live in one household. Presbyterians and Congregationalists, with their traditions from Great Britain, have a different perspective from continental Reformed churches. Therefore, the best direction for the Reformed Church was to look toward closer union with the Christian Reformed Church[55] and the German Reformed Church in the United States. Steffens stated his hesitancy not on theological grounds, but on the practical question of whether the historical characteristics of

---

[53]  Ibid.
[54]  Steffens had pointed out already in 1878 that there was a great difference between the Dutch and the German Reformed churches in Europe. The first is decisively Calvinistic while the second had more the spirit of Melanchton, "De Eisch des Geloofs end de Leer der Gereformeerde Kerk," *De Hope*, February 27, 1878.
[55]  There were serious conversations about unity going on between the Christian Reformed Church and the midwestern leaders between 1887-1893.

the Dutch and German churches were such as to allow them to live together comfortably.[56]

In January 1892, Steffens attacked the plan for a federal union on grounds of theology and church order. He objected that the German church was confessionally deficient because it held to the Heidelberg Catechism but not the Belgic Confession and the Canons of Dort. Steffens argued that the Belgic Confession is the central confession for the Reformed Church, with the Canons of Dort being a further statement giving more precision to the confession. The Heidelberg Catechism, he wrote, is not really a confession. It is rather a teaching tool designed for the instruction of the youth rather than a full statement of the theology of the church. The catechism does not contain clear teaching about predestination, or more particularly the doctrine of reprobation. It is open to the Arminian interpretation that had to be corrected and condemned by the Synod of Dort. Church unity must be based on confessional unity; without confessional agreement serious new tensions can arise that can lead to schism.[57]

His second objection was that the plan provided that each entering denomination could maintain its own identity and creeds under its continuing General Synod, but that there would be an assembly above the synods.[58] Just as each church already had a church

---

[56]   The Steffens family was German. He had been born in Emden, Germany, and had come to America in 1872 to serve the German-speaking Reformed Church in America congregation in German Valley, Illinois.

[57]   Steffens, "Wekelijksch Budget," *De Hope*, January 6, 13, 1892. Steffens's claim that the Belgic Confession is the central confession may have some merit, but in the life and worship of the denomination the catechism has played a far more important role.

[58]   Steffens objected to the following provisions in the Plan of Federal Union:
   Article III: For the management of certain common interests of these federated churches, an Ecclesiastical Assembly is hereby constituted, which shall be known by the name and style of "The Federal Synod of the Reformed Churches."
   Article VI: The Federal Synod may advise and recommend in all matters pertaining to the general welfare of the Kingdom of Christ, but shall not exercise authority except such as is expressly given it under this Constitution. Whenever anything recommended by the Federal synod shall have received the assent of each of the General Synods, it shall have the force of law in both Denominations.
   Article VIII. The Federal Synod shall not interfere with the creed, cultus or government of either Denomination. Also matters of discipline shall be left to the exclusive and final judgment of the ecclesiastical authorities of the Denomination in which the same may arise, *Acts and Proceedings*, 1891, 352-54.

order that carefully delineated the responsibilities of consistories, classes, and synods, so the federal plan delineated the relationship of the assembly to the other bodies in the new organization. Steffens objected that the plan proposed a union of denominations without asking the congregations to consent. This is new because it changes the role of congregations in the classes. Steffens here was making the same point that he had made when he complained about the action of the Reformed Church in America's decision in 1884 to make the General Synod a *continuing body*. It brought a hierarchy back into the church order. Steffens wanted to guard against any action that would call into question the fact that the local congregation with the Word and sacraments and discipline is fully the church.[59]

Egbert Winter rejected both of the arguments of Steffens. He and John Karsten both contended that acceptance of the Heidelberg Catechism by itself is already sufficient confessional grounds for entering into the union. The catechism is sufficiently clear on matters of human depravity, grace, and salvation so that Arminianism is ruled out. It is not necessary that the doctrine of reprobation be spelled out clearly. One must be careful about saying too much about that or getting into theological debates about the merits of infra- and supra-lapsarianism. The blessings of the union would far outweigh any deficiencies of doctrinal definition.[60]

[59]  Steffens, "Wekelijksch Budget," *De Hope*, January 6, 1892.

[60]  Winter, "Federale Vereeniging," *De Hope*, January 6, 1892. Karsten, January 13, 1892. After Steffens accepted a call in 1895 to teach in the Presbyterian seminary in Dubuque, Iowa, Winter became his successor at Western Theological Seminary. James Bratt, in his study of Dutch Calvinism in America, implies that Steffens became disenchanted with his midwestern Reformed Church colleagues because they "had little use for principial analysis of 'the spirit of the age' or for any other Kuyperian tool" (*Dutch Calvinism*, 46). However, Geerhardos Vos, in a July 12, 1890, letter to Abraham Kuyper, suggested that Steffens's isolation from his colleagues was related to his fierce opposition to merger with the German Reformed Church while Winter, Moerdyk, and Karsten all wrote in favor of it. Vos wrote,

> Dr. Steffens, who still sees the situation in the Reformed Church the clearest, is rather isolated and has heard much opposition already. *De Roeper* [a secessionist church paper in the Netherlands] is mistaken when it thinks that Freemasonary is the only point of difference between us and the Reformed Church. The question at issue is much deeper. Our simple people have felt by a sort of instinct the seriousness of the trend in which the large American churches move (James T. Dennison, Jr., *The Letters of Geerhardus Vos* (Phillipsburg, N.J.: P & R Publishing, 2005), 142.

The Rev. Egbert Winter, D.D.
(1836-1906)

*Courtesy of Western Theological Seminary*

"As a preacher he always aimed to *teach* his people. As a teacher he ever sought to *indoctrinate* his pupils. Possessed of a clear intellect he loved the orderly statement of the truth. Ardently loving the doctrines of our Reformed Church he delighted to present them as the only foundation on which a sinner could build a hope of forgiveness and salvation." –John W. Beardslee, *Leader*, December 19, 1906, 120.

Winter also defended the Federal Union plan with the provision for an assembly in addition to the General Synods of each denomination. He agreed with Steffens that the original authority of the church lay with the consistory. Winter quoted extensively from the plan to show that the federal union concept does not undermine the role of the local congregation or change the basic order of the Reformed Church in America. Moreover, Steffens's objection that a new concept was being introduced into the church order does not carry much weight. Reformed polity has always been open to change.[61]

Later in the year, Steffens wrote another article in which he explained the real reason he was against the union. He was a Calvinist who objected to Arminianism and feared that it was present in the German Reformed Church, which had only the Heidelberg Catechism and not the Belgic Confession or the Canons of Dort as its standard. This opened the door to Arminianism and liberalism, as well as Romanism and liberalism.[62] Steffens wrote that it is not separation

[61]    Winter, *De Hope*, January 20, 1892; January 27, 1892.
[62]    Consideration of Mercersburg theology is postponed to the chapter on the relation of the midwestern leaders to development in American Protestant theology in the nineteenth and twentieth centuries. Between 1844-1854,

into denominations that keeps division and unrest in the church. Unrest comes when liberals deny the essential nature of the faith.[63] Steffens's arguments carried the day in the midwestern Reformed Church. Following the defeat of the plan, the close relationship that the two Reformed churches had enjoyed since American independence began to fade. The Reformed Church lived thereafter more within the Presbyterian orbit. The German Reformed Church in the United States went through a series of unions that ended with the merger in the United Church of Christ in 1957.

Four major intertwined issues shaped the controversies that were occasioned by the union efforts. All of them came to the fore in the debate between Steffens, on the one hand, and Winter, supported by Peter Moerdyk and John Karsten, on the other. One issue was the extent to which the desire to strengthen relationships with the Christian Reformed Church should trump efforts to form a closer union with other denominations. A second was the extent to which union with other denominations would make a real difference to the Reformed congregations that lived in the "Dutch colonies" in the towns and villages in the Midwest. In the case of the German church, there was little midwestern geographical overlap. Moreover, the German-language congregations in the Midwest had made a conscious decision to be members of the Reformed Church in America rather than the German Reformed Church in the United States. With regard to the Presbyterians, the difference in languages and customs between denominations whose origins were in Great Britain on the one hand and the European continent on the other meant that there would be many practical issues to overcome in the event of union. In view of the fact that prior to 1900 most of the midwestern Reformed churches still worshiped using the Dutch language, it was probably only their strong sense that in Christ there is only one church that led them to consider union at all.

---

suspicion of Nevin and Schaff was perhaps greater in the eastern Reformed Church in America than in the Midwest, where it was less well-known. Joseph Frederick Berg, who had grown up in the German church and served pastorates in that denomination, was called to teach theology at New Brunswick Theological Seminary, 1861-1871. He was a persistent foe of Mercersburg theology. For a history of the suspicion of Mercersburg Theology in the Reformed Church in America, 1844-1854, see Gregg Mast, "A Decade of Hope and Despair: Mercersburg Theology's Impact on Two Reformed Denominations," in *A Goodly Heritage*, Jack Nyenhuis, ed., 163-80.

[63]  Steffens, "Verdeel en Heersch," *De Hope*, November 9, 1892.

The two issues of church order and theology were closely related. Steffens put his finger on the heart of the matter. After approximately 1885, the real issue was how closely the congregations in the Reformed Church in America should be linked with denominations in which Protestant liberalism and modernism were tolerated. However much those who favored union complained that it was "nontheological factors" (such as ethnicity, desire to maintain the status quo, "bekrompenheid," provincialism), theological objections always were put forward by opponents to union.

Shifts in Steffens's position between 1875 and 1886 indicate how important theology was. In 1875, when classical Reformed theology was still dominant in Presbyterian churches, Steffens favored moving forward in discussions looking toward church union. By 1886, when the "New Theology" as taught at Andover Theological Seminary was making inroads in the Presbyterian churches, he was becoming cautious. In the 1890s, when biblical higher criticism was making inroads in Union Theological Seminary in New York City, Mercersburg theology was strong in sections of the Reformed Church in the United States but as such was not raised as an issue by Steffens. Revision of basic Christian doctrines of the Trinity, depravity of humankind, and the virgin birth and resurrection of Jesus Christ was being proposed by some in other denominations. Steffens came out in strong opposition to union efforts. His November 1892 statement that liberalism was the essential issue remained central to discussions of church union.

Issues of church order were closely related to the theological concerns. Memories of the persecution of the Afscheiding ministers by the Directorate of the liberal Dutch church remained strong. The midwestern leaders remained suspicious of all appearances of hierarchy among the assemblies of the church. They remained adamant that the Belgic Confession's horizontal church order could not be compromised. Union into a larger denomination with a strong General Synod or Assembly opened the door to bureaucratic hierarchy and new forms of ecclesiastical oppression.

## Ecumenical Relationships and Plans of Union after World War II

The failure to unite with the German Reformed Church did not end ecumenical interest on the part of the Reformed Church in America. It continued to relate to the Presbyterian Alliance and became a charter member of the Federal Council of Churches in 1906. From time to time the General Synod dealt with various invitations to enter into discussions about union with one or another Presbyterian denomination. However, it was not until after World War II that the issue of church union gained central stage again.

After World War II, the midwestern Reformed Church in America stood at a fork in the road with regard to its ecumenical position. Three roads were open between 1946 and 1950. One was to follow the road of full cooperation with American Protestant denominations that had been walking together since the founding of the Evangelical Alliance in 1873 and that were together in the Federal Council of Churches (FCC).[64] The second road was to become associated with the National Association of Evangelicals (NAE) that was organized in 1943. It was necessary to choose between those two roads because the NAE did not allow any denomination that was a member of the FCC to become a member of the NAE. The third road opened with the proposal that the Reformed Church in America unite with the United Presbyterian Church to become the United Presbyterian Reformed Church.

Had the decision been simply one of confessional unity, union with the United Presbyterian Church should have been the road chosen. The Westminster Confession and Catechisms were compatible with the Reformed Church in America's Standards of Unity. The United Presbyterian Church was as conservative theologically as the Reformed Church in America. The United Presbyterian Church, with the center of its population in Pennsylvania and Ohio, would have filled in the geographical gap between the eastern and midwestern regions of the Reformed Church.

In early 1947, the *Church Herald* printed letters that suggested that serious efforts be made to formulate a liturgy and statement of doctrine to be agreed upon prior to proceeding to vote on the merger with the United Presbyterian Church.[65] Some pastors called for reconciling differences in the confessions and the church orders.[66] For example, the Reverend Henry Fikse pointed out that the United Presbyterian

---

[64]  The Federal Council of Churches was reorganized to become the National Council of Churches of Christ in the USA in 1950.

[65]  Bert Van Malsen, "Letters to the Editor," *Church Herald*, February 14, 1947, 10; Jerome De Jong, February 7, 1947, 8; John S. Ter Louw, "A Tentative Draft Before We Vote," January 31, 1947, 10.

[66]  Henry Fikse, "The Bible and Church Union," *Church Herald*, March 21, 1947, 8. The Rev. Albert W. De Jonge, "Letters to the Editor," March 25, 1949, also objected to the difference between the two denominations regarding the formula of subscription. See also the response to Fikse's article by Lester Kuyper, "The Bible and the Confessional Standard of the United Presbyterian Church," *Church Herald*, April 18, 1947, 11, 14. See also Henry Bast, "Priorities in Church Union," April 29, 1949, 13.

Church had changed its position on the authority of the Bible from "*the* rule of faith and life" to "*an* infallible rule of faith and practice." Fikse also objected that the Reformed Church's form of subscription requiring ministers to be loyal to the confessions was stronger than was that of United Presbyterian Church. In spite of the call for more careful outlining of the confessional stance of the proposed new denomination, no discussion took place in the *Church Herald* following publication of the proposed confessional statement, "The Revised Confession for Church Union" in the May 21, 1948, issue.

In their accounts of the course of events leading up to the failure to unite, Lynn Japinga and Herman Harmelink III have shown that nontheological factors had greater weight than specifically theological objections.[67] Herman Harmelink III provides a detailed account of the events and history of proposals for union between the Reformed Church in America and other denominations. His conclusion is that the failure of all efforts to unite with another denomination was due to nontheological factors.

> While its opposition to union is often couched in theological terms, and while it claims to be truer to the Bible than the ecumenical group, non-theological factors carry the greatest weight. Among them are the Dutch heritage, and doubts about the non-Dutch; the "come-outer" separatist tradition, which thinks in terms of dividing rather than uniting; a contentment with the status quo made possible by isolation from mainstream America.[68]

In light of the above discussion about the failure of the merger with the German Reformed Church in America, it can be contended

---

[67]   Japinga deals with the issues related to membership in the Federal Council of Churches as well as with the history of the attempt to merge; see her "On Second Thought: A Hesitant History of Ecumenism in the Reformed Church in America," in John W. Coakley, ed., *Concord Makes Strength: Essays in Reformed Ecumenism*, Historical Series of the Reformed Church in America, no. 41 (Grand Rapids: Eerdmans, 2002), 10-34. Japinga also deals with the failed attempt to unite with the (Southern) Presbyterian Church in the United States in 1969. Since the latter vote lies outside the time frame of this book and the issues were much the same as in the plan of union with the United Presbyterian Church, please to refer to the chapter by Japinga for further information.

[68]   Harmelink, *Ecumenism and the Reformed Church*, 88-89. For Harmelink's more recent reflections on Reformed Church ecumenism, see his "Ecumenism and the Reformed Church Revisited," in Coakley, *Concord*, 87-88.

that Harmelink and Japinga paint with too broad a brush when they conclude that *in all cases* the failure to unite was due to the midwestern separatist tradition, Harmelink's and Japinga's charges carry more weight when they write about twentieth-century ecumenical and merger efforts. Nevertheless, one must ask whether opposition was due to "isolation from mainstream America" or whether it was occasioned by opposition to what was perceived as mainstream liberal American Protestantism. Attention must be paid to midwestern attitudes toward the Federal Council of Churches and the National Association of Evangelicals in the 1940s. By that decade, midwestern Reformed churches had shifted from their earlier Dutch Reformed piety to the practices of American evangelical piety as reflected in the theology and practice of the NAE rather than in the FCC. The issue was not so much to preserve the Dutch heritage as to avoid American Protestant liberalism.

At the fork in the road in the years 1946-1950, there was pressure on the General Synod of the denomination to choose between membership in the National Association of Evangelicals and the Federal Council of Churches. The Reformed Church had been a member of the Federal Council since it had been organized in 1908. It was the major avenue of cooperation with "mainline" denominations. To withdraw would have meant the loss of strong historic ties not only with churches within the United States, but also with churches in Asia that were established through the evangelistic efforts of Reformed Church missionaries.

However, many in the Midwest had long been suspicious of the FCC because it had some of its origins in the Social Gospel Movement of the late nineteenth century.[69] Midwestern Reformed Church members objected that there were many in the council who did not accept biblical accounts of the virgin birth, the vicarious atonement, the deity of Christ, the bodily resurrection of Jesus, and crucial doctrines of the faith. The council defended itself by pointing out that the Unitarians were not accepted into its membership because they did not hold the doctrine of the Trinity. The confession of the FCC that Jesus is "divine Lord and Savior" affirmed the deity of Christ. It was not a "super-church" but a council of churches that respected the responsibility of its member denominations to hold to their own confessional bases and forms of liturgy and church order. Ecumenicity was understood in terms of

---

[69] Sydney Ahlstrom, *A Religious History of the American People* (New Haven: Yale Univ. Press, 1972), 802-804.

visible relationships among churches where the Word is preached and the sacraments administered, rather than as an invisible spiritual unity among individuals.[70]

The National Association of Evangelicals was an association of those who had a spiritual unity in Christ and accepted seven basic creedal points, including the inspiration and infallibility of the Bible, the doctrine of the Trinity and the deity of Christ, the virgin birth, vicarious atonement, bodily resurrection, the necessity of regeneration by the Holy Spirit, and the visible return of Christ. Individuals as well as church assemblies could become affiliated with it.[71] Because the association had a rule that no denomination that was a member of the Federal Council was eligible to affiliate with it, the question of Reformed Church membership in the NAE became moot when the General Synod refused to withdraw from the Federal Council.[72] By remaining in the Federal Council, the Reformed Church reaffirmed its loyalty to the Belgic Confession, which taught that unity must take place in the visible church around the preaching of the Word and celebration of the sacraments as well in the spiritual unity of individual believers.

Paul Fries has shown recently that both the advocates of spiritual unity and those who called for church union should be understood to have deep roots in the Reformed tradition. He points out that it is a misunderstanding to say that when John Calvin "writes of the universality of the church and the call and regeneration of the believer, he is referring only to the invisible church of the truly elect. This is not the case; there is no salvation apart from the visible church. The means of grace do not appear in the invisible church; here there is no preaching

---

[70]  The attack on the Federal Council of Churches was launched by the Rev. Henry Bast, who published and sent "An Appeal to the Ministers and Laymen of the Chicago and Iowa Synods." Samuel Cavert's response to criticism of the Federal Council of Churches entitled, "The Purpose and Plan of the Federal Council of Churches," was published in the *Church Herald*, April 30, 1948, 12. Cavert was general secretary of the Federal Council of Churches.

[71]  See James DeForest Murch, *Cooperation without Compromise* (Grand Rapids: Eerdmans, 1956), 39, 66. See also Rutherford L. Decker, "The Purpose and Plan of the National Association of Evangelicals," *Church Herald*, May 7, 1948, 12. Decker was president of the NAE in 1946.

[72]  For the report on the reasons that the Reformed Church in America should remain a member of the Federal Council of Churches of Christ rather than become associated with the National Association of Evangelicals, see *Acts and Proceedings*, 1948, 141-45.

of the gospel, no administration of the sacraments."[73] Along with this "church-to-church" ecumenism, one must also recognize the "heart-to-heart ecumenism" that holds that "formal agreements between denominations are far less important than the fellowship rising out of spiritual experience. Hearts warmed by Christ find unity regardless of church affiliation and allow believers from various backgrounds to ignore the issues that historically divided them."[74]

[73] Paul Fries, "The Theological Roots of the RCA's Ecumenical Disposition," in Coakley, *Concord*, 39. Paul Fries was academic dean and professor of theology at New Brunswick Theological Seminary at the time he wrote the chapter.

[74] Ibid., 42.

CHAPTER 4

# Reformed Pietists: The Way of Salvation

When the leaders of the Protestant Reformation rejected the Roman Catholic doctrine that in the celebration of the Holy Communion the bread and wine are actually changed into the body and blood of Christ, it became necessary to articulate how Christ is present in the life of the believer. In chapter 2, it was noted that Luther taught that Christ is present "in, with, and under" the bread and wine, while the followers of Zwingli spoke of the Lord's Supper as a memorial feast.[1]

In the Reformed tradition it was emphasized that Christ the ascended Lord is seated at the right hand of God, where he is our advocate before the Father and where his body is God's pledge that we will also be taken up to be with him. Thus the absence of his body on earth is a sign of God's faithfulness that we have an eternal future with Christ at the right hand of God. In this present age, we live with the dual experience of the absence of his body among us and of the presence of his Holy Spirit who abides in the church, maintains the scriptures as God's living Word among us, makes effective the sacraments as a means

[1]   See p. 35-41.

of grace, and regenerates our hearts.[2] The practice of piety in Reformed churches has its roots in this dual experience of the absence of Christ's body and the presence of the Holy Spirit of Christ. The Heidelberg Catechism articulates the nature of Reformed piety in its answer to the question, *"What does it mean to eat the crucified body of Christ and to drink his shed blood?"*

> It is not only to embrace with a trusting heart the whole passion and death of Christ, and by it to receive the forgiveness of sins and eternal life. In addition it is to be so united more and more to his blessed body by the Holy Spirit dwelling both in Christ and in us that, although he is in heaven and we are on earth, we are nevertheless flesh of his flesh and bone of his bone, always living and being governed by one Spirit, as the members of our bodies are governed by one soul.[3]

With this understanding of the Lord's Supper as set forth in the Heidelberg Catechism, Reformed piety does not concentrate its attention solely upon Christ's presence at the Lord's Table but persistently shifts its attention to the activity of the Spirit of Christ in the heart of the believer and to the presence of the Spirit of Christ active in the church and in course of history. Christ's presence in Holy Communion is not separated from the theology of faith and the life of faith. Such faith includes both knowledge and trust. True faith is

> not only a certain knowledge by which I accept as true all that God has revealed to us in His Word, but also a wholehearted trust which the Holy Spirit creates in me through the gospel, that, not only to others, but to me also God has given the forgiveness of sins, everlasting righteousness and salvation, out of sheer grace solely for the sake of Christ's saving work.[4]

The leaders of the Second Reformation (*Nadere Reformatie*) in the Netherlands sought to hold together the orthodox theology of the Reformed tradition with the faith as they experienced it in their devotional life. After the Synod of Dort, orthodox theology, with its emphasis on doctrine, had its focus on God's decrees and predestination. Individual piety emphasized the new birth, conversion,

---

[2]    Heidelberg Catechism, Q. 49-54, 70, 76. See also Steffens, "Niet meer met ons en toch met ons," *De Hope*, April 22, 1884.

[3]    Ibid., 76.

[4]    Ibid., 21.

and "the sanctification of the believer so that he might acquire an experiential or personal knowledge of Christ's saving grace."[5]

The midwestern leaders followed the pattern of the Second Reformation leaders in holding together orthodox Reformed theology and experiential preaching. They could call upon the Belgic Confession, the Heidelberg Catechism, and the Canons of Dort to justify their position. They believed that the seventeenth-century Protestant scholastic systematic theology manuals were consistent developments of the theology of the confessional documents.[6] The order of articles in the Belgic Confession was almost the same as the order of topics in their theology manuals. Similarly, the warm personal tone of the questions and answers of the Heidelberg Catechism provided a firm basis for the very personal ways in which they addressed the congregation, calling for repentance and for more holiness in daily living. Since all of the theological professors at Western Seminary were pastors of congregations before they were called to teach, they combined within themselves the close relationship between theology and preaching.

In the remainder of this chapter the systematic Reformed theology that was taught by the theological leaders of the midwestern Reformed Church will be examined. In doing so, we will see how orthodox theology, with its focus on the doctrine of God and the divine decrees, was intended to provide assurance of the providential care of God and confidence that believers would persevere in the faith to the end of their lives, in spite of their sins and weaknesses. Then attention

---

[5]    M. Eugene Osterhaven, "The Experiential Theology of Early Dutch Calvinism," *Reformed Review*, 27/3 (1973-4), 180. Many studies of the history of Protestant pietism have focused on events in Germany. In contrast to the leaders of the Second Reformation in the Netherlands who sought to hold personal piety together with Reformed scholastic theology, the German pietists of the eighteenth century reacted against the dry, intellectualistic German Protestant scholasticism of the seventeenth century. Men such as August Hermann Francke, Gottfried Arnold, Phillip Jakob Spener, Count Zinzendorf, and others emphasized the new birth. They separated themselves from the national church by meeting in pietistic "conventicals." The emotional aspect of religious life tended to be set in contrast to orthodox theology and the structures of the national church. For further development of this point, see Peter C. Erb, ed., *Pietists: Selected Writings* (New York: Paulist Press, 1983), 1-14; Joel R. Beeke, *The Quest for Full Assurance* (Carlisle, Penn.: Banner of Truth Trust, 1999), 294.

[6]    Given the strong negative overtones that the term "scholastic theology" has acquired in Protestant circles, it is well to be reminded again that the term refers to a method of teaching theology. Like any method, it can be used to sharpen our theological awareness or be misused to suck the life out of the faith.

will be given to how midwestern Reformed Church preachers sought to strengthen the faith of the members of their congregations through their preaching the way of salvation. Preaching the "way of salvation" (*ordo salutis*) was intended to encourage members of the congregation to examine their progress or lack of progress in their own spiritual growth.

### The Doctrine of God in Systematic Theology

The first teacher of theology at Hope College was Cornelius Eltinge Crispell.[7] He had been born in Marbletown, New York, in 1820. He graduated from New Brunswick Theological Seminary in 1842 and served three pastorates in New York before he was called to teach at Rutgers College in New Brunswick, New Jersey. He taught at Hope College from 1866-1877. His class notes are no longer available, but in 1868 *De Hope* published a lecture that he had given in the First Reformed Church in Holland, Michigan. The lecture provides an outline of what he taught ministerial students. It shows his dependence on the systematic theologies developed by the seventeenth-century Protestant theologians. This lecture is of fundamental importance to an understanding of the theology of the midwestern Reformed Church. Every professor of systematic theology at the seminary from 1866 to the end of World War II taught in his tradition. Although one discovers subordinate points of disagreement among them, there is no major dispute about doctrine or any fundamental departure from his methodology.[8]

Like his successors, Crispell did not seek to be original or creative in his theological teaching. His lecture was little more than an abbreviated exposition of the three Standards of Unity. As his

[7]    Theological education of ministers was offered at Hope College beginning in 1866. Western Theological Seminary was separated from Hope College in 1886 and became a separate institution in that year.

[8]    The professors of systematic theology at Western Theological Seminary prepared course notes for their students rather than requiring them to buy textbooks. With the exceptions of Crispell and Nicholas Steffens, whose notes are no longer available, some or all of their course notes are in WTS/ JAH. The professors of systematic theology were Egbert Winter, Gerrit H. Dubbink, Evert J. Blekkink, John E. Kuizenga, and John R. Mulder. The systematic course notes of Albertus Pieters, who normally taught English Bible and missions, are also available. The course notes of all of the teachers are remarkably similar in organization, theological definitions, and methodology. They show little originality or creativity. It is clear that in matters of systematic theology they, like Charles Hodge at Princeton, did not intend to introduce new ideas at Western Theological Seminary.

**The Rev. Cornelius E. Crispell, D.D. (1820-1910)**

*Courtesy of Western Theological Seminary*

Cornelius E. Crispell, born in Marbletown, New York, was the son of a French Huguenot father and a Dutch mother. He served as a pastor in the Reformed Church in America for forty-seven years and as a professor for sixteen years. "We see him instructing the youth in the simpler studies of the preparatory school and at the same time a professor of history to young men at Rutgers College; and afterward professor of mathematics, philosophy and astronomy in Hope College, and then at the bidding of the Church a Professor of Didactic and Polemic Theology to which was soon added the department of pastoral theology, and in this variety of service displaying the well-equipped and competent man." "This dear man of God was equally at home and appreciated as a preacher and pastor."—*Acts and Proceedings,* 1911, 256-57.

exposition is followed below, footnotes are provided to show how his successors continued his way of doing theology.

### God's Perfections

Crispell opened his lecture by stating, "God is a Spirit of infinite perfections—consisting in three persons—and the cause of all things apart from Himself."[9] God's ultimate purpose is to reveal God's own perfection. All of the divine works are designed to implement this goal. Even those actions that appear to be contrary to that goal, such as the actions against Pharaoh (Exod. 9:16), and the man born blind (John 9: 3), are designed for the revelation and glory of God. In harmony with this goal, the ultimate purpose of human beings is "to glorify God and to enjoy him forever."[10]

[9]   C.E. Crispell, "Ware Godgeleerdheid," *De Hope*, Sept. 30, 1868.
[10]  Ibid. Although the phrase, "to glorify God and enjoy him forever," is

Crispell's reference to the "perfections" of God indicates that he was using abstract theological language inherited from medieval and Protestant academic scholars rather than strictly biblical language. In using abstract language, he followed the Belgic Confession, which speaks of God as "eternal, incomprehensible, invisible, unchangeable, unending, almighty; perfectly wise, righteous, good, and a very abundant fountain of all good."[11] God is therefore unchangeable in every respect, without beginning or end.[12] God is everywhere present, all-knowing of all past and future events, the cause of all good.[13]

the answer to the first question in the Shorter Westminster Catechism, it was as fully appreciated in the Reformed Church in America as in the Presbyterian tradition. Nicholas Steffens taught that the glory of God, not predestination, is the central Reformed principle. Christ came to earth to glorify the Father ("The Principle of Reformed Protestantism and Foreign Missions," *Presbyterian and Reformed Review*, Vol. 5/18 [April, 1884], 244-45). The glorification of God is also the central principle of foreign missions (ibid). Professor Gerrit Dubbink. who taught at Western Theological Seminary from 1904 to 1910, taught that humans have been placed in this world as free moral beings to glorify God. The subordinate end is the happiness of God's creatures. We must insist on both. Gerrit Dubbink, unpub. and undated class lectures on systematic theology (JAH, WTS), 13.

[11]  Belgic Confession, 1.

[12]  "By the immutability of God we mean that attribute in virtue of which there can be no change in God, either in His essence, or in any of His attributes, or purposes...any change in the essence of God would be irreconcilable with the very idea of Deity....If there were any change, such change would have to be for better or worse, but either would exclude the idea of absolute perfection," Egbert Winter, *Dogmatics*, II (JAH, WTS), 62.

Evert Blekkink agreed that God as sovereign is unchangeable. "There is no external power to change the Almighty. There is no possible internal reason for change. He is the perfection and fullness of Being" (Blekkink, *The Fatherhood of God* (Grand Rapids: Eerdmans, 1942), 19. Nevertheless, Blekkink was open to the possibility that God was free to be flexible. "There is a flexibility in the Divine Government that must be reckoned with if we are to know God as he is. As recorded in the Scriptures God frequently changes his dealings with men and nations as the circumstances and conditions call for it....In all his relations to man, the race, and the universe, he remains free in his activities at all times, under all circumstances and conditions," ibid., 23.

[13]  "God's knowledge is that perfection in the Divine intellect whereby He understands Himself, and all things possible and actual—past, present, and future—in a Divine manner, by one simple act without succession," Dubbink, *Knowledge of God* (JAH/WTS), 12.

By the knowledge of God we mean that attribute in virtue of which

God is also merciful, patient, gentle, and gracious. God eternally hates all moral evil. God is a God of truth[14] and is always free to do his good pleasure, absolutely unlimited by anything outside the divine being.[15]

Professors of theology at Western Theological Seminary continued to teach students the list of attributes of God. At the end of the period reviewed in this book, M. Eugene Osterhaven wrote a series of articles on the Belgic Confession. In relation to Article I, he gave a pastoral interpretation of the attributes.

> His invisibility (John 1:18) reminds us that we walk by faith and not by sight (2 Cor. 5:7).

> His immutability means that He is "the same yesterday, today, and forever" (Heb. 13:8); that the heavens and the foundations of the earth may perish but He remains the same (Heb. 1:10ff.); and that He will remember His covenant forever (Psalm 105:8).

> His infinity is His limitlessness, the confession of which reminds us that we cannot flee from his presence (Psalm 139:7).

> His justice is His maintenance of the right and is best exhibited when He remains just and justifies those who believe in Jesus (Rom. 3:26).[16]

### God's Providence and Assurance of Salvation

God's decision to reveal his glory began in the work of creation[17] and continued in the work of providence and redemption. Crispell understood the order of providence and redemption to be Trinitarian.

> The Father appears as the protector of divine governance, and the maintainer of God's reign, appoints and sets out the duties

---

God knows himself, and all outside of Him—all things past, present, and future—all things actual, possible and certain—by an eternal, original, intuitive perception," Winter, *Dogmatics* II, 76-77.

[14] "By the truth of God we mean that perfection in the Divine essence in virtue of which God is and remains forever in perfect harmony with Himself, and His words, and works—and hates all that is false, and loves all that is true" Winter, *Dogmatics*, 133.

[15] Crispell, "Ware Godgeleerdheid."

[16] M. Eugene Osterhaven, *Our Confession of Faith* (Grand Rapids: Baker, 1964), 26-27. Osterhaven (1915-2005) taught at Western Theological Seminary from 1953 until he retired in 1986.

[17] "The supreme end of creation is the glory of God. Man exists because of God, but God does not exist because of man," Dubbink, *Knowledge of God*, 26.

of the Mediator, and with the Son, sends the Holy Spirit. The Son appears as the Mediator that includes the offices of prophet, priest and king, and with the Father sends the Holy Spirit. The Spirit appears as the Sanctifier, sent by the Father and the Son.[18]

Crispell taught that we know God's providence and redemption through the two books of nature and of scripture, as taught in the Belgic Confession:

> We know him by two means. First, by his action of creating, sustaining, and directing the whole world, seeing it is before our eyes as a beautiful book, in which all creatures, great and small, are as so many letters that give us to *see the invisible things of God, namely his eternal power and deity,* as the Apostle Paul says, Romans 1:20. All these things are sufficient to convince men and leave them without excuse. Secondly, to his glory and our salvation, he makes himself more clearly and fully known, so far as we need to know in this life by his holy and divine Word.[19]

Providence and assurance of salvation were focal points for the faith of the Dutch immigrants. Crispell and his successors emphasized both. In spite of human beings' fall into depravity, God did not forsake them. God's mercy and righteousness appear in the fact that the message of salvation is offered to all without distinction. God's benefits for natural life, for seedtime and harvest, are also available without distinction.[20]

Few doctrines played such a vital role in the piety of the Dutch colonies as that of the providence of God. Their understanding of the doctrine must be distinguished from Enlightenment and Romantic American leaders' use of the word "Providence" in place of the word "God." They vigorously rejected Paley's idea of God as the watchmaker who does not interfere with the world after it has been created.[21] Dubbink defined providence as the action of God whereby all

---

[18]   Crispell, "Ware Godgeleerdheid."
[19]   Belgic Confession, 2.
[20]   Crispell, "Ware Godgeleerdheid." Providence is "the almighty and ever-present power of God whereby he still upholds, as it were by his own hand, heaven and earth together with all creatures, and rules in such a way that leaves and grass, rain and drought, fruitful and unfruitful years, food and drink, health and sickness, riches and poverty, and everything else, come to us not by chance but by his fatherly hand" (Heidelberg Catechism, Q. 27).
[21]   The Rev. Meinhart. D. Van der Meer, "De Groote Daden Gods" *De Hope,* February 12, 1929.

**The Rev. Adrian Zwemer
(1823-1910)**

*Courtesy Joint Archives of Holland*

"Brother Zwemer was an earnest, conscientious and consecrated pastor, a practical, instructive and edifying preacher, a spiritually minded man, and his labors were owned and blessed of God. Besides his labors in the pastorate he sought to be useful through the Press. Under the general caption 'The Home and the Heart,' he contributed many highly edifying articles to 'De Hope.' Possessing the poetic gifts he has left behind a volume of poems."—*Acts and Proceedings*, 1910, 835.

impersonal fate or chance is excluded. "Providence is the work of God whereby the whole world and all that is in it, is preserved and governed with power and wisdom, according to his will, unto his glory, the happiness of his creatures, and the salvation of his people."[22]

After America entered World War I in 1917, John Kuizenga wrote passionately about God's providential activity:

If God is only outside, our only hope is in the miracle, which does not seem to happen. If God is only inside, we are forced to the monstrous proposition that all is right with the world....There are forces, and aims, and greeds, and hatreds, and so-called "divine rights" which God does not want, which clash with his will; but he shall bend them all to accomplish the goal, which is his, and not theirs....That holds because God is in his world. But he is also more than his world. Hence we may look for new influences that are not now at work; we do look for a new era and a better world, which is to come by a more complete introduction of the power of our Lord Jesus Christ.[23]

[22]   Dubbink, *Dogmatics*, 30-31.
[23]   John Kuizenga, "The Fullness of Time," *Leader*, December 19, 1917, 2.

The pastoral importance of the doctrine of providence came to the fore in Adrian Zwemer's 1881 New Year editorial in *De Hope*. The lives of his readers had been filled with uncertainty in such matters as personal health, deaths of children, mothers dying in childbirth, and family finance as well as in public disasters such as the Civil War, the Holland fire of 1871 and other fires, and the financial panics of 1857 and 1873. Reflection on God's providence enabled them to cope with such uncertainty.

Zwemer expressed his confidence that God would not forget or abandon his people, but this did not mean that their lives would no longer be filled with troubles. God would strengthen them through testing and suffering. Those whom God loves, God chastens. "There are dark days before us. God leads us through dark valleys that are unknown. That is the way God works in the world, sowing the seeds of the living word of truth that will provide the harvest of righteousness in the time of harvest."[24]

God's providence and assurance of salvation sustained the Dutch Reformed immigrants as they went through the difficult first three decades in America. Johan Stellingwerff's collection of letters exchanged by immigrants to Iowa during the period 1849-1873 provides insight into the way God's providence sustained them. The letters of Diedrich Arnold Budde and his wife, Christina Maria Budde-Stomp, are particularly helpful in providing insight into the nature of their trust in God's providence and assurance of salvation.[25]

[24] Adrian Zwemer, "Onze Nieuwjaarsgroeten," *De Hope*, January 12, 1881. Adrian Zwemer was born in the Netherlands in 1823 and ordained to the Reformed Church in America's ministry in 1858 without having attended a theological school. He was the father of James Frederick Zwemer, who served as pastor, principal of Northwestern Academy in Orange City, Iowa, and as professor of theology in Western Theological Seminary. His second son, Frederick James Zwemer, served as missionary pastor in South Dakota, Illinois, and in Wisconsin. His third son, Samuel M. Zwemer, became world renowned as the "Apostle to Islam." His fourth son, Peter John Zwemer, died in Oman while serving as a missionary there. His daughter Nellie served as a missionary in China from 1891-1930. Adrian Zwemer was one of the leaders among the midwestern ministers who stimulated the strong foreign mission interests in the midwestern Reformed Church.

[25] The Budde family, like the Wormser and Scholte families, was originally Lutheran from Germany. During the 1820s they had joined the Nederlandse Hervormde Kerk. They became part of the Afscheiding of 1834 and were subjected to government persecution and then became independent from the new Christelijke Afgescheiden Kerk when Scholte was deposed. The Buddes left the Netherlands after Scholte with the intention of joining him in Iowa. However, they decided to remain in Burlington, Iowa, rather

The letter written by Dietrich Budde to Johan A. Wormser on the day of their anticipated departure to America, March 27, 1847, expressed his assurance of salvation and trust in God's providence.

> May the Lord reward all your friendship, love, and benevolence bestowed us. We are after all children of the same heavenly father, purchased by the blood of his only begotten son to be his eternal possession and bound to the spiritual head, our Lord Jesus Christ. We are of good cheer; until now we are lacking in nothing. The throne of grace is open to us; we are free to approach God in prayer, unitedly entrusting ourselves to his care and faithfulness, asking that he will prosper our faith.[26]

Christina M. Budde-Stomp often expressed her confidence in God's faithfulness in the face of the many misfortunes that came to them in America. In 1861, when she and her husband were suffering through days "of sickness and adversity," she wrote, "As we increase in years and in weakness of the body, his promise is that he will not abandon nor forsake us; even in our old age we will still be bearing fruits that were planted in the house of the Lord."[27]

The following year, Mrs. H.M. Bousquet-Chabot of Pella wrote to Budde-Stomp that two of her sons had joined the Union Army in the Civil War. She was grieved to see her youngest son, Herman, leave, but she was comforted by the fact that his going off to war "had its blessing for me and mine [and] could only be attributed to God's fatherly governance over us."[28] Herman had been involved in a spiritual struggle for two years, but "now before he left his parental home to go into military service, [the Spirit of God] empowered him freely to confess that he belonged to the Lord Jesus. You can imagine what a relief this was for us at such a sad departure."[29]

---

than proceed to Pella. They were instrumental in establishing a Dutch Reformed congregation in Burlington. When the Dutch Reformed church closed, they joined the German Reformed congregation. Much of their correspondence was with members of the Wormser families in Amsterdam, the Netherlands. See Johan Stellingwerff, *Iowa Letters: Dutch Immigrants on the American Frontier*, ed. Robert P. Swierenga, trans. Walter Lagerwey, The Historical Series of the Reformed Church in America, no. 47 (Grand Rapids: Eerdmans, 2004), xviii-xix.

[26]   Ibid., 54.
[27]   Ibid., 490-91.
[28]   Ibid., 496.
[29]   Ibid.

Christina M. Budde-Stomp's trust in the providence of God included confidence of eternal life and gave her patience to endure her present sorrows and suffering. She was ready to "leave the future to the Lord. From our earliest years he has been our hiding place in dangers, etc. (Psalm 90). Things may be ever so good for us here below, but there always remains a void until we enter the rest that is laid away for the people of God."[30] At a time when she was suffering from a rapid heartbeat and rheumatism, when her husband's chest gave him trouble during a stormy winter, she asked God to give her patience to endure while she looked ahead to her eternal abiding place.

> May the Lord grant us patience and meekness to bear what he lays upon us. The world is a vale of tears, nothing but sorrow and trouble. We have no abiding peace here, and when the battle is done, the course is run, God will wipe away all tears from our eyes, and there will be no more trouble and grief, but we shall praise and glorify him through all eternity.[31]

### Predestination, God's Foreknowledge, and Eternal Decree

After dealing with providence and assurance of salvation in his 1868 lecture, Crispell went on to deal with God's foreknowledge and plan of redemption.[32] He and his successors insisted that God's foreknowledge was based in God's predestination and eternal decree. Professor Egbert Winter in his class lectures provided a clear and succinct statement of the doctrine. He understood the scriptures to teach that God has decreed all things that come to pass, down to the smallest details.

> By the doctrine of Predestination we mean the predetermination of all events in history, and all the destinies of God's creatures in accordance with God's definite, unfailing, independent, unchangeable and all-inclusive purposes, which, as to their final character, are holy, just, wise, and good.[33]
>
> As such He wills the welfare of His creatures in strict accordance with His own glory, and moral character. His moral character, then, must assert itself in history, when and where He reveals Himself. And such assertion demands definite and all-

---

30    Ibid., 586.
31    Ibid., 607.
32    Crispell, "Ware Godgeleerdheid."
33    Winter, *Dogmatics*, Vol. 3, II, 17–18.

inclusive plans or purposes.[34]

When they taught the doctrine of predestination, the midwestern professors could not avoid meeting the objection that God must then have ordained the fall of humankind into sin; therefore, not humanity but God is ultimately responsible for sin and evil in the world. All of the midwestern professors denied that God is responsible for sin. They distinguished God's *prescriptive* will from the divine *permissive* will. Thus God effectively prescribed all that is good and right in creation and by divine good pleasure[35] gave the original human beings freedom to disobey as well as to obey.

> ...God does not stand related to good and evil precisely in the same way....
>
> Even though He took up in His eternal world plan the evil as well as the good, the former he took up in the way that He willed that it should come on the basis of His permitting it—not as working it efficiently, or as constraining or compelling men thereof either by direct inworking upon their mind, or by ordering providence so as to deprive them of the proper exertion of their own will. He never would tempt or force to sin.[36]

Although the midwestern leaders usually resisted attempts to speculate on why God permitted the fall into sin,[37] Crispell did explore the issue. He said that insofar as we can see, God's permitting the fall into sin was wise because it was the best means to reveal God's mercy, benevolence, and righteousness. We must remember that creation is for the sake of the glory of God through the revelation of the divine perfections. God redeems Christ's elect and forgives their sin, the angels

---

[34] Ibid., 19. The first Q & A of the Heidelberg Catechism includes the clause, "that he protects me so well that without the will of my Father in heaven not a hair can fall from my head; indeed, that everything must fit his purpose for my salvation."

[35] By "divine good pleasure," Reformed theologians meant that God is free to do what God wills in accordance with divine justice and mercy. Thus God was free either to create or not create the world, free to decree whether and whom to save or not to save. By using this phrase they rejected pantheism and Stoicism and all other philosophies that would undermine the freedom of God. God was also free to give Adam and Eve the choice to obey or disobey. Therefore God cannot be held responsible in any way for the choice they made.

[36] Winter, Vol. 3, II, 23.

[37] See Winter, *Dogmatics* Vol. 3, IV, 88-90.

in heaven are led to break out in songs of praise (Luke 2:13-14), and there is great rejoicing in heaven (Rev. 4:11; 5:9, 13). In the punishment of the wicked who do not come to faith God's hatred of sin and evil, as well God's retributive justice, is manifested.[38]

The midwestern ministers accepted the teaching of the Synod of Dort concerning election and reprobation. The Canons of Dort teach

> that in the course of history God graces some with the gift of faith and others not proceeds from his eternal decree, *who has made these things known from of old* (Acts 15:18), and *who accomplishes all things according to the counsel of his will* (Ephesians 1:11). In keeping with this decision he graciously softens the hearts of the elect, although they are hard, and disposes them to faith; but in his righteous judgment he leaves the non-elect to their ill-will and obstinacy.[39]

The midwestern leaders agreed with Dort: "As all men in Adam have sinned and brought upon themselves God's judgment and eternal death, God would have wronged no one had he willed to leave the whole human race in sin and disfavor."[40] They also agreed that the reason for the gracious election of some to salvation is "only the good pleasure of God, good not because he selected out of all possible conditions certain qualities and works of men as a prerequisite of salvation, but because it pleased him out of the common mass of sinners to adopt some for his own possession."[41]

Gerrit Dubbink defined reprobation as "the predestination of certain men whom God leaves in their sinful estate to eternal condemnation on account of their sins" (see Jer. 6:30; Matt. 7:23; 1 Pet.

---

[38]   Crispell, "Ware Godgeleerdheid," 1. Crispell's suggestion follows the Canons of Dort, which teach that God "also purposed, for the showing forth of his mercy and for the praise of the riches of his glorious grace, to give the elect to Christ for saving and to call and draw them by his Word and Spirit effectually into fellowship with Christ, or, to grace them with true faith in him, justification, sanctification and being effectually kept in fellowship with Christ, at last glorification," I/7.

[39]   Canons of Dort, I/6.

[40]   Ibid., I/1.

[41]   Ibid., I/10. The most recent books written by a midwestern Reformed Church in America minister in full defense of Dort's doctrine of predestination are Harry Buis, *Historic Protestantism and Predestination* (Grand Rapids: Baker, 1958), and *The Doctrine of Eternal Punishment* (Philadelphia: Presbyterian and Reformed Publishing, 1957). He emphasized the importance of the doctrine of election as providing the strongest grounds of assurance for the elect.

2:8; Jude 4).[42] Although they found this to be a disconcerting doctrine, they believed that scripture taught it. The resistance to the gospel and law of God on the part of many hardened sinners could not be denied. Preaching the doctrine of reprobation is without positive impact on the reprobate. "Sinners are entirely willing to be passed by....While God leaves them alone, they hate and oppose him. All sinners resist common grace. In so far as God has dealings with them, they show themselves to be his enemies." [43]

Because expositions of the Canons of Dort have often been outlined by the acronym TULIP, standing for Total Depravity, Unconditional Election, Limited Atonement, Irresistible Grace, and the Perseverance of the Saints, the central concern of the Canons of Dort that the gospel must be preached indiscriminately to all is often ignored by those who study the canons. The canons constantly point out that the doctrine of election is important because it comforts believers with assurance of their salvation in Christ. [44]

## God's Covenant of Works and Covenant of Grace[45]

The doctrine of election can easily be understood individualistically when considered solely in relation to the eternal decree of God, in contrast to much biblical language that relates God's election to Israel and the church. Lambert J. Hulst recognized the problem and called attention to the fact that the principles of Reformed church order must be grounded in God's covenant with Abraham rather than in election or regeneration.[46] According to God's covenant with Abraham, his descendants through Isaac remained in the elect covenant community

42  Dubbink, *Dogmatics*, 21.
43  Ibid., 21.
44  For a balanced evaluation of the Canons of Dort, see M. Eugene Osterhaven, *The Faith of the Church* (Grand Rapids: Eerdmans, 1982), 77-83. Gordon Girod, pastor of the Seventh Reformed Church in Grand Rapids, Michigan, gave a vigorous defense of TULIP in a series of sermons that were also published in his book, *The Deeper Faith* (Grand Rapids: Reformed Publications, 1958).
45  John R. Mulder, professor of theology at Western Theological Seminary, gave a standard definition of a covenant when he taught that "a covenant is a contract, an agreement between two parties on a certain matter. Conditions are clearly delineated and rewards and punishments fixed," course notes on "Anthropology" (WTS/JAH, 1948 and prior years), 11.
46  Lambert J. Hulst served as a pastor in the Reformed Church in America from 1874-1881. He was a frequent contributor to *De Hope*. During the controversy about Freemasonry, he was deposed from the ministry in the Reformed Church in America when he with his congregation changed over

until by their actions they cut themselves off. Hulst wrote that the same applied in the baptized community in the New Testament.[47]

### The Covenant of Works

According to the professors of systematic theology at Western Theological Seminary, the covenant with Abraham was set within the context of two covenants—the covenant of works and the covenant of grace. The covenant of works was made with Adam as the representative or "federal" head of the whole human race. It promised life to him and all his posterity upon condition of perfect and personal obedience. When Adam disobeyed God's command not to eat of the fruit of the tree of the knowledge of good and evil, Adam's sin was "imputed" or reckoned to every descendant in the whole human race. Through his fall, the whole human race became totally depraved, not in the sense that the race and every individual were as bad as possible, but in the sense that they could never do any works that would overcome the guilt of their sin or merit salvation in any sense of the word.[48]

The covenant of works as taught at Western Seminary explained how all humanity has come to be fallen. "The covenant of works was never abrogated, for God does not change his will for man."[49]

---

to the Christian Reformed Church. He became a minister in the Christian Reformed Church where he had a very distinguished ministry. For an excellent account of his life and ministry, see James D. Bratt, "Lambert J. Hulst: The Pastor as Leader in an Immigrant Community," in Hans Krabbendam & Larry J. Wagenaar, eds., *The Dutch-American Experience: Essays in Honor of Robert P. Swierenga* (Amsterdam: VU Uitgeverij, 2000), 209-221.

47   Lambert J. Hulst, "Waarheid: Toegepast op het Kerkelijk Leven," *De Hope*, August 21, 1878. More recently, Richard A. Muller, professor of theology at Calvin Theological Seminary, has pointed out that the five points of TULIP distort our understanding of Reformed faith when they leave the impression that "God's electing grace [comes] as an unmediated bolt from the blue" ["How Many Points?" in *Calvin Theological Journal*, vol. 28, (1993), 428]. Muller contends that five points in the Canons of Dort were set forth in response to the five points of the *Remonstrance* of the Arminian party (426). He rightly points out that "the Reformed doctrine of grace—the irresistible grace of the five points—not only identifies God's grace as unmerited but also locates the primary working of that grace in the covenanting community of believers, where it is presented through the means of the Word and sacrament" (429).

48   John R. Mulder, "Anthropology Class Notes,"1948 and prior years (WTS/JAH), 14-24; Dubbink, *Dogmatics*, 49; Bastian Kruithof, *The High Points of Calvinism* (Grand Rapids: Baker, 1949), 33-38. Cf. also Winter, *Dogmatic Theology, Second Part*, 152-59.

49   Mulder, "Anthropology," 24.

It remains in force throughout the history of the human race. In maintaining that it was a contract mutually entered into by Adam and God, it showed why God could not be held responsible for the sinful conditions of fallen mankind. Adam was not a naïve innocent child, but a fully responsible human being. It recognized the representative principle, whereby the father in the family acted on behalf of the whole family. Biblical support was found for each of the points made in the previous sentences. The fact that the doctrine of the covenant of works substituted contractual legal language for the personal relationship language of Genesis 2-3 was minimized or ignored.[50]

### The Covenant of Grace

Because the human race was hopelessly lost under the conditions of the covenant of works, God instituted the covenant of grace for the sake of the elect. The conditions of the covenant of grace had been summarized by the writers of the Westminster Confession:

> Man, by his fall having made himself incapable of life by that covenant, the Lord was pleased to make a second, commonly called the Covenant of Grace: whereby he freely offereth unto sinners life and salvation by Jesus Christ, requiring of them faith in him, that they may be saved; and promising to give unto all those that are ordained unto life his Holy Spirit, to make them willing and able to believe.[51]

According to the covenant of grace, the Son of God agreed to atone for the sins of God's elect by bearing the necessary punishment and to meet the demands of the law upon them. Jesus Christ thus became the guarantor of the salvation of the elect, the number of whom is fixed. Christ did not die for all, but for the elect only.[52]

---

[50] For a discussion of how Thomas Boston in Scotland expounded the covenant of works, see McGowan, A.T.B., *The Federal Theology of Thomas Boston* (Edinburgh: Rutherford House, 1997), 9-16, and Donald J. Bruggink, *The Theology of Thomas Boston, 1676-1732*, thesis ms. (Univ. of Edinburgh, 1956; located in Beardslee Library at Western Theological Seminary); and Bruggink, "Calvin and Federal Theology," in Richard C. Gamble, *An Elaboration of the Theology of Calvin* (New York: Garland, 1992), 37-44.

[51] Westminster Confession, chapter VII. See also Dubbink, *Dogmatics*, 54.

[52] Egbert Winter, "Part IV: God Revealed in Objective Soteriology," *Dogmatic Theology*, Vol. III, 3. Winter distinguished between the covenant of redemption that was the agreement between the Father and the Son in eternity and the covenant of grace between God and the elect that is

An issue that had threatened to divide those who came together at the Synod of Dort was that of the order of the eternal decrees in relation to the covenant of grace. It is not necessary to follow the intricacies of this controversy between the "supralapsarians" ("before the fall") and the "infralapsarians" ("after the fall"). Ultimately the synod favored the infralapsarians without condemning the supralapsarians. The synod's position also became that of most of the midwestern leaders.[53]

The infralapsarian position was favored for two reasons. The first is that the supralapsarian position is somewhat vulnerable to the idea that since God is absolutely sovereign, God is ultimately responsible for human sin. No theologian wanted to allow that conclusion. The second is that the infralapsarian argument makes it clearer that election is "in Christ." Election does not come about because of a naked eternal decree apart from the saving work of Christ. Steffens taught that even God's punishing righteousness is not bereft of fairness and mercy. There is no chasm between God's righteousness and God's grace in Christ.[54] Winter wrote that because our election is "in Christ," we need not try to search out that which is hidden in God, but we need only to preach Christ and look to Christ for our salvation.[55] In preaching, we can offer a serious call to sinners to repentance and faith, rather than simply declare what God has decreed for the elect.[56]

---

executed in the process of history. The intent of the distinction between the two was to protect the doctrine of election from any taint of Arminian teaching that Jesus died for all rather than for the elect alone and to avoid any possibility of the error that God's election is on the basis of a foreseen faith or human action on the part of those who come to faith. Winter's successor at the seminary, Gerrit Dubbink, seems to have agreed with Winter. On the other hand, John R. Mulder rejected the distinction between the two covenants; Dubbink, *Dogmatics*, 54; Mulder, "Anthropology," 12. On the whole, midwestern Reformed Church theologians took the position summarized by the Christian Reformed Church theologian Louis Berkhof, who wrote, "The covenant of grace and redemption are two modes or phases of the one evangelical covenant of mercy," *Systematic Theology* (Grand Rapids: Eerdmans, 1949), 265. Berkhof's first edition was published in 1939 and was virtually unchanged in successive printings. Although Berkhof was Christian Reformed, his *Systematic Theology* was widely used in the midwestern Reformed Church. Berkhof has a clear, concise statement of the history and significance of the issues, 264-71.

[53]   A succinct exposition of the issues is to be found in Berkhof, *Systematic Theology*, 118-25.
[54]   Steffens, "De Eenheid Gods," *De Hope*, October 18, 1876.
[55]   Winter, "De Weg naar den Hemel," *De Hope,* July 10, 1901.
[56]   Winter, *De Hope,* June 5, 1901. In the early 1920s a serious controversy

*The Covenant with Abraham*

God's covenant with Abraham was established within the covenant of grace. The covenant with Abraham clearly means that election is primarily corporate, *with Abraham and his descendants* rather than with individuals, according to the promise of God: "I will establish my covenant between me and you and your offspring throughout their generations, for an everlasting covenant, to be God to you and to your offspring after you" (Gen. 17:7).[57] As the sign of the covenant, God instituted the practice of circumcising all the male descendants

erupted in the Christian Reformed Church concerning what came to be called "the well-meant gospel offer." The Rev. Herman Hoeksema insisted that preaching consists of a general declaration of the truth that God saves the elect and condemns the reprobate. However, the gospel is not offered to everyone, for that would again place the ultimate decision of salvation in the hands of human beings rather than in the hands of God. Hoeksema submitted the following proposition for discussion: "The preaching of the gospel is as such neither a blessing nor a curse. It addresses man as a rational, moral being who is therefore responsible before God. God, however, uses also that preaching to realize his counsel of predestination, both of election and reprobation, so that he, without nullifying the ethical nature and responsibility of man, calls the one unto salvation and hardens the other. The preaching of the gospel is therefore never grace for the reprobate, neither is it ever intended to be such by God," quoted in Gertrude Hoeksema, *Therefore Have I Spoken: A Biography of Herman Hoeksema* (Grand Rapids: Reformed Free Publishing, 1969), 251; and in A.C. De Jong, *The Well-Meant Gospel Offer: The Views of H. Hoeksema and K. Schilder* (Franeker, Netherlands: T. Wever, 1954), 49. The position of Herman Hoeksema was condemned by the Christian Reformed Church Synod in 1924 (*Acta der Synode 1924 van de Christelijke Gereformeerde Kerk,* 113-37, especially the "three points" on 124). For a historical review and evaluation, see John Bolt, "Common Grace and the Christian Reformed Synod of Michigan (1924)" *Calvin Theological Journal,* vol. 35, (April 2000), 7-36. Herman Hoeksema was the major force in the formation of the Protestant Reformed Church. The controversy was watched with interest by leaders of the midwestern Reformed Church.

57   Western Theological Seminary teachers gave priority to the covenant with Abraham over the covenant with Israel through Moses. They taught that the covenant with Abraham remains in force through all generations and makes Abraham to be "a channel of blessing to all the families of the earth." "The introduction of the Mosaic Dispensation may be regarded as the putting into effect of what God had said to the patriarchs, and serves to illuminate the words of promise spoken to them rather than to present new facts" (John W. Beardslee, *Notes on Messianic Prophecy* (Holland, Mich.: privately printed, located in special collections, Beardslee Library, Western Theological Seminary, 1908), 28-29.

of Abraham through Isaac and Jacob. The covenant was maintained through the people of Israel and then the church was grafted into it following the death and resurrection of Jesus (Rom. 4:1-25). On the basis of the continuity of the one covenant with Abraham, the midwestern leaders accepted the practice of infant baptism as the sign of the covenant just as circumcision was that sign in the Old Testament.[58]

### The Covenant with Abraham and Infant Baptism

It was the practice in the Netherlands Hervormed Kerk at the time of the Afscheiding of 1834 to baptize all children of baptized members of the church who were brought for baptism. When the seceders began to organize under their General Synod, a difference of opinion arose over several points with regard to the practice of infant baptism. Since many of the baptized parents who brought their children for baptism in the Netherlands Hervormde Kerk had but nominal faith at best, some of the seceders maintained that only children of confessing members should be baptized. Others argued that this brought a subjective element into the decision to baptize. Baptism must be on the basis of God's covenant with Abraham and his descendants. So long as the parents have not cut themselves off from the covenant by denying their faith either by word or deed, they and their children are to be recognized by the church as members of the covenant.

[58]  See for example the sermon entitled, "De Kinderen des Verbonds en hun Deel aan den Heere," in A. Zwemer and B. Van Ess eds., *Nagelatene Leerredenen van Roelof Pieters* (Grand Rapids: Eagle Printing, 1881), 187-204. Roelof Pieters was born in Havelle, Drenthe, March 2, 1825. Following his immigration to the United States, Van Raalte came to know him and encouraged him to become a minister. In March 1855 he began to study in Holland Academy. In 1858 Pieters entered New Brunswick Theological Seminary and graduated in 1861. He served as pastor of congregations in Drenthe and Graafschap in Michigan and in Alto, Wisconsin, before accepting a call to the First Reformed Church in Holland, Michigan, succeeding Van Raalte there. He was a strong advocate for Christian schools and served on the editorial committee of *De Hope*. In a time when tensions about the Masonic Order were great between the eastern and midwestern sections of the denomination, his appreciation for the solid Reformed education he had received at New Brunswick helped maintain denominational unity. He died February 14, 1880, following an operation; see Zwemer and Van Ess, *Nagelatene Leerredenen*, x-xviii. His son, Albertus Pieters, became an outstanding Reformed Church missionary in Japan and teacher at Hope College and Western Theological Seminary.

The issue was raised in the Classis of Holland in 1854. The classis adopted the position that Van Raalte had already held in the Netherlands before coming to America. It decided that the children of nonconfessing baptized parents should be baptized on the basis of their participation in the covenant of grace, not primarily on the basis of the faith of their parents. Such children are to be regarded as members of the church. [59] In a later meeting, the classis voted not to favor allowing another confessing member, rather than the parents, to answer the questions of the liturgy regarding the baptism of the child. That should be the responsibility of the father even if he was not a confessing member.[60]

Lambert J. Hulst was a strong defender of the decision of the Classis of Holland. He pointed out that one does not become a member of the church through baptism but that one is already a member of the church on the basis of the covenant.[61] He quoted Johan A. Wormser, Sr., who had admonished the church in the Netherlands not to stop

---

[59]   *Minutes of the Classis of Holland*, 166-67. See also Johan A. Wormser, *Een Schat in Aarden Vaten in Twee Werelddeelen: Het Leven van Albertus Christiaan Van Raalte* (Nijverdal: E.J. Bosch, 1915), 190-91; Dosker, Henry E. *Levensschets van Rev. A.C. Van Raalte, D.D.* (Nijkerk: C.C. Callenbach, 1893), 172-73.

[60]   Ibid., 201. The issue of the baptism of children of nonconfessing members of the church among the separatists in many cases was not about the lack of faithful church attendance or about the parents' agreement that the faith proclaimed by the church was true. In many cases, nonconfession was due to the fact that the parents had not yet come to experience their conversion or to recognize in themselves the "marks" or signs of their election by God. They were not yet ready to agree with the admonition in the Heidelberg Catechism that the gift of faith is "not only for others, *but for me also*," Q. 21 (emphasis mine). They considered it presumptuous to make confession of faith prior to receiving the marks of their election. In 1932, Professor Siebe Nettinga wrote that the Classis of Holland avoided the problems of the "half-way covenant" in New England so long as the church's consistory maintained careful pastoral care and discipline, Nettinga, *De Hope*, March 8, 1932. An additional factor in the New England controversy about the "half-way covenant" was that the right to vote in civil elections was contingent upon being a confessing member of the church.

[61]   Hulst, *De Hope*, March 29, 1876; September 4, 1878. Hulst became a minister in the Christian Reformed Church when the Reformed Church in America continued to allow elders to accept freemasons as members. The Christian Reformed Church continued until 1898 the practice of permitting the baptism of infants of noncommunicant members. See James A. De Jong, *Henry J. Kuiper: Shaping the Christian Reformed Church, 1907-1962*, Historical Series of the Reformed Church in America, no. 55 (Grand Rapids: Eerdmans, 2007), 1-2.

baptizing infants, but instead to nurture them in the understanding of their baptism.[62]

The book by Johan A. Wormser, *De Kinderdoop Beschouwd met Betrekking tot het Bijzonder Kerkelijke en Maatschappelijke Leven (Infant Baptism with reference especially to the life of the Church and Society)*, which had been published first in the Netherlands was republished in America by the Hope College Press in 1873.[63] Wormser argued that infant baptism must be on the basis of membership in the covenant. The covenant has two sides: the first is the objective assurance of God's grace; the second is the obligation to live in accordance with one's baptism. The biblical example is the prodigal son who was welcomed and forgiven by his father through no merit of his own but then was expected to fulfill his role again as a son in the family. Infant baptism anticipates that the children will live godly lives.[64]

Wormser objected to those who confused issues of baptism with predestination. Those who have been baptized must not go about asking, "Have I been predestined?" Instead, they must remind themselves, "I have been baptized; I have died and risen in union with Christ. I belong to the covenant-keeping trinitarian God."[65] By making this declaration instead of asking about whether one really has faith or is really elect, there is assurance of salvation. To question our faith or election is to return to the slough of doubt. Assurance is not to be found through the search for individual spiritual experience.[66]

Wormser placed heavy emphasis upon nurture and pastoral care of those who had been baptized. Baptized children are tender shoots to be cared for and prayed for by the church. They have been grafted in but not yet fully rooted. The child who is baptized soon becomes engaged in the life-long struggle to overcome the temptations of Satan

[62]    Hulst, *De Hope*, March 1876.
[63]    Johan A. Wormser had been a close associate of members of the Afscheiding, including especially the Rev. Hendrick Scholte and some of those who immigrated to Iowa. For information about the Wormser family, see Stellingwerff, *Iowa Letters*, 3-8, and the role of the Wormser "society" in relation to the Secession of 1834, 22-31. Jan Peter Verhave, *Afgescheiden en Wedergekeerd: Het Leven van J. A. Wormser en zijn gezin* (Heerenveen, Netherlands: Uitgeverij Groen, 2000), provides many details about Wormser's relationships to those who emigrated. He was especially related to H.P. Scholte during his youth and the 1830s and early 1840s. For Wormser's understanding of baptism, see ibid., 629-31.
[64]    Wormser, J.A. *De Kinderdoop Beschouwd met Betrekking tot\het Bijzonder Kerkelijke en Maatschappelijke Leven* (Holland, Mich.: De Hope College Drukkerij, 1873), 76-87.
[65]    Ibid., 120.
[66]    Ibid., 62-64.

and the enticements of the world and to remain faithful to God. In the long struggle, the true weapons are the redemptive and sanctifying grace of God. This grace promises to deliver us through the church rather than being one that leads us constantly to seek new individual experiences.[67]

The decision of the Classis of Holland continued to be reaffirmed from time to time by the midwestern leaders. When Abraham Kuyper maintained in the late nineteenth century that infant baptism is to be administered on the grounds of "presumptive regeneration," he was vigorously opposed by Egbert Winter, who held that the covenant had the promises of God rather than an infant's "presumed regeneration" as its basis.[68] It was reaffirmed again by "J.B." in *De Hope's* "Question box" column. J.B., in answer to a question, responded that children of nonconfessing members may be baptized if the child is viewed (1) as a child of the church and in the covenant and (2) there is good evidence that it will be taught the Reformed faith.[69] John R. Mulder reaffirmed it in his inaugural address on becoming a professor at Western Theological Seminary in 1930, when he said, "The position of our Reformed Church is that the privilege of infant baptism does not rest upon communicant membership of the parents. The Church believes that to require communicant membership is to set an unscriptural limitation upon the privilege of baptism."[70]

The first regularly installed professor of systematic theology at Western Theological Seminary who challenged the practice of permitting infant children of noncommunicant members to be baptized was M. Eugene Osterhaven. He wrote,

> the office of baptism includes questions which only a believing Christian parent can answer affirmatively....This writer believes therefore that parents who have been baptized in infancy but who have not been willing to assume the privileges and obligations of the covenant when they have come to maturity, do not have the right to have their children baptized.[71]

[67]  Ibid. 120-23.
[68]  Winter, *Dogmatics* VI, 156-160.
[69]  J.B. *De Hope,* May 29, 1928. "J.B." was the Rev. John Bovenkerk (1880-1951), who wrote "De Vragenbus" ("The Question Box") in *De Hope*, 1920-1933. He was born in the Netherlands and graduated from Western Theological Seminary in 1916. During the years he wrote the column he was serving as pastor of the First Reformed Church in Muskegon, Michigan.
[70]  John R.Mulder, "Servants of the Message," *Leader*, December 17, 1930, 9.
[71]  M. Eugene Osterhaven, "Youth Forum," *Church Herald*, June 20, 1952.

The Reformed Church in America eventually came to agree with the conclusion set forth by Osterhaven. In 1976, the Reformed Church in America amended its *Book of Church Order* to make it mandatory that the congregation's board of elders "shall consider requests for infant baptism, providing at least one parent or guardian is a confessing member of the church to which the request is presented."[72]

## Preaching the Way of Salvation

In the teaching about the covenant with Abraham and his descendants, the corporate nature of the doctrine of election was emphasized, with the result that children of believers were baptized. On the other hand, according to the Canons of Dort, God's election pertained to individuals, since God

> freely willed as his good pleasure, to elect to redemption in Christ from the whole human race a certain number of persons, neither better nor more deserving than others, but with them involved in a common misery, fallen through their own fault from their original uprightness into sin and perdition. God also ordained Christ from eternity to be a Mediator and Head of the elect and a foundation for salvation.[73]

The individual character of election as taught in the Canons of Dort became a source of doubt for a significant number of the Dutch immigrants to America. Pastors had to deal with the lack of assurance of salvation and fears of those who had concluded that perhaps they were not among the elect. Such people would say that they believed "all that God has revealed to us in his Word" and that God's salvation is for others, but they could not be sure that "*to me also* God has given the forgiveness of sins, everlasting righteousness and salvation." [74] They believed that it would be presumptuous to become communing members of the church before they received signs of their election.

The comment of Jesus, "You shall know them by their fruits" (Matt. 7:16), was at times used by pastors to admonish members of their congregations to examine their hearts and lives to see whether they were fruitful. The Reverend Roelof Pieters, for example, urged people to ask whether they really loved the law of God and meditated on it the whole day. He asked whether they really loved God and whether they could say that they have kept the commandments. Were they ready to deny

---

[72]   *Book of Church Order*, I.1.5, Sec. 2a, p. 20 ; 2006 edition; *Acts and Proceedings*, 1975, 82-83; 1976, 46.

[73]   Canons of Dort, I/7.

[74]   Heidelberg Catechism, Q. 21.

**The Rev. Roelof Pieters
(1825-1880)**

*Courtesy of Joint Archives of Holland*

"He was loyal to the Confession of the Reformed Church because he was fully convinced that it was faithful to the Word of God. Original and independent as he was in his manner of preaching, he nevertheless allowed no difference with the accepted doctrines of the church. The doctrine of the Covenant occupied a central place in his heart and therefore also in his ministry. He courageously opposed sins; he earnestly called sinners to repentance; and when they testified to their conversion, he demanded, "Bring forth fruits worthy of repentance."—Adrian Zwemer, *Nagelatene Leerredenen van Roelof Pieters*, xvii.

themselves? [75] As pastoral admonitions to those who were becoming careless in their faith such questions could lead to spiritual awakening, but those of a more tender conscience were led easily to doubt their election.

The Reverend H.H. Dieperink Langereis tried to give words of reassurance to believers in his sermon on the text, "Surely his salvation is at hand for those who fear him" (Psalm 85:9a). He preached that increased awareness of sin was not to be a cause for alarm; it could be a mark of being among the elect. Grief over one's guilt did not mean that one was a greater sinner than others. Having the appearance of godliness without deep feeling does not always indicate hypocrisy. One must overcome doubt about election by looking to Christ for salvation. [76]

[75]  Roelof Pieters, *Nagelatene Leerredenen*, 41-42.
[76]  H.H. Dieperink Langereis, "Waarom Gods Volk zoo weinig verzekered is van zijn genadestaat," *De Hope*, June 1, 1887.

The constant attention given in sermons and articles to the issue of assurance provides evidence that there was widespread doubt among members of the midwestern Reformed churches about the sincerity of their own faith.[77] Pastors had to provide reassurance for those who were disturbed about their own lack of spiritual progress and perseverance in the faith.[78] John Karsten comforted them by acknowledging that the forces of unrighteousness are many, he but assured them that our Redeemer God has power over the forces of unrighteousness.[79] Derk Broek told them that those who lack assurance while on earth have a wonderful surprise awaiting them when they enter heaven in spite of their unworthiness.[80] Egbert Winter comforted those who worried about whether the young people would persevere to the end by saying that we must encourage them to believe in Christ, to make use of the means of grace, and to trust in the internal testimony of the Holy Spirit.[81] John De Haan quoted many verses, such as Matthew 17:5; John 3:14-16, 10:27-29, 14:6; Romans 6:4, etc., to show that we can be sure of our perseverance until death by the grace of God.[82]

The problem of the assurance of salvation was particularly acute among the Reformed Dutch pietists of the Second Reformation and those who came to America following the Secession of 1834 in the Netherlands. They emphasized the importance of remaining loyal to the

[77]  For a graphic account of the nature of their doubt, see Sheeres, *Son of Secession*, 93-100, which describes the faith crisis through which Gerritdina Ten Brummelaar went in 1851. In 1859, she married the Rev. Douwe J. Vander Werp, who became a strong leader in the Christian Reformed Church.

[78]  The need to provide reassurance to those who were worried about their election to salvation was also present in the eastern region of the Reformed Church, especially in the eighteenth century; see James Tanis, *Dutch Calvinistic Pietism in the Middle Dutch Colonies* (Hague: Martinus NIjhoff, 1967), 122-23.

[79]  John Karsten, "Waarom zou ik vreezen in kwade dagen, als de ongerechtigen die op de hielen zijn, mij omringen—Ps. 49:6," *De Hope*, March 24, 1914.

[80]  Derk Broek, "De Verrassing van het Hemelsche Leven," *De Hope*, August 14, 1895. The Rev. Derk Broek (1836-1903) was born in the Netherlands and graduated from New Brunswick Theological Seminary in 1864. He served pastorates in Michigan and Ohio. His sermons and articles were often "experiential" in nature.

[81]  Egbert Winter, "Hoe Blijf ik in mijn Geloof?" *De Hope*, December 10, 1890.

[82]  John De Haan, "De Mogelijkheid der Zekerheid in ons Heengaan," *De Hope*, December 15, 1914. The Rev. John De Haan served Reformed Church pastorates in Illinois and Michigan, 1898-1917, until he accepted a call to serve in the Christian Reformed Church. A sermon on the certainty of faith by Roelof Pieters is to be found in Pieters, *Nagelatene Leerredenen*, 157-69.

The Rev. John R. Mulder, D.D.,
(1893-1964)

*Courtesy of Western Theological Seminary*

When John Mulder retired as president of Western Theological Seminary in 1960, the General Synod resolved that: Whereas the church has been blessed by the far-reaching effects of his faithful and fruitful administration, knowledge and radiant personality, spanning two generations of students, and Whereas a deep debt of gratitude extends to him from every corner of our denomination, Therefore be it resolved: that we extend to Dr. John R. Mulder the undying appreciation of the church for his many illustrious years of service to Christ through the Reformed Church in America"— *Acts and Proceedings*, 1960, 56.

teachings of the Reformed confessions, especially the Canons of Dort. The doctrine of election defended in the Canons of Dort emphasizes the election of individuals while almost totally ignoring the covenantal roots of the doctrine related to God's covenant with Abraham and the church in the New Testament. In spite of the constant admonition in the Canons of Dort that the Holy Spirit gives faith through the hearing of the Word of God (I/3, 14; II, 5; III/IV, 8; V/10, 14), the emphasis upon the election of individuals to salvation and the decree of reprobation for others provided strong encouragement to many to focus on whether God's decree of election applied to them and therefore to examine their own spiritual progress or lack thereof constantly.[83]

In their efforts to help members of the church become more aware of their spiritual progress, midwestern pastors were helped by

[83]  The focus of attention to the five-point TULIP acronym, with its initial emphasis on human depravity and predestination, tends to underestimate the Canon's fifth article on perseverance and assurance.

the theological exposition of the *ordo salutis* ("order of salvation"). Theological conversation about the *ordo salutis* sought to define more precisely the activity of the Holy Spirit in bringing sinners to salvation. The doctrine emphasized that from first to last salvation is God's work. Whatever cooperation there is between God and individuals[84] at certain stages in the process is due entirely to God's grace. In the activity of the Holy Spirit, a personal relationship is established between the sinner and Christ with whom the sinner is brought into union.[85]

With slight variations, all of the midwestern professors and ministers were in agreement about the order of the steps in the way of salvation (*ordo salutis*). As taught by Egbert Winter, the steps were (1) election, (2) effectual calling, (3) the internal call, (4) regeneration, (5) conversion, (6) faith, (7) union with Christ, (8) justification, (9) adoption, (10) sanctification, (11) preservation and perseverance, (12) certainty of salvation.[86] John R. Mulder taught a slightly simpler order that was essentially the same as that of Winter: (1) election, (2) mystical union, (3) calling, (4) regeneration, (5) conversion, consisting of repentance and faith, (6) justification, (7) sanctification, (8) perseverance.[87]

The *ordo salutis* was very useful as a tool for helping members of the congregation understand what was happening in their lives when

---

[84]   The strong emphasis upon the experience of the individual in the way of salvation encouraged those who immigrated to America to look favorably upon American revivalism and the work of American evangelists such as Dwight L. Moody, who stressed the need for conversion and personal sanctification. American revivalism encouraged Arminian tendencies in the practice of the Reformed Church in America. It is ironic that the emphasis on the *ordo salutis*, which was intended to support Dort's high doctrine of predestination, instead created a practice of piety that opened the way to evangelical revivalism among the Reformed in America.

[85]   Winter, *Dogmatics*, part V, chapter 3, 17-18.

[86]   Ibid., 19-87. "He works in the heart by irresistible grace—takes resistance out of the will, and makes willing, and brings men thus willingly to Christ. This work of the Holy Ghost consists of various influences and phases. It has a process. And this process is described under the general terms *ordo salutis*," 18.

[87]   John. R. Mulder, *Soteriology* (class notes located in Mulder file, JAH/WTS), 16. For an example of the use of the *ordo salutis* in preaching after World War II, see Gordon H. Girod, *The Way of Salvation* (Grand Rapids: Baker, 1960). Girod taught that the order is based on the presuppositions that God alone is sovereign, that human beings are totally depraved in the state of sin, and that salvation is by grace alone, 7-9. He concluded his series of sermons with an invitation: "Hear, therefore, the invitation of Christ. Come, confessing your sin; come in faith believing. Enter into life now, that you may live through all eternity," 157.

the Holy Spirit entered their hearts. It encouraged them to know that they had been called from the degradation of sin to new life in Christ. By emphasizing that the regenerating work in the new birth (regeneration) given by the Holy Spirit preceded their conversion and entrance into faith, they were confirmed in the Reformation teaching that salvation is by grace alone, without any of their own works of merit. It taught that justification is an act of God by which the righteousness of Christ was "imputed" or reckoned to them while they were yet sinners. It enabled the pastor and other believers to walk with them in the long and arduous road of sanctification, looking to final assurance and ultimately glorification with Christ.

The *ordos salutis* can be a helpful means for considering the various ways in which God works redemptively with sinners. It can be misleading if it is understood to be a ladder by which one must step by step ascend until one is finally glorified.[88] Rather than deal with all of the elements distinguished in the *ordo salutis*, it is sufficient here to note what the midwestern professors and pastors taught about justification, regeneration, conversion, and sanctification. Although the Protestant Reformers under the leading of Martin Luther had placed justification by faith through grace alone at the center of their teaching concerning salvation, the midwestern professors gave regeneration a more central role.

Gerrit Dubbink taught that regeneration is solely the work of God, whereby the human being becomes a renewed person, "born again," with a new life principle.[89]

> ...regeneration is that act of God whereby He imparts new spiritual life to a sinner dead in trespasses and sins. The life is new, not in the sense that it is inhuman, or unhuman, or other than human, but it is new in quality, direction, aim, etc., in harmony with the nature and the will of God.[90]

According to Evert Blekkink, the regenerating activity of the Holy Spirit occurs in the subconscious, in the unseen and unfelt depths of the soul, so that the person is born again. "He is as unconscious of his spiritual rebirth as of his natural birth."[91]

---

88  For a criticism of the *ordo salutis* as a series of steps, see Karl Barth, *Church Dogmatics*, trans. G.W. Bromiley (Edinburgh: T. &. T. Clark, 1997), Vol. 3/2, 505-20.

89  Gerrit Dubbink, *Outline of Christian Ethics* (file located in JAH/WTS), 10-11.

90  Dubbink, *Dogmatics*, 69.

91  Evert Blekkink, *The Fatherhood of God*, 77.

Midwestern teachers sometimes taught that the regenerative work of the Holy Spirit went on throughout the whole lifetime of the believer. At other times they emphasized that it was the gift of the new birth, to be followed by conversion and faith. Nicholas Steffens wrote a series of articles in which he described the course of the new life in Christ. The new life in the individual goes through a long development comparable to the growth of a tree. God's plan for the regenerate person is nothing other than the complete restoration of the image of God. That life does not flow smoothly, for the prince of darkness attacks like a roaring lion. The existence of sin continues throughout this life, and the struggle against sin requires that the regenerate sinner attend constantly the preaching of the Word and the celebration of the sacraments.[92]

Conversion had to be seen as subsequent to the prior regenerating work of the Holy Spirit. The midwestern Reformed Church leaders opposed firmly all Arminian tendencies as well as American revivalists who opened the door to the possibility that conversion could precede regeneration in the *ordo salutis.* Egbert Winter taught that conversion and faith cannot be the foundation for the new birth. Only those who are already regenerated come to conversion and faith.[93] He wrote that the conversion fixes attention on the active human agency in the way of salvation. It "is the conscious, purposed, voluntary and active turning of the sinner to the Lord and His service."[94] Repentance from sin is the content of conversion, but it can never come without prior regeneration and the working of the Holy Spirit. "Evangelical repentance is that inward, heartfelt sorrow over sin, and conscious turning therefrom to Christ and his service, which follows from, and upon the inworking of the Holy Ghost in the heart." [95]

Midwestern congregations with their pastors often supported efforts of evangelists who called sinners to conversion and repentance, but they also believed that conversion is an on-going lifestyle for believers who must daily repent and turn away from sin. Derk Broek taught that conversion is a continual characteristic of the new life of the regenerate one. The old man and the old woman are dying to sin and fight against it with tears. In turning away from sin, the new life becomes joy in God through Christ.[96]

---

[92]   Nicholas Steffens, "De Geschiedenis van het Nieuwe Leven," *De Hope*, March 15, 1882.

[93]   Winter, "De Weg naar den Hemel," *De Hope*, November 20, 1901.

[94]   Winter, "*Ordo Salutis,*" *Dogmatic Theology*, Fifth Part, 39.

[95]   Ibid., 42.

[96]   Derk Broek, "De Natuur der Bekeering," *De Hope*, October 27, 1885.

In contrast to regeneration and conversion as the process of growth of the new life in Christ by the power of the Holy Spirit, the justification of the sinner in Christ was understood to be a declarative act of God. On the basis of Christ's atonement, God has pardoned the guilty sinner and sins have been forgiven. As a forensic or judicial act, God's declaration of pardon is instantaneous, complete, and final.[97] Justification is not a process; it takes place only once and gives title to eternal life.[98]

In the *ordo salutis*, justification by faith could never be separated from its close relation to sanctification as a work of God's free grace. Gerrit Dubbink defined sanctification as "the work of God's free grace, whereby we are renewed in the whole man after the image of God, and are enabled more and more to die unto sin, and live unto righteousness."[99] In the process of sanctification we come to will what God wills. It is a gradual, progressive process that never reaches completion in this life. Christ who is our justification is also our sanctifier through the indwelling and activity of the Holy Spirit.[100]

John Karsten summed up the attitude of midwestern leaders when he wrote that God has redeemed human beings in order that they would become holy. Not only would they come to have an actual, personal experience of the grace of God in their hearts, but they would fulfill their Christian calling to love and live according to the commandments of God.[101] Because God's purpose was not only that human beings be saved but also that they be sanctified and lead holy lives, the preaching in the midwestern Dutch enclaves bore the stamp of the call to holiness and the disciplined life at least as much as it included the call to repentance and faith.

Reformed Church pastors rejected the teaching of those in the Wesleyan and Holiness traditions who taught a doctrine of complete sanctification or perfectionism. Perfectionists taught that it is possible for one to be entirely sanctified and to be filled with the love of God, so that one no longer lives with conscious or deliberate sin. Reformed pastors found no grounds in the Bible for the perfectionist doctrine.

---

[97] Dubbink, *Dogmatics*, 75.
[98] Mulder, *Soteriology*, 32.
[99] Dubbink, *Dogmatics*, 80.
[100] William J. Van Kersen, "Jezus Ons Heiligmaking Geworden," *De Hope*, November 4, 1924. The Rev. William Van Kersen (1873-1949) graduated from Hope College and Princeton Theological Seminary. He served Reformed churches in Wisconsin, Illinois, and Iowa. From 1910-1940 he was the district secretary for the Board of Foreign Missions.
[101] John Karsten, "Heiligmaking," *De Hope*, August 18, 1885.

On the contrary, those who believe in Jesus Christ know that they have within themselves a constant battle against sin and a longing to grow in holiness in Christ.[102]

Midwestern pastors constantly called upon the members of their congregations to be diligently faithful to Christ in their daily lives. For example, a sermon by James Wayer on Ephesians 5:15a, "See then that ye walk circumspectly," considered the nature, necessity, and purpose of the Christian life.[103] Wayer wanted to encourage his congregants to be on their guard to "remain faithful at their posts" and "never be found wanting" lest their lives "prove inconsistent with our profession and the will of Him who said, 'If ye love me, keep my commandments.'"[104] He reminded his people that they were always being watched by those outside the church who wanted an opportunity to criticize, by Satan who was looking for a point to attack, by their own consciences that accused them, by the omniscient eye of God who sees all, and finally by the "hungry eyes" of those who are looking for encouragement from the strong, consistent Christians.[105]

Wayer stressed the importance of being faithful in walking circumspectly. He preached that a consistent Christian life is a rebuke to the world. It also "strengthens the cause of the gospel and of our Savior Jesus Christ."[106] A consistent Christian life encourages other believers and strengthens those who are weak. Above all, the supreme purpose in walking circumspectly is "to glorify God and enjoy Him forever." The sermon ends with a benediction, "May God give us grace and strength to glorify Him and to extend his gospel among the children of men by 'walking circumspectly' all the days of our life."[107]

---

[102]  Derk Broek, "De Christelijke Hoop en...tot Heiligmaking," *De Hope*, May 8, 1889.

[103]  James Wayer, "Walking Circumspectly," in James F. Zwemer, *Messages from the Word: Sermons by Ministers of the Reformed Church in America* (Holland, Mich.: Holland Printing, 1912), 42. Comparatively few of the sermons by midwestern ministers at the beginning of the twentieth century expounded an extended passage of scripture. Their texts often considered a single verse or part of a verse. It was not unusual for them to treat only a brief clause or phrase, such as "walk circumspectly." The Rev. James Wayer (1871-1965) was born in the Netherlands and graduated from Hope College and Western Theological Seminary. He served churches in Michigan and Wisconsin. The sermon discussed here was probably preached at the Bethany Reformed Church, Grand Rapids, between 1907 and 1912.

[104]  Ibid., 44-45.

[105]  Ibid., 45-49.

[106]  Ibid., 50.

[107]  Ibid., 52.

Emphasis upon the holy life of obedience and prayer was kept in the foreground in the midwestern church by virtue of the provision in the church order that the Ten Commandments and the Lord's Prayer as taught in the Heidelberg Catechism be preached every year or at least one time in four years. Many congregations also included the reading of the Ten Commandments or at least Jesus' summary of the law in their weekly worship. James Wayer summed up the mindset of the great majority of midwestern ministers when he wrote,

> The bed-rock in God's great moral program for mankind is the Ten Commandments. No life can be morally safe that does not rest on the principles it contains. Neither can any aggregate of human lives, be it a single community or a nation, long endure unless these fundamental principles of the Decalogue rule therein. Why have nations gone to ruin and disappeared from the face of the earth? There is but one final explanation: God was not in all their thoughts and they corrupted and destroyed themselves. The Decalogue has never been repealed.[108]

The life sanctified in Christ by the activity of the Holy Spirit was understood to be one of thankfulness and service guided by God's commandments. The maxim, "Love God and do what you will," left people rudderless on the road of sanctification. The midwestern Reformed Church members were thankful for the presence among them of God's law revealed to Israel of old.

> But God did not leave Israel to its own devices. He revealed his will through his law and bound them to himself, not to subject them to a new bondage, but to guarantee their freedom. For only in the obedience and service of their true Lord could they enjoy any enduring freedom. The Decalog, therefore, was "a document of freedom which Jehovah gave to his people whom he had redeemed from Egypt."[109]

---

[108] James Wayer, "Young Peoples Prayer Topic: The Ten Commandments in the Life of Today," *Leader*, August 10, 1921, 44

[109] I. John Hesselink, "The Law of God," in *Guilt, Grace, and Gratitude*, ed. Donald J. Bruggink, 198. The quotation is from J.J. Stamm, *Der Dekalog im Lichte der neueren Forschung* (Bern: Verlag Paul Haupt, 1958), 55.

CHAPTER 5

# The Practice of Piety: A Godly Community in a Christian Land

While the followers of Albertus Van Raalte firmly held to the doctrine that each person is called to be regenerated and converted to Jesus Christ, they also believed that they were a covenant community. They were not individualistic in their faith or in their life together. They had agreed with Van Raalte that their first mission in America was to create a colony that was Christian, with Christian government, "in order to uphold the law of God which is the foundation of every state."[1] The new Dutch colonies were expected to be godly communities in a Christian nation. Loyalty to God and patriotism in a Christian nation were held together in their practice of piety.

They sought to glorify God in all that they did, not only as individuals but also as a community. It is not by accident that two of their favorite evangelical hymns came to be "Holy, Holy, Holy" and "Blest Be the Tie that Binds." On the sixtieth anniversary of the founding of the Holland colony, Matthew Kolyn spoke in Zeeland, Michigan, about the character of the midwestern Reformed Dutch communities who remained true to the vision of Van Raalte:

[1] Quoted in Hinte, *Netherlanders in America*, 124.

This town and colony and every Dutch community ought to be recognized as such, not by the wearing of wooden shoes, or the insistence upon the use of our language, beautiful as it is, upon the streets and in business, but by that sobriety and love of order and respect for law and appreciation of the noblest things of life, that belongs to the best Dutch traditions; by dignified and simple manners, by placing education and character above and before appearances and possessions; by reverent observance of Divine ordinances, and the cultivation of all those virtues, for which our ancestors in Holland and here have been so favorably known.[2]

## Nurturing American Life and Faith  Through Cooperation with Voluntary Societies

The Reverend Dr. Herman Bavinck, who became the theological leader in the Christelijke Gereformeerde Kerk, looked back upon what happened after the Secession of 1834 and criticized the seceders' practice of a separatistic piety that led them to withdraw from the life of their nation and society. He wrote:

Satisfied with the ability to worship God in their own houses of worship, or to engage in evangelism, many left nation, state, and society, art and science to their own devices. Many withdrew completely from life, literally separated themselves from everything, and in some cases, what is even worse, shipped off to America, abandoning the Fatherland as lost to unbelief.[3]

Although Bavinck's criticism of the narrow pietism of the "many" who "withdrew completely from life" and even "shipped off to America, abandoning the Fatherland," applies to some of those who emigrated, events in America soon proved that those who united with the Reformed Church in America did not seek to separate themselves from American life. Settled together in their colonies, they retained for a long time their distinct ethnic flavor, just as other Europeans who immigrated to America did in the nineteenth century.

The leaders of the midwestern Reformed Church accepted rapidly the responsibilities of life as an American church by cooperating with many of the Christian voluntary societies in the country. Every week *De*

---

[2]    Matthew Kolyn, "The Hollander in America," *Leader*, September 4, 1907, 27/2.

[3]    Quoted in "Catholicity of Christianity and the Church," trans. John Bolt, *Calvin Theological Journal*, 27/2 (1992), 246.

*Hope* included articles about foreign mission societies, home mission societies, Jewish missions, temperance movements, Sunday school associations, tract societies, Christian Endeavor societies, and other Christian welfare societies. The voluntary societies became a means by which lay women as well as men could cooperate for the spreading of the gospel, improving the personal morality of individuals, and promoting a just order of society without being hampered by confessional boundaries and regulations. They resisted the slogan, "In isolation is our strength," that some of immigrants brought with them from the Netherlands.

The American Sunday School Association was one of their links to the world of American Protestantism. By 1866, the American Sunday School Association was playing a vital role not only in evangelistic outreach but also in promoting Christian morality in American life. The association was gaining strength among midwestern Reformed churches as well. Its annual publication of suggested topics and Bible passages to be studied during the four quarters of the year became the basis for the weekly exposition of the Sunday school lesson in *De Hope*. Sunday schools were an American innovation for the Dutch immigrants, who ever since the Synod of Dort had been reared in the tradition of catechetical instruction as their basic method of passing on biblical and theological understanding of the faith. However, the Sunday school movement became so popular that it threatened to surpass catechetical instruction.[4]

The Sunday school movement presented a problem for the immigrants. On the one hand, catechism was the basic tool used by ministers to teach children the essential doctrines of the Reformed faith. On the other hand, lay members of the congregation taught the Sunday school lessons, which used short passages of scripture chosen

---

[4]    The Rev. James Zwemer, stated clerk of the Classis of Holland, was an enthusiastic promoter of the Sunday school movement. In 1875, he reported that four more Sunday schools had been organized by congregations in the classis. He stated that it was important for children to learn to read the Bible itself as well as memorize the answers in the catechism. "Verslag van den Godsdienstigen Toestand der Gemeenten Behoorende tot de Classis van Holland," *De Hope*, April 21, 1875. Twenty-four years later he was still promoting Sunday schools. He gave a list of six points on how to prepare children for Sunday school attendance, including teaching children to find the verses in the Bible, requiring obedience to their teachers, giving them money for the offering, listening to them sing their songs, and encouraging prayer, "Huiselijke Voorbereiding Voor de Zondagsschool," *De Hope*, March 22, 1899.

by the International Sunday School Association.[5] Nicholas Steffens wrote that Sunday school is not to be rejected; it has evangelistic and nurturing power because it reaches more children and therefore is better than nothing. However, Sunday school does not reach the goal of providing a systematic understanding of the great doctrines of the faith. His suggestion was that there should be more teaching of doctrine in the Sunday school.[6]

The debate about the relative importance of Sunday school in relation to catechetical instruction touched a vital issue with regard to the future stance of the midwestern Reformed Church in America. If catechism training and instruction in doctrine was neglected, it was likely that the Reformed identity of congregations would slowly erode. The emphasis upon short biblical passages and memorizing the Sunday school's "golden text" for each week was likely to result in an understanding of the faith that was allied closely with nineteenth century American evangelicalism. For that reason the debate continued into the twentieth century.[7]

Although the nature of the midwestern Reformed Dutch communities retains some of the characteristics listed by Matthew Kolyn in 1906, the midwestern Reformed Church in America never adopted the slogan, "In Isolation is Our Strength," that had been coined in the Netherlands by the great friend of the seceders of 1834, Groen Van Prinsterer.[8] The editors of De Hope had encouraged participation in American life beginning with its first issue by including two weekly columns with news and comments, one about events in the United States and one about foreign countries.[9] The result was that the

[5]    Roelof Pieters, "Opvoeding," De Hope, July 6, 13, 1871.
[6]    Steffens, "Sabbathschool en Catechtsatie," De Hope, October 16, 1883.
[7]    See articles in De Hope by James Zwemer, March 15, 22, 1899; John Karsten, February 25, 1903; Peter De Pree, November 9, 1904; and William Moerdyk, October 17, 1911. The Midwestern Reformed Church Sunday schools were enabled to retain their Reformed identity with the help of the weekly exposition of the biblical lesson in the columns in De Hope and the Leader. Beginning in the 1930s the Sunday School Guide was a crucial Reformed Church resource for Sunday school teachers.
[8]    The slogan played a role in the Christian Reformed Church, which was far more hesitant to assimilate into American culture than was the midwestern Reformed Church. On the deliberate cultural and ecclesiastical isolation of the Christian Reformed Church prior to World War II, see John Kromminga, The Christian Reformed Church, 91-124.
[9]    Often there was another column and/or editorial comments about events in the Netherlands, which was neither American nor foreign in the minds of the editors.

dominant religious and moral issues facing Americans also became important issues for the church.

Reformed Church members living in Dutch immigrant enclaves in America did not understand taking action on the religious and moral issues facing Americans to include matters of economics, governmental programs of social welfare, or equal rights for all. They were, however, intensely interested in issues that concerned personal morality, sexual ethics, maintaining a strict observance of the Sabbath, and the use of alcoholic beverages. After 1900 they were also challenged to respond to issues of social and economic justice being raised by leaders of the Social Gospel movement.

## Family, Marriage, and Sexuality

In the theology of midwestern Reformed Church pastors, the family was the link between the individual believer and society; therefore, they were concerned not only about good relationships in the home, but also about maintaining customs and legal provisions to support marriages and families. The midwestern theologians wrote little during the nineteenth century about the theology of marriage. At the turn of the century, Henry Dosker placed a letter from President Theodore Roosevelt in *De Hope*. Roosevelt wrote opposing the attitude among young men that led them to postpone getting married in order to enjoy their freedom and avoid the financial burdens of marriage and family. Roosevelt insisted that having children is an important part of a good marriage. Childless couples are more prone to divorce. Dosker agreed with Roosevelt that in their desire to enjoy the material benefits of life, marriage was being avoided. Both agreed that good citizenship involved raising a family. Dosker was strongly opposed to conception control and to abortion; these things are a curse on natural life.[10]

By 1920 a number of leading intellectuals and social critics in America were advocating more liberal divorce laws, birth control, eugenic sterilization of mentally retarded people, and even more liberal abortion laws. Midwestern Reformed Church leaders were almost unanimous in objecting to the trend. Evert Blekkink's undated lecture notes about marriage and the family are consistent with the doctrine of other midwestern leaders prior to 1920.[11] Blekkink taught that the family was instituted by God with the creation of Adam and Eve, with

[10]  Henry Dosker, "Wekelijksch Budget," *De Hope*, February 18, 1903. Roosevelt was much admired in the Dutch enclaves, especially since he was a member of the Reformed Church.

[11]  "Lectures on Theology," located in the WTS/JAH, John R. Mulder file, Box

monogamy as the divinely appointed form. Polygamy first appeared among the Canaanites. Adultery is a damnable sin against society and God. The purity of the home is fundamental to society. Sexual relations outside marriage are to be rejected and houses of prostitution suppressed. There must not be a double standard for men and women with regard to sexual relations.[12]

In the order of the family, the father and mother must be held in equal honor in the home. The father is to be the provider for the family, for he is stronger. Parents are responsible to the state, society, and God for the training of their children. Parents and children should love each other. Children are to honor and obey their parents so long as they live. To dishonor parents is the second greatest crime, next to murder. Divorce in the United States is a bigger problem than Mormonism. The only two scriptural grounds for divorce are adultery and desertion. Blekkink opposed the additional grounds that were recognized in some states.[13]

Issues of marriage, sexual relations, and divorce became more pressing as the twentieth century went on. The most extensive treatment of these issues is to be found in the class notes for the course on ethics given by John R. Mulder in 1950. He echoed Blekkink in teaching that

> the purpose of marriage is to secure the preservation and perpetuation of the race....In sex the marital relationship reaches a stage which has its fruition in the sacred privilege of bringing forth new life. A trust like that calls for a most strenuous discipline of the sex life....Marriage may not be regarded as the mere legalization of a natural appetite....We are not trying to suggest that within the marital state, sexual satisfaction should transpire only at such time as reproduction is desired, for we believe that the sex act can also be the highest expression of love and devotion for each other....[14]

---

1. Blekkink taught systematic theology at Western Theological Seminary, 1913-1928, and it is possible that Mulder received these notes in a course that he studied under Blekkink. Mulder graduated from Western Seminary in 1921.

[12] Blekkink, "Purity of the Home," "Lectures on Theology," n.p.

[13] Ibid. The sentences in this paragraph are either direct quotes or close paraphrases.

[14] Mulder, "Sexual Morality," VI, WTS/JAH, Box 1, Mulder papers. Unfortunately, there are no page numbers for the ethics course notes. To locate the references, one should look for the section title and the Roman numeral in the outline.

The correct attitude toward sexual relations within marriage is consecration, not suppression.[15]

Since the purpose of marriage and human sexuality is that of procreation and perpetuation of the race, Mulder taught that birth control militates against the divine purpose of marriage. "Except for reasons that appear legitimate in the light of this divine purpose for marriage, any limitation of conception shows refusal to co-operate with God's purpose. Christians who are willing to marry, but unwilling to become parents, show themselves to be ready to take the benefits of marriage, but unwilling to accept its duties."[16]

After Mulder had made his strong opposition to birth control known, he made several concessions that opened the door to its practice by a married couple. Like almost all of the midwestern leaders, he had a strong desire to avoid "legalism," by which the church made rules to be followed by individuals. Therefore he told his students that in individual cases, "this is not a matter to be determined by rule, but by moral principle, every Christian being convinced in his own heart what is the proper, God-honoring use he makes of the bodies that have been created by God and redeemed by Jesus Christ."[17] Moreover, there are some legitimate reasons for birth control. These can be listed as an effort to prevent frequent pregnancies that may jeopardize the health of the mother, chronic health conditions of the mother, financial insecurity that makes for oppressive poverty, and "duties whose discharge is obstructed by pregnancy and child birth."[18]

Like all their predecessors, Mulder and Blekkink were strongly opposed to sexual relations outside marriage. That opposition included all types of incest, homosexuality, and masturbation, as well as adultery and fornication. However, they made a distinction between adultery and fornication so far as the church's discipline is concerned. The young couple who consummate the sex act prior to marriage should be dealt with gently. "Adultery is iniquitous, personally and socially and Scripturally, whereas [the fornication of the young couple—eph] is a sex irregularity, not to be condoned because it is offensive, but forgivable because it is not a perversion."[19]

[15] Mulder, "Sexual Morality," III.
[16] Mulder, "Birth Control," II, III.
[17] Mulder, "Birth Control" VIII.
[18] Ibid., IX..
[19] Mulder, "Sexual Morality," III, 4. See also J. B. "Vragenbus," *De Hope*, November 4, 1930.

Mulder and Blekkink both show that they were men of their times. They were cautiously open to limited eugenic sterilization while vigorously opposed to abortion and infanticide. However, they were ready somewhat reluctantly to accept "legislation by states to prevent propagation by those mentally or physically insufficiently equipped to assure the desired hereditary qualities. This is society's manner of practicing birth control. It may be necessary, and it may be broadly Christian, but it should be a practice closely guarded by such judgment as shall obviate indiscriminate sterilization."[20]

**The Role of Women**

Midwestern leaders taught that the man is the head of the house and that the woman was the "weaker vessel." Henry Dosker wrote a poem in 1881 about the relation of a man and his wife. The poem describes the man as the head, the woman the neck. The man has the scepter and the crown. He is the strong cedar; she is the climbing rose. She supports and trusts him and wins his love. They are one in the Lord, with one faith and hope.[21] It was agreed by almost all that a woman's place is in the home. Homemaking and motherhood are their most crucial roles and calling from God. "W." in 1924 wrote that this role must not be underestimated. It may be even more difficult than the man's role and some women may even prefer to escape to the man's world.[22]

At the end of World War II, John R. Mulder was still teaching senior students at the seminary that, according to 1 Timothy 2:12 and 15, the woman may not usurp authority over the man. He objected to a feminism that "has brought her upon such equality as to jeopardize the realization of the rich promise of 1 Tim. 2:15. Suppose that the women of Israel had been feminists and contraceptionalists! It is still the seed of the woman that must fight against the serpent."[23]

[20]    Mulder, "Birth Control" X, 4.
[21]    Henry Dosker, "Man en Vrouw," *De Hope*, February 9, 1881. Steffens agreed with Dosker. In 1881 he wrote a series of three articles opposing the American emancipation of women movement. He contended that women should count the blessings they enjoy because of the gospel, in contrast to the deplorable conditions under which they live in countries that are under the domination of Muslim, Hindu, Chinese, and pagan religions. His articles contain graphic details. American women should further the cause of women in other countries by supporting foreign missions rather than political emancipation movements. "Het Leven der Vrouwen op Aarde," *De Hope*, November 23, 30, December 7, 1881.
[22]    W. "De Moeder in het Huisgezin," *De Hope*, January 15, 1924.
[23]    John R. Mulder, "Birth Control," VI. The strong language used here by

Some of the men were more ready to give women a wider role in the society than in the church. "N." in 1888 presented a strong case for educating women as well as men.[24] In 1874 Jacob Van Der Meulen attended a meeting in Muskegon at which the woman's suffragist Elizabeth Cady Stanton presented a lecture advocating giving women the right to vote. The issue had been placed on the ballot in Michigan. Van Der Meulen was not only impressed by her presentation, but he was making speeches in favor of the proposition.[25]

When efforts were being mounted in America in 1912 to amend the American Constitution to give women the right to vote, Henry Geerlings, managing editor of *De Hope* and the *Leader*, presented a strong argument in favor of such an amendment.

> The great argument in favor of woman suffrage is in the fact that no nation can ever be really free if the women who give it its men are not free. The mother is the matrix of the race. Free women will give us free men. Strong, brave, high-minded, self-reliant mothers will put those marks upon their sons. And the day when woman will take her place as the equal of man will mark an epoch in the history of the human race. It will be the beginning of the time when free women will be nature's assurance that this nation will be a nation of free men. [26]

William Moerdyk, one of the editors of *De Hope*, resisted giving the suffrage to women. He was not convinced by the argument of some that woman's suffrage would strengthen the move for prohibition because women would vote against the saloons. In Phoenix where more women than men voted, the saloons won by 252 votes out of a total of 4,400 voters. "Let the women hold to their householding calling."[27]

The men were even more hesitant to allow women to vote and hold office in the church than in society. They believed that women should make their contributions to the life of the church through the

the normally judicious and careful Mulder displays the depth of feeling present in the issues at the end of World War II.

24   N. "De Dochter niet Uitgesloten," *De Hope*, February 28, 1888.
25   Jacob Van Der Meulen, "Mrs. Stanton's Voorlezing," *De Hope*, June 17, 1874. The proposition was defeated in the statewide election.
26   Henry Geerlings, "Current Events," *Leader*, November 27, 1912, 95.
27   William Moerdyk, "Het Vrouwen Stemrecht," *De Hope*, July 1, 1913. William Moerdyk was a brother of Peter Moerdyk. He was born in the Netherlands in 1843 and was a member of the first class to graduate from Hope College in 1866. He served pastorates in Wisconsin, Michigan, and Illinois from 1869-1913. He died in 1914.

ladies' aid and missionary societies and by teaching children in the Sunday school.[28]

Women were permitted to attend General Synod as guests beginning in 1895. The editors of *De Hope* were cautiously favorable to the move, saying that it was helpful to have them present. However, they saw a danger that the practice would lead to some who (like the liberals and Methodists) would begin to advocate for women in the offices of the church.[29] The editors' fears were well founded. It was not long before a movement began to give the women the right to vote in congregational meetings. Just three years later, F. Van Driele, a Grand Rapids elder who was a frequent contributor to *De Hope,* had contended that in light of what Paul says about Phoebe in Romans 16, the men of the church must be more open to accept the service and gifts of women in the church.[30]

Men were quick to recognize that when women had the right to vote in congregational meetings there would also be agitation for the right to hold office. The Reverend Henry J. Pietenpol wrote that Paul taught clearly that man is created in the image of God and woman is created in the image of man. Women may not rule over men and therefore may not hold office in the church. To vote is to rule, so acceptance of the right to vote logically entails the right to hold office.[31]

**Worldly Amusements**

Living the godly life meant that it was necessary not only to abstain from evil but also to abstain from becoming a stumbling block for others. Because the godly life involved setting an example for others, personal morality could not avoid becoming public morality for the community. In the nineteenth century, the list of "worldly amusements" to be avoided in the Dutch communities closely resembled the issues of

[28] Helen Assewoude, "De Betrekking tot en het Werk van de Vrouw in de Sabbatschool," *De Hope*, November 1, 1893. This is one of the very few articles written by women to appear in *De Hope*. Other articles by women were written by missionaries or on the subjects of family life and faith. It may be significant that the author of this article was unmarried.

[29] Editors, "Wekelijksch Budget," *De Hope*, July 3, 1895.

[30] F. Van Driele, "Vrouwen kunnen ook Dienstbaar zijn in des Gemeente De Heeren," *De Hope*, June 15, 1898.

[31] Henry J. Pietenpol, "Het Vrouwen Kiesrecht in onze Gemeenten," *De Hope*, June 13, 1920. See also J.B. "Vragenbus," *De Hope*, April 5, 1921. Henry J. Pietenpol served pastorates in Michigan, Wisconsin, Iowa, and Illinois

public morals in evangelical American Christianity, with prohibition of dancing, card playing, gambling, and the theater or movies high on the list.[32]

An unnamed pastor in 1910 warned against the evils of a whole list of worldly amusements.

> Behold in our generation of boasted enlightenment, progress and culture, the sorry spectacle of pleaders for the saloon, the dance, the theatre, the nude in art, divorce, suicide, erotic realism in fiction, smoking of cigarettes by women (never ladies), even licensed prostitution, or the common brothel! Men hold briefs for relics of paganism and barbarism; for war, for the quiet extinction of the insane, the idiot, the incurables, and those with dotage.[33]

The items on the lists can be placed in several categories. Most important were those amusements that could lead to sexual immorality. These included dancing, movies, theater, and attendance at roller skating rinks where young men and women mingled and skated together. Another category was activity that tempted people to ignore the real purposes of the Sabbath, including holding Sunday school picnics on Sunday.[34] Some members of the churches addressed letters to the "Question Box" regarding the permissibility of a variety of activities, such as going to beauty parlors,[35] having a radio in the home,[36] and what criteria would make a movie "good" and worthy of attendance.[37]

---

from 1893-1928. He died in 1947. He was the father of Henry Pietenpol, for many years the highly respected dean of Central College in Pella, Iowa.

Women were not permitted to hold the office of elder or deacon in the Reformed Church in America until 1979. However, the first woman was ordained as minister in the Reformed Church in America was Joyce Stedge, who was ordained by the Classis of Mid-Hudson in 1973, Russell L. Gasero, ed., *Historical Directory of the Reformed Church in America 1628-2000*, Historical Series of the Reformed Church in America, no. 37 (Grand Rapids: Eerdmans, 2001), 373.

[32] See George Marsden, *The Evangelical Mind and the New School Presbyterian Experience* (New Haven and London: Yale Univ. Press, 1970), 18-19.

[33] "Pastor," "Pleading for Baal," *Leader*, November 23, 1910, 82-83.

[34] L.J. Hulst, "Picnic en Excursie," *De Hope*, August 4, 1880. Hulst's objection is that such picnics detract from the real purposes of Sunday school.

[35] J.B. "Vragenbus," *De Hope*, December 17, 1929.

[36] Ibid., January 27, 1925.

[37] Ibid., June 11, 1929. J.B. answers that movie companies are in the business to make money and have few intentions to improve morality. There may

A distinction was also made between necessary and unnecessary work on Sunday. That distinction could lead to discussions about how long milk could be kept fresh. The Classis of Wisconsin apparently had concluded that it could be kept in cans in cool water overnight. At its meeting June 19, 1878, it advised farmers to hold their Saturday milk overnight and deliver it with the Sunday milk to the cheese factory on Monday morning.[38]

In contrast to the Synod of the Christian Reformed Church, which had made a legislative decision about "worldly amusements" to be avoided,[39] the Reformed Church in America refused to make a decision prohibiting members from certain associations or activities. The midwestern leaders were in full agreement that "legalism" is not the road to take. John R. Mulder in 1950 articulated for his students what had long been the basic position of midwestern leaders. He made a distinction between a rule and a principle. "A moral principle is the formulation of a moral obligation without reference to any given situation. A principle always leaves the application of itself to the judgment of the persons concerned. A principle always rests in the very nature of man and of his social relationships, and is universally and permanently applicable."[40] Within that framework the conscience of the individual Christian must be respected.

In 1959, Mulder gave a clear statement of the Reformed Church in America's position when he wrote,

> First off, let us get it before our minds that the Reformed Church does not legislate on matters of personal conscience. We have no legislation on smoking, eating, drinking, social life—only the stipulation that we must remember that we belong to Christ. That means that Reformed Theology believes that conduct is to become an expression of Christian faith which parallels Christian belief. The purpose of the Christian community is to try to edify one another, and to be helpful to one another....We do not try to legislate one into goodness.[41]

---

be some good movies such as *King of Kings* and *The Ten Commandments*, but even these are made to entertain and entice people to attend other movies. But J.B. does not lay down any fast rule about attending "good" movies.

[38] H. Borgers, Stated Clerk, "Eene Verdaagde Zitting van de Wisconsin Classis," *De Hope,* July 3, 1878.

[39] *Acta der Synode 1928 van de Christelijke Gereformeerde Kerk,* 86-89; see also James A. De Jong, *Henry J. Kuiper,* 59-66.

[40] Mulder, "The Scriptures as a Guide to the Christian in matters of ethics" II (Class notes on file in WTS/JAH).

[41] Letter to Mr. A. Wassink from John R. Mulder, September 8, 1959 (located in Mulder file, Box 6, in WTS/JAH).

J.B.'s answers in the "Question Box" always were given in terms of a principle. Thus with regard to whether it is permissible for Christians to play cards, he wrote that there is no command, "Thou shalt not play cards," but card playing easily leads to a desire for "good luck." "Good luck" is suspect to a Calvinist.[42] Again, with regard to having a radio set in the house, there is no law for or against it; the issue is how it is used in the home.

No one fought harder against "legalism" than did Albertus Pieters, who insisted that the Ten Commandments were given to Israel in the Old Testament and ceased to exist as law when the law was fulfilled in Jesus Christ. He taught that there is a common morality given in the creation. The New Testament provides guidance for Christian conduct within the framework of God's grace. The church and its leaders also have the duty in the preaching of the Word and pastoral care to provide instruction in the faith and guidance for moral conduct, but

> it is not within the authority of any church to decide what is right or wrong in personal conduct. I have never smoked tobacco, and do not desire to smoke, but if my church should be so ill advised as to forbid it, I should make a bee line to a tobacconist and turn myself into a smoke stack, as do others, in indignant protest against such an invasion of Christian liberty.[43]

## Temperance and Prohibition

The enactment of prohibition laws in the twentieth century appeared to be one of the great success stories in the Christianization of Protestant America. Midwestern leaders had taken a stand against immoderate use of alcoholic beverages. Most of them favored the passage of the 1854 Maine Law, the first prohibition law in America. The prohibition campaign was one of the reasons they believed that their policy of cooperation with other Protestants was better than that of establishing separate societies on a strictly Calvinistic basis. They were particularly opposed to the saloons in every community because, as they charged, the only reason men go there is to get drunk. Innumerable references to the evils of strong drink appeared on the pages of De Hope. Sunday school temperance lessons were expounded once every quarter in De Hope and the Leader.

---

[42] J.B. "Vragenbus," De Hope, March 30, 1926.
[43] Albertus Pieters, The Seed of Abraham (Grand Rapids: Eerdmans, 1950), 120-21.

Steffens was a voice of caution regarding the campaign. He worried about how to enforce prohibition[44] but insisted on opposing the saloons. He defended the General Synod of the Reformed Church in America when it did not agree to organize temperance societies. Consistent with his understanding of the separation of the responsibilities of the church from those of state, he wrote that the General Synod must confine its actions to ecclesiastical matters. Civil laws are the responsibility of civil authorities. He pointed out that there were seventeen million Protestant church members in the United States, who had sufficient power and ability to organize for prohibition. He wanted room left for respecting the consciences of those who stood for moderation rather than abstinence.[45]

Local option was one of the strategies employed against the saloon and the liquor trade. John Karsten exposited faithfully the biblical teaching for the Sunday school temperance lesson in each quarter of the year. He urged support for action that would give local communities the right to vote "that no saloon should be tolerated in that division."[46] The saloon must be put out of existence.

What the law can do, that must it do in order not to become indirectly an ally of the worst element of society. It must address itself to *public institutions* which breed moral miasma. The right to send an evil doer to prison involves the right to prevent the evil act in so far as a public institution, like a saloon, can be charged as the occasion of it. In every other department of life the law asserts its authority for the public weal."[47]

William Moerdyk complained in 1913 that the people of Holland were not as active in supporting the campaign against the saloons as they should be. Households were being laid waste, prisons, mental institutions, orphanages, and poor houses were full because the saloons were allowed to remain open. He pointed out that Ottawa County (within which Holland was located) with its many Christians and churches should have succeeded in closing the saloons by now.[48]

When prohibition came into force, opposition to it came quickly; illegal trade in strong drink increased rapidly, accompanied by crime and gangsterism. Peter Moerdyk, along with other leaders, appealed

[44]  Steffens, "Weg met de Saloons," *De Hope*, March 9, 1887.
[45]  Steffens, "De Maatscappij in Het Licht van Gods Woord," *De Hope*, October 17, 1894.
[46]  Karsten, "Local Option" *Leader*, April 24, 1907, 402.
[47]  Ibid., 403.
[48]  William Moerdyk, "Wekelijksch Budget: Wiens Schuld," *De Hope*, September 9, 1913.

for obedience to the law and its enforcement by authorities, lest the anarchists take over. He pointed out that God has given laws for the regulation of society. The prohibition law must not be allowed to be violated with impunity and thereby become dead letters.[49] In spite of the rise in crime and opposition to the prohibition laws, the editors of *De Hope* and the *Leader* did not waver. When Al Smith ran for president in 1928, both papers rallied their readers against his campaign to repeal the prohibition laws.

Opposition to the use of alcoholic beverages continued after the repeal of the prohibition laws. The quarterly Sunday school temperance lesson remained a feature in the *Sunday School Guide*, which was used in the majority of the midwestern churches. The General Synod was called upon frequently to urge abstaining from alcoholic beverages, and the editor of the *Church Herald* highlighted consistently the evils of "alcohol's harvest." "When will we awaken, and rise to action? When will we do what we can, where we can, as we can to hold back this flood-tide of destruction? Or is it already too late?"[50]

## The Sabbath as a Gift of God

Celebration of the Sabbath as a gift of God linked the church to the sphere of labor and God's work of creation, redemption, and sanctification.[51] In the midwestern Reformed Church, it was understood that the Sabbath was a gift of God in creation and therefore was a gift of God to every human being. It was not to be understood as a gift only for Jews and Christians.[52] Human beings as the image of God need one day in seven to rest from their labor. They have a God-given right to rest as God rested on the seventh day. The rhythm of the Sabbath days also gives dignity to human labor both before and after the Fall. Therefore, the Fourth Commandment included the command to work for six days and rest on the seventh.[53]

---

[49] Peter Moerdyk, "Handhaving der Wet," *De Hope*, January 17, 1922.

[50] Louis Benes, "Alcohol's Harvest," *Church Herald*, January 8, 1954, 6.

[51] The Rev. J.W. Poot, "De Christelijke Rustdag en Zijne Waarneming," *De Hope*, October 16, 1895. J.W. Poot was born in the Netherlands, received into the Reformed Church from the Congregational Church, served Reformed Church congregations in Michigan, Illinois, and Iowa before being dismissed in November, 1913, to serve in a Lutheran church.

[52] Adrian Zwemer, "Huiselijke Woorden," *De Hope*, January 20, 1875.

[53] Nicholas Steffens, "Eene Nieuwe Reeks van Brieven over Verschillende Onderwerpen," *De Hope*, May 1, 1895.

Poot explained that the Sabbath has three biblical roots: the creator root in God's creative activity, the Redeemer root in the Jewish rest day, and the Christian rest day in God the sanctifier and glorifier.[54] In the late nineteenth century, it became necessary to clarify the relationship among the three roots because the Seventh Day Adventists and Seventh Day Baptists were insisting that according to the Bible Saturday, not Sunday, is the God-ordained day of rest. Poot did not quote the Fourth Commandment specifically in either Exodus 20:8-11, which refers to God's activity in creation, or Deuteronomy 4:12-16, which bases the command on God's redemption of Israel. However, he interpreted the command to rest on God's taking the Israelites out of their slavery in Egypt, where they never had any rest. Then he went on to say that the Christian day of rest must give preference to Sunday because God raised Jesus Christ from the dead on Sunday.[55] Moreover, because the Resurrection and Ascension point forward to Christ's coming again, the Christian observance of the day of rest is already a sign of the restoration of the whole creation in the new age.[56]

Midwestern Reformed Church leaders wrote constantly against the danger of legalism in Sabbath observance. Nicholas Steffens insisted that the Fourth Commandment was an aspect of the Jewish age that was done away with when Jesus Christ fulfilled the Old Testament Law given to Moses. Because believers are justified by faith alone and not by the works of the law, Christians are now free from the law given to Moses. Steffens warned against the practice of the Roman Catholic Church that added church laws to the Old Testament laws. He also warned against the practice of the Puritans, because they had allowed themselves to be ruled by a legalistic spirit. Thereby they had changed the Sabbath as a day of joy into a day of duties and obligations.[57]

The Fourth Commandment, according to Steffens, must not be understood as a commandment, but it does hold a universal principle about the nature of humanity as created by God. Therefore, it is a gracious confirmation of our original nature as created in the image of God for the welfare of humanity. The Christian church must uphold the importance of celebrating the Sabbath rest on Sunday as a day of worship, of rest from labor, and of doing acts of mercy. The Sabbath rest is a blessing for all humankind.[58]

---

[54]  Poot, ibid. "Sanctifier and glorifier" is my translation of the Dutch word, *voleinder*, which literally translated is "completer."

[55]  Ibid.

[56]  Ibid.

[57]  Steffens, "Eene Nieuwe Reeks van Brieven," *De Hope*, May 1, 1895.

[58]  Ibid. In another article, Steffens contrasted the interpretation of the

Midwestern Reformed believers were generally in agreement with American Protestant society, which tried to stem the tide against encroachments on Sunday as a day of rest and worship. They opposed legislation that would have permitted stores to be open and recreational events to be staged on Sunday. They often based their objection on the fact that it is the very nature of human beings to need one day of rest in seven and that requiring some people to engage in unnecessary work on Sunday is to go against their nature and deprive them of the blessings of the day.[59]

Steffens felt something of the dilemma that faced the American nation with regard to writing Sunday laws and using the powers of the state to enforce them on Jews, unbelievers, and a variety of Seventh-Day advocates. Some radicals of his day opposed all Sabbath legislation on that basis. On the other hand, if the very nature of humanity is such that a day of rest is needed on a regular basis, then it is possible to defend such laws on the basis of our common humanity. Steffens saw no other way than to choose between the two positions.

Steffens observed that the deeper issue is the right of the state to bind the conscience. He asked, "Who gave the state the right to bind the conscience if God has not laid that burden upon it?"[60] He said that he was hesitant to allow the state to punish anyone for disobeying Sunday laws that on a rather arbitrary basis distinguish between what is permissible and what is not. But that was not his final word. It was also a question of whether America is to be an atheistic nation or a religious one. If it is to be atheistic or neutral, then all such laws should be abolished. If it has a religious basis, then it has the right to write and enforce legislation consistent with the very nature of created humanity. At that point Steffens brought his article to a close. He wrote that he might come back to the problem at some time in the future.[61] Since the consensus in the Reformed Church at the end of the nineteenth century was that America is a Protestant Christian nation, almost all

Westminster Confession, which he says led to the Puritan Sabbath, with the interpretation of the Fourth Commandment in the Heidelberg Catechism, Q. 104, which stresses the Sabbath as a day of worship and doing works of mercy. See also Adrian Zwemer, "Huiselijke Woorden," January 20, 1875.

59  John Karsten, "De Zondags Kwestie," *De Hope*, March 6, 1889. The distinction between necessary and unnecessary work on Sunday was basic to Reformed Church members' decisions about what they should or should not do.

60  Steffens, "Eene Nieuwe Reeks van Brieven," *De Hope*, May 1, 1895.

61  Ibid. I have not discovered whether he ever did come back to deal further with resolving his dilemma.

of its members believed that laws governing conduct on Sunday were not only permissible, but even the obligatory responsibility of the civil government.

## Common Schools vs. Christian Schools in America

In spite of the contention that the United States is a Protestant Christian nation, it is a fact that God is not mentioned in the American Constitution. Since much of the cooperation of Reformed Church members with other institutions and activities in American society was legitimated on the basis of the nation's Christian character, the charge that America is not a Christian nation had to be taken seriously. The issue became central in the controversy about whether it was necessary to send their children to Christian schools rather than public schools.

In 1619-19, the Church Order of Dort had made the establishment of Christian schools a responsibility of each consistory.[62] In accord with this provision, the seventeenth- and eighteenth-century schools in the Netherlands taught in accord with Reformed theology. In the United States, the Reformed Church modified the article in light of American conditions, where it was geographically and financially impossible to provide Christian schools in each place. In such places, the provision of Dort was to be met by instructing the children in the faith at home and by praying daily with them. The people were to avoid having their children educated by teachers who were immoral or who scoffed at the Holy Scriptures.[63]

Albertus Van Raalte believed that it was important to establish Christian schools at every level from elementary education through college. The Classis of Holland went on record for parochial Christian schools.[64] However, due to the people's poverty in the early years, most of them sent their children to the public schools. Since the public school boards in the new Dutch immigrant colonies could be controlled by the Dutch themselves and Bible reading and prayer were permitted, many could not see any good reason that they should have

---

[62] *Church Order of Dort*, 21; Daniel J. Meeter, *Meeting Each Other In Doctrine, Liturgy, and Government*, Historical Series of the Reformed Church in America, no. 24 (Grand Rapids: Eerdmans, 1993), 68-69.

[63] *Explanatory Articles*, 56; Meeter, *Meeting Each Other*, 133-34. For an account of the Reformed Church in America's implementation of this provision of Dort in the American colonial era, see Norman Kansfield, "Education," in Van Hoeven, ed., *Piety and Patriotism*, 130-48.

[64] *Minutes of the Classis of Holland, 1847-1857*, 174-75; Van Hinte, *Netherlanders in America*, 391.

to incur the additional expense involved in maintaining a Christian school for their children.[65]

Most members of the midwestern Reformed Church in the nineteenth century came to favor sending their children to public schools, although there always remained a residual interest in establishing Christian schools.[66] At the end of the century, the Reformed Church pastor Peter Moerdyk wrote that it was wrong to try to keep children from relating to the American community by keeping them in Dutch language schools.[67] The editors of *De Hope* opposed establishing Christian schools as long as the American school did not become "neutral."[68]

The debate grew sharper in the first decades of the twentieth century when several ministers who had been born in the Netherlands were called to serve Reformed Church in America congregations. The Reverend Jacob Van Houte insisted that "principles carry themselves through." America, he wrote, was founded on the principles of the European Enlightenment. It was not founded on Christian principles; therefore, it is not a Christian nation. One cannot depend on the public schools to remain Christian or to give a Christian education. The public school, as a creation of the state, is therefore not really a Christian school, however Christian it may appear to be at the moment.[69] In making this argument he was repeating the complaint of the Reverend Marinus E. Broekstra, printed a decade earlier. Broekstra charged that arguments in favor of the Christian character of the public schools

[65]    Many of the first generation of leaders of the colonies continued to hold the Christian school as the ideal, but were ready to accept the "common schools" so long as they remained inclined toward the Christian faith; see Adrian Zwemer, in *Nagelatene Leerredenen van R. Pieters*, xv-xvi; see also R. Pieters, "Belijdenis en Praktijk," *De Hope*, March 17, 1869.)

[66]    Nicholas Steffens favored the support of Christian schools; see "Eenhied en Opvoeding,"
        *De Hope*, June 4, 1907; "De Ontkerstening der Openbare School," July 26, 1910. For a history of the efforts to establish Christian educational institutions for higher education, high school, and elementary schools in the Midwest, see Elton Bruins, "The Educational Endeavors of the Reformed Dutch Church, 1628-1866," *Reformed Review*, Winter 2005-2006, esp. 176-83.

[67]    "Parochial Scholen," *De Hope*, January 23, 1878.

[68]    Editor, "Wekelijksch Budget," *De Hope*, March 1, 1893.

[69]    Jacob Van Houte, "Is de Dusgenaamde Christelijke School Overbodig? *De Hope*, October 6, 1914; "Is de Publieke School een Christelijke School?" *De Hope*, July 4, 1914. Van Houte was born in the Netherlands in 1845. He served Reformed churches in Ohio, Illinois, Michigan, Iowa, and New Jersey between 1884 and 1916. He died in 1919.

were based on the "utilitarian idea." The schools lacked the theological foundation that would sustain their Christian character.[70]

Broekstra contended that the public schools under the direction of the state violated the principle of "sovereignty in its own sphere." Education of children is the responsibility of the sphere of the family. Parents of baptized children have promised to give them a Christian education, not only in the way of salvation but also for their life in the world. It is therefore a violation of the baptismal promise when they send their children to public schools.[71] The arguments set forth by Van Houte and Broekstra summarized the basic arguments in favor of Christian schools.[72]

An article by Gerhardus De Jonge, one of the editors of *De Hope,* is representative of the position of the public school proponents. He began by pointing out that the public schools are under the administration of local districts and serve all children without discrimination. The public school is a purely American institution designed to meet specifically American needs. In the areas where many of the Dutch immigrants were located, the schools followed the provisions of the old Northwest Territories Act that set aside section 16 of each township for the purpose of public education. That act provided that "religion, morality, and the knowledge necessary to good governance and welfare of the people shall be encouraged through the means of education."[73]

Due to the fact that America is made up of a great many people with many different languages, customs, and religious preferences, coming in great numbers from Europe, he argued, it was essential to educate children together in the common schools for the sake of their being integrated into the life of the nation. De Jonge believed that

---

[70]  Marinus E. Broekstra, "Eenige Bedenkingen," *De Hope,* December 24, 1902. Broekstra was born in the Netherlands in 1872, graduated from the theological school in Kampen in 1893 and Western Theological Seminary in 1897. He served as pastor of Reformed churches in Iowa, Michigan, Illinois, and New Jersey from 1897 until his death in 1940.

[71]  Ibid. On the basis of "sovereignty in its own sphere," Christian Reformed leaders also objected to "parochial schools" under control of the church. Christian schools had to be under the direction of an association of Reformed parents who could not allow their responsibility to be transferred to the church any more than to the state. Henry Zwaanstra, *Reformed Thought and Experience in a New World* (Kampen, Netherlands: J.V. Kok, 1973), 139-44. See also the article by Reformed Church minister John Van Der Beek, "Reply to Mr. Aue" *Leader,* February 6, 1918, 3.

[72]  For a detailed exposition of the history of the discussion in the Christian Reformed Church about Christian elementary schools, see Zwaanstra, *Reformed Thought,* 132-56.

the American nation was founded on Christian principles; therefore, Christians have a civic responsibility to educate their children in the public schools that are a bulwark of American freedom.[74]

Five decades later, Isaac Rottenberg contributed an article to the *Reformed Review* that went to the heart of the debate. He wrote that the Christian school issue must be considered in the context of "the historical-eschatological acts of God and the Kingdom." The education of children is not exclusively a parental responsibility. Not only the family, but also the whole society and the state have a stake in developing a child for civic, economic, and social maturity. One cannot on the basis of "sovereignty in its own sphere" or the baptismal promise or the "antithesis" between the regenerate and unregenerate insist upon parental control of the education of the child.[75] At the time Rottenberg wrote, the decisions of the Supreme Court concerning the role of education in the public school recognized that Americans are a "religious people." Therefore, the Constitution permits teaching about religion in the public schools, but worship is not within the provenance of the schools. Rottenberg maintained on that basis that the Bible has a place in the public schools.[76] In view of the fact that the state and society as well as parents and the church have a vital interest in providing quality education to children, the public school is to be given priority, but Christian schools must be accepted as an emergency measure when the public schools do not adequately fulfill their responsibilities.[77] Difference of opinion on what is adequate is at the center of public debate and parental decision today.

## Two Challenges to the Nature of Midwestern Reformed Church Participation in American Society

At the beginning of the twentieth century, the midwestern Reformed Church was challenged to deeper reflection on the theological basis and nature of its participation in American society. On the one hand, the movement of Neo-Calvinism in the Netherlands under the leadership of Abraham Kuyper sought to provide a new understanding of Reformed theology that could be a basis for Reformed participation in the modern cultural and scientific life. On the other hand, the Social Gospel movement under the leading of American ministers such

[74]   Ibid.
[75]   Isaac Rottenberg, "Public School versus Christian School," *Reformed Review*, 9/3 (April 1956), 9-16.
[76]   Ibid., 13.
[77]   Ibid., 15.

as Washington Gladden and Walter Rauschenbusch was becoming prominent in the United States.

### (1) The Neo-Calvinism of Abraham Kuyper

The midwestern Reformed Church was affected by developments in the Netherlands where Abraham Kuyper, the Reformed political leader, journalist, theologian, and educator was teaching a "neo-Calvinism" that defended traditional Reformed theology while also providing a theoretical foundation for Christian participation in society. He made an impact on the English-speaking world in the United States when he gave a series of lectures on Calvinism at Princeton Theological Seminary in 1898. Following his time in Princeton, he gave lectures to the Reformed communities in Grand Rapids and Holland, Michigan, and Chicago, Illinois.[78]

Abraham Kuyper challenged American Christians to see that there is a deep divide between those who have been born again or "regenerated" by the Spirit of God and those who remain unregenerated. The two classes of people work on different principles and are building conflicting systems of science and culture. Although at a given moment the two classes may be working together to achieve a goal in science, culture, or political life, they will eventually come into conflict. In his historical context in 1898, he recognized the two conflicting systems to be Calvinism and Modernism:

> From the first, therefore, I have always said to myself, "If the battle is to be fought with honor and with a hope of victory, then *principle* must be arrayed against *principle;* then it must be

---

[78] The Christian Reformed Church and the midwestern Reformed Church in America vied with each other in offering hospitality and homage to the great leader from the Netherlands. Although his impact on the Christian Reformed Church was eventually to outstrip his influence in the Reformed Church, at the time of his visit he enjoyed friendships in both denominations. For an enthusiastic report by a Reformed Church leader about Kuyper's visit, see Henry Dosker, "Onze Gast," *De Hope*, November 2, 1898.

Henry E. Dosker translated Kuyper's second Stone lecture into English for presentation at Princeton, and Nicholas Steffens translated lecture three. For a full study in English of the contribution of Kuyper, see Peter S. Heslam, *Creating a Christian Worldview: Abraham's Kuyper's Lectures on Calvinism* (Grand Rapids: Eerdmans, 1998). Heslam's book is an extended commentary and evaluation of Kuyper's Stone *Lectures on Calvinism*, given at Princeton Theological Seminary 1898. Kuyper's *Lectures on Calvinism* continue to be influential, especially in the more Reformed wing of the evangelical community in America.

felt that in Modernism the vast energy of an all-embracing *life-system* assails us, then also it must be understood that we have to take our stand in a life-system of equally comprehensive and far-reaching power. And this powerful life-system is not to be invented nor formulated by ourselves, but is to be taken and applied as it presents itself in history."[79]

Three ideas of Kuyper came to play an important role following his lectures at Princeton and visit to western Michigan. The first was that there was an "antithesis" between the regenerate and unregenerate who on principle were building separate systems. Therefore, it was essential that Christian organizations be established who could think and act on a distinctively Reformed theological basis. In the Netherlands this involved establishing separate Christian schools, labor unions, bakers' associations, and even separate goat breeders societies.

The second idea was that in spite of the antithesis between the systems of the regenerate and the unregenerate, there were whole areas of society where it was possible for cooperation on the basis of God's common grace. Common grace was God's gracious action whereby God restrained the consequences of the fall into sin and depravity. By God's common grace that was present for all, human beings were still able to think scientifically, build cultures, and maintain social organization. Common grace was a restraining influence but not saving grace. God's special, or saving grace, was given only to those whom God had elected to salvation.[80]

[79] Kuyper, *Lectures on Calvinism*, 11-12. Kuyper used the phrase "life system" in his lecture because his American friends told him that it would be more easily understood as a translation of the German technical term *Weltanschauung*. At many points in the lectures, he used the phrase "life and world view" that became the more accepted terminology by the Kuyperians in America; see *Lectures on Calvinism*, 11, n1.

   "Modernism" took many forms in Europe and America. In the Netherlands two of its primary representatives were Cornelis Willem Opzoomeer and Jan Hendrik Scholten. "Certainly, they continued to talk about the 'divine,' but by that they meant that the divine revealed itself *in* the human, in his particular thinking, willing, and feeling, and was not directed *to* the human from without. 'God' does not stand over and against nature, but is the center of all reality—that is itself the revelation of God" (Blei, *Netherlands Reformed Church*, 68).

[80] For a clear exposition of the doctrine of common grace within the Kuyperian tradition, see the Christian Reformed Church theologian Louis Berkhof, *Systematic Theology*, 432-46. The distinction between special grace and common grace was also taught by theological professors at Western Theological Seminary. Blekkink wrote, "There is a sense in which it is

A third idea of Kuyper was that of "sovereignty in its own sphere." In his *Lectures on Calvinism,* Kuyper also set forth his understanding of "sphere sovereignty" in contrast to "popular sovereignty" and "state sovereignty." Popular sovereignty was what was proposed in Paris in 1793 at the height of the French Revolution. It dethroned God and put people on the throne. "It ignores God. It opposes God."[81]

Kuyper maintained that the various social spheres of society, including the family, religion, business, science, and art do not owe their existence to the state or derive the law of their life from the state. "They obey a high authority within their own bosom; an authority which rules, by the grace of God, just as the sovereignty of the State does."[82] Therefore the church must be separate from the state. Each has its own sphere and responsibility. The highest duty of the government is to maintain justice and provide security for the people. It must make law in accordance with justice. It may not impose its laws (1) in the social sphere; (2) on the corporative sphere of universities, guilds, associations, etc.; (3) in the domestic sphere of the family and married life; and (4) in communal autonomy. "In these four spheres it must reference the innate law of life."[83]

Midwestern Reformed Church writers welcomed Kuyper's contribution to a theology for Christian participation in American society, but they responded with greater enthusiasm to some of Kuyper's issues and vocabulary than to others. They adopted his use of the term "common grace" as available to unregenerate and regenerate alike. With regard to the life of the family, educational institutions, the state, and science they accepted with modifications his teaching that each is "sovereign within its own sphere." They agreed that with regard to salvation there is a chasm between the regenerate and the unregenerate, but they did not agree that the chasm exists across

---

true that the whole world shares in the sacrifice of Christ. It is the basis of common grace as it is of saving grace. God is longsuffering with the wicked, causes rain to fall on the unjust, holds in check the destructive forces in nature and humanity, brings to fullest development the hidden possibilities, in both man and beast, through his Spirit and for the sake of the mediatorial work of Christ." "Limited Atonement," *Leader,* July 5, 1916, 594. See also John R. Mulder, "Christology," 15; "Anthropology," 26.

   Blekkink differed from Kuyper. Blekkink wrote that the sacrifice of Christ "is the basis of common grace as it is of saving grace." Louis Berkhof wrote, "As far as we know, Dr. Kuyper does not posit "a connection in any way between the atoning work of Christ and common grace" Berkhof, *Systematic Theology,* 437.

[81]   Kuyper, *Lectures on Calvinism,* 85, 87.
[82]   Ibid., 90.
[83]   Ibid., 96.

every aspect of society. They were not ready to accept his contention that, since principles carry through, there is an antithesis so stark that believers and nonbelievers are building separate houses in areas of the state, education, and science.

The Reverend Dr. John Kuizenga, professor of theology at Western Theological Seminary, presented an articulate response to Kuyper's ideas in articles published in the *Leader* between 1917 and 1922. He vigorously opposed the slogan, "In isolation lies our strength." He quoted Herman Bavinck, who had written, "Isolation is not always a proof of strength, it may also be a sign of bigotry (*bekrompenheid*)." [84] Kuizenga wrote that it is a fatal mistake to use the term, "Calvinism," to limit our church fellowship to a narrow circle. It is the duty of all of us to tell people how much "Calvinism" has in common with Methodism and all the other Christian churches, including the Roman Catholics and even with theists. "So it is misrepresenting Calvinism if we insist on church fellowship and practical cooperation only with those churches which are identically of the same confessional Calvinism as our own. Here isolation is not strength but bigotry." [85]

Leaders in the Christian Reformed Church spoke frequently of what made their Calvinistic denomination "distinctive" on the American scene. Kuizenga and his colleagues rejected that approach to denominational understanding. In the final article in his long series, "What We Stand For," he wrote that since we stand for the same things

---

[84]  John Kuizenga, "What we stand for, XI," *Leader*, Dec. 26, 1917. Herman Bavinck belonged to the second generation of the leaders of the Christelijke Gereformeerde Kerk and had been a professor at its theological seminary in Kampen. When under the leading of Kuyper the Free University was established, Bavinck became a theological professor there. Like Kuyper, he had studied under Modernist teachers at the University of Leiden and received his doctor's degree there. He and Kuyper gave leadership uniting the *Afscheiding* and the *Doleantie* churches in 1892. For the history of events leading to the merger, see Hendrik Bouma (Theodore Plantinga, trans.) *Secession, Doleantie, and Union: 1834-1892* (Pella, Iowa: Inheritance Publications, 1995). For an essay on the relation of Bavinck to the Reformed Church in America minister Henry Dosker, see George Harinck, "'Something That must Remain, If the Truth is to be Sweet and Precious to Us': The Reformed Spirituality of Herman Bavinck," *Calvin Theological Journal*, 38 (2003), 250-51. On the whole, leaders in the Reformed Church in America were theologically closer to Bavinck than to Kuyper. Beginning in the 1950s the theological writings of G. Berkouwer, professor of theology at the Free University, were much appreciated in the midwestern Reformed Church. In his theological activity he carried on in the spirit of Bavinck; see John Bolt, "Nineteenth and Twentieth Century Dutch Reformed Church and Theology," *Calvin Theological Journal*, 38 (1993), 441-42.

[85]  Kuizenga, "Playing fast and loose with Calvinism," *Leader*, Nov. 27, 1918, 9.

The Rev. John E. Kuizenga, D.D.
(1876-1949)

*Courtesy of Hope College Alumni Magazine,*
*October, 1949, 14.*

"His soul reveled in beautiful statements, and he called from literature, both poetry and prose, its choicest lines, and gathered them into the rich storehouse of his memory so that he could use them at appropriate moments. His mind delighted in the marshaled thoughts of philosophers and theologians, and he followed their ideas with lucidity of understanding. But, best of all, his spirit responded to the truth of God's Word, and he feasted his soul on the Living Word. When he rose to teach, or to preach, all this wealth of material became available, and he laid strong hands on immortal truth to make it the 'sword of the Spirit' that converts men's souls."—John R. Mulder, *Hope College Alumni Magazine*, October 1949, 14.

that the best evangelical churches stand for, our mission cannot have a distinctive theology or form of polity. He said that for now there still is a distinct Dutch religious psychology that includes thriftiness and soberness in life, conservatism, ingrained virtues of individual morality, "churchiness" with its light and shadowed sides, deep love of the Word and things of the Spirit, and efficiency of administration and organization.[86] However, we must not protect this Dutch psychology by cutting ourselves off from the broader horizons of American evangelical churches.

Kuizenga also attacked Kuyper's understanding of the "antithesis." He agreed that there is an antithesis between the regenerate and the unregenerate on the way of salvation. He also agreed that without the working of the Holy Spirit in our hearts there is no hope of being born

[86]    Ibid., January 9, 1917, 8-9.

again. Regeneration is God's work, not ours. But Kuizenga charged that Kuyper had overstated the position. "To overstate a position is often as fatal to orthodox thought as to understate it...."[87] The antithesis is to be found not simply between believers and unbelievers; it is also present within the heart of every believer and cuts across the whole society in a nation. Kuizenga agreed with Benjamin Warfield of Princeton Theological Seminary, who rejected the idea that there are two kinds of science. Warfield, who played host to Abraham Kuyper when he gave the *Lectures on Calvinism*, maintained that scientists are not erecting two different buildings on two different sets of principles, one by the regenerate and the other by the unregenerate. Warfield held that:

> science was an objective, unified, and cumulative enterprise of the whole humanity. There could be no difference in kind between the work of the regenerate and unregenerate scientists....He did not wish to deny that there was a difference between the results produced by Christian and non-Christian scientists, but for him this was not a difference between two types of science but in the quality of their findings.[88]

Scientists are not erecting two different buildings, but "one edifice of truth."[89] Most of the midwestern leaders as well as the professors at Hope College accepted the view of Warfield rather than of Kuyper on this matter.[90]

In his long 1922 series of articles, "Grace, Special and General Culture," Kuizenga wrote, "The purpose of special grace in Jesus Christ is redemption, but we should conceive of this redemption in broad

---

[87]  Kuizenga, "As to the Absolute Antithesis," *Leader*, December 10, 1919, 9. Kuizenga's sharply worded articles against a number of elements in Kuyper and his followers must not be understood as one more example of the polemics between leaders in the Reformed and Christian Reformed churches. During those same years he published articles against the Kuyperians "principialism" in the *Christian Journal*, edited by members of the Christian Reformed Church. James Bratt calls Kuizenga the "rising star" in the Reformed Church; see Bratt, *Dutch Calvinism in Modern America*, 99-101. For information on "principialism" and the "antithesis" as advocated by Kuyperians such as Klaas Schoolland within the Christian Reformed Church, see Henry Zwaanstra, *Reformed Thought and Experience in a New World*, 108-118.

[88]  Heslam, *Creating a Christian World-View*, 186.

[89]  Ibid.

[90]  See M. Eugene Osterhaven, professor at Western Theological Seminary, for a critique of the doctrine of the antithesis, "Quia Semper Reformanda Est, "*Reformed Review*, 11/1 (1957), 10-13.

terms."[91] Jesus Christ came to redeem the whole creation. It is world redemption. The only thing lost through sin is individual lives, whether fallen angels or human lives. Inanimate and animate creation apart from humankind has a future in God's hands.[92] Kuizenga maintained that truth must be conceived of in a wider significance than Christians often do. He believed that there is such a thing as specifically Christian science that takes into account God's creative and providential activity, in contrast to materialistic science, and similarly that there is Christian art, Christian sociology, and Christian sport.[93] But in carrying out such activities, the Christians must not become separatist in their endeavors.

His 1920 article, "The Puritan and Calvinistic Ideal," summarized what Kuizenga and other leaders in the midwestern Reformed Church believed when they taught that America was founded on Christian principles. Although he was less certain than some of his colleagues that America is a "Christian nation," he wrote that "the spirit of the pilgrim ideals still leavens our national life to an extent that it is not possible in Europe."[94] The Reformed Church has the task not only to evangelize, but also to make America as Christian as we can. In carrying this out, we must not compel the consciences of those outside the faith or discriminate against them legally. We must uphold the right to dissent and permit atheists to speak, but we ought also to preserve the tradition that in America religion has the right of way over atheism. But Christians must be Christian in every aspect of life. "A Christian cannot be neutral, as a business man, as a teacher, as a citizen—He is Christian in everything or in nothing."[95]

### (2) The Social Gospel Movement

The Social Gospel movement became an important challenge to the nature of midwestern Reformed Church participation in Protestant witness and mission in American society. One of the fathers of the movement was Josiah Strong (1847-1916), whose book, *Our Country*, was heartily endorsed by the midwestern leaders.[96] He was

[91]  *Leader*, May 17, 1922, 9.
[92]  Ibid.
[93]  Ibid.
[94]  Kuizenga, "The Puritan and Calvinistic Ideal," *Leader*, October 10, 1920, 9.
[95]  Ibid.
[96]  For an excellent description of the Social Gospel movement see Sydney E. Ahlstrom, *A Religious History of the American People*, 785-804. Josiah Strong's book had been translated into Dutch by John H. Karsten and recommended by five leading midwestern ministers (Peter De Pree, Adrian

"the dynamo, the revivalist, the organizer, and altogether the most irrepressible spirit of the Social Gospel movement."[97] In 1885, Strong had come to believe that the new industrial city was the greatest crisis facing the nation and the American church. In 1898, he was forced out of the Evangelical Alliance on account of his advanced social views and his liberal theology that was heavily influenced by Horace Bushnell.[98] He then organized the League for Social Service (later the American Institute of Social Service) that became an interdenominational agency of national scope.

The midwestern leaders were not enthusiastic about the liberal theology of the Social Gospel movement. They did not share the optimism of the leading theologian of the movement, the Reverend Walter Rauschenbusch (1861-1918), who taught the perfectibility of human nature under the power of the gospel. On the final page of his book, *Christianity and the Social Crisis*, he wrote, "Humanity is gaining in elasticity and capacity for change....The swiftness of our own country proves the immense latent perfectibility in human nature."[99] The language of the perfectibility of human nature went against the grain

---

Zwemer, Balster Van Ess, Peter Moerdyk, and John Kremer) and two professors (G.J. Kollen and G. Hempkes) as the best statement of reasons for a vigorous program of evangelism and foreign missions [Josiah Strong, trans. J H. Karsten, *Ons Land: Deszelfs Mogelijke Toekomst en Tegenwoordige Crisis* (Grand Rapids: Hollandsche Boek-Drukkerij van H.A. Toren, 1889), 283-86].

97  Ahlstrom, *A Religious History*, 799.
98  Horace Bushnell (1802-76) is sometimes called the father of American theological liberalism. He is best known today for his book, *Christian Nurture*, published in 1847, in which he argued that revivals and conversion experiences are unnecessary when faithful Christian nurture is carried out. Bushnell held that human language about God must be metaphorical or figurative rather than literal. "Words get their significance, I have insisted, under conditions of analogy, and never stand as a direct and absolute notation for thought" (Horace Bushnell, *Christ in Theology*, Hartford: Brown and Parsons, 1851), 40. His understanding of the nature of human language encouraged the New Theologians to use language that the midwestern leaders rejected as ambiguous. His rejection of the Anselmic doctrine of the atonement as being "the simplest form of absurdity" (229) was especially offensive to those who maintained strict loyalty to the language of the Reformed confessions. For a clear introduction to the thought and life of Bushnell, see John M. Mulder, "Introduction," in Horace Bushnell, *Christian Nurture* (Grand Rapids: Baker, 1979), vii-xxx.
99  Walter Rauschenbusch, *Christianity and Social Crisis* (New York: MacMillan, 1908), 422. He had become convinced of the need for a social gospel during his eleven-year ministry with the German Baptist congregation (1886-87) near "Hell's Kitchen" in New York City.

because all of the midwestern leaders had long fought against Wesleyan "perfectionism" as contrary to their doctrine of total depravity and their recognition of the continuing power of sin even in the life of the most ardent believer.

They also objected to the Social Gospel movement's argument that social salvation precedes individual salvation, both temporally and in importance. Rauschenbusch complained that the call by evangelists for individual decisions at times only left "men worse by getting religion."

> We are not disposed to accept the converted souls whom the individualistic evangelism supplies, without looking them over. Some who have been saved and perhaps reconsecrated a number of times are worth no more to the Kingdom of God than they were before. Some become worse though their revival experiences, more self-righteous, more opinionated, more steeped in unrealities and stupid over against the most important things, more devoted to emotions and unresponsive to real duties.[100]

Conversion had to be social because sin was essentially social. Rauschenbusch objected to the traditional view of original sin as responsible for the biological transmission of sin from Adam to each member of the human race. The doctrine "has diverted our minds from the power of social transmission, from the authority of the social group in justifying, urging, and idealizing wrong, and from the decisive influence of economic profit in the defense and propagation of evil."[101]

Because sin is primarily social rather than individual, conversion is most valuable "if it throws a revealing light not only across our own past, but across the social life of which we are a part, and makes our repentance a vicarious sorrow for all. The prophets felt so about the sins of their nation. Jesus felt so about Jerusalem, and Paul about unbelieving Israel."[102] Rauschenbusch asked, "If we are converted, what are we converted to?" His answer was, "If we are regenerated, does the scope of so divine a transformation end with our 'going to heaven.' The nexus between our religious experience and humanity seems gone when the Kingdom of God is not present in the idea of regeneration."[103]

---

[100]  Walter Rauschenbusch, *A Theology for the Social Gospel* (New York: MacMillan, 1917), 96.

[101]  Ibid., 67.

[102]  Ibid., 99.

[103]  Ibid., 100-101.

The Social Gospel advocate, the Reverend Washington Gladden, was optimistic that under the fatherhood of God we can look forward to the ultimate triumph of the kingdom of heaven that is already present among us, "just as the spring is here when the crocuses open and the violets and the spring beauties are first in evidence."[104] He wrote,

> Every department of human life—the families, the schools, amusements, art, business, politics, industry, national policies, international relations—will be governed by the Christian law and controlled by Christian influences. When we are bidden to seek first the kingdom of God, we are bidden to set our hearts on this great consummation; to keep this always before us as the object of our endeavors; to be satisfied with nothing less than this. The complete Christianization of all life is what we pray for and work for, when we work and pray for the coming of the kingdom of heaven.[105]

The midwestern Reformed Church leaders did not agree that the "complete Christianization of all life in the coming of the kingdom of heaven" is a realistic expectation. Evert Blekkink, who was more optimistic than most, rejected the simple slogan of those who declared that the essence of the gospel is "the fatherhood of God and the brotherhood of man." He taught that God is father of all by creation, but by redemption God is father only of those who are reborn of the Spirit. The fatherhood of God in creation "constitutes the brotherhood of man." The fatherhood of God by redemption established the brotherhood of believers.[106] He agreed with Kuyper that there is a deep cleavage running through the human race from the dawn of human history.

---

[104] Washington Gladden, *The Church and the Kingdom* (New York: Revell, 1894), 8. Gladden's lecture, "The Church and the Kingdom," was presented before the State Association of the Congregational Churches of Ohio May 9, 1894.

[105] Ibid.

[106] Evert J. Blekkink, *The Fatherhood of God*, 85. Blekkink's teaching on this subject was adopted by most other midwestern Reformed Church leaders. Osterhaven accepted the phrase as biblical but objected that it was misused by liberal theologians following Harnack. Osterhaven wrote, "But when the New Testament speaks about God as Father it is usually in the special, redemptive sense" ("Youth Forum," *Church Herald*, April 29, 1949, 11). Louis Benes, editor of the *Church Herald*, attacked the slogan, saying that the phrase must be used for the family of God and brotherhood of believers. Within the family of God, it is unthinkable that there should be segregation of the races ("Brotherhood and Race," *Church Herald*, February 15, 1952, 6).

The Rev. Evert J. Blekkink, D.D.
(1858-1948)

*Courtesy of Western Theological Seminary*

Evert Blekking was a delegate to the World Missionary Conference, Edinburgh, 1910. "He was true to the highest principles of the Reformed Church and the spirit of his Lord and Master so permeated his character that he will be remembered as a living example of what it means to be a Christian. He was always a helpful writer in our denominational publications. He published 'Our Father in Heaven,' a discussion of the fatherhood of God. He was one of the founders of the church paper, 'The Leader,' and served for a considerable time as its editor."—*Acts and Proceedings,* 1949, 200.

In the dawn of recorded history we find the righteous and the wicked. In the first psalm this line of demarcation is drawn: "Blessed is the man that walketh not in the counsel of the ungodly, nor standeth in the way of sinners, nor sitteth in the seat of the scornful. But his delight is in the law of the Lord. The ungodly are not so, but are like the chaff which the wind driveth away."[107]

Blekkink believed that the line is drawn even more sharply in the New Testament, where Jesus spoke of the wise and foolish virgins, the wheat and the tares, and the sheep and the goats. Blekkink insisted that it was necessary to call individuals to repentance.

Individual salvation is the keynote of the gospel music. Without it social redemption is impossible. The one preceeds the other as the foundation the superstructure. Air-castles can exist in the

---

[107]  Blekkink, ibid., 85.

mind's eye but they have no enduring value. Salvation is primarily personal: essentially individual. 'What must I do to be saved?'[108]

However much Blekkink would have liked to believe that everyone would come to repentance and salvation, he believed that there could be no hope for that. "The race will be saved, but not every individual of the race, 'There is a great gulf fixed...'"[109] In spite of the great gulf fixed, however, the midwestern ministers believed that it is premature to draw the line solidly in the present age by creating separate Christian organizations in each sphere. The wheat and the tares grow together for a time. Blekkink did not appeal to a doctrine of common grace as the basis for cooperation with unbelievers. He simply called upon followers of Christ to act in the world on the basis of the love of Christ.

> Like the Master the servant must go about doing good. We are in a world in need. The underprivileged—the deformed in body, the broken in health, the blind, the feeble minded, the ignorant, the hungry, and the inadequately sheltered; the inmates of almshouses, asylums for the insane, hospitals, and other institutions for suffering humanity—are a vast multitude. And the spiritual needs are even greater than physical and mental.[110]
> The love of Christ constraineth us. Christians share in the sufferings of Christ for the salvation of the world. We must take the cross and follow him; like him we shall rejoice in the cross for the joy that is set before us in the life of good works for the glory of God and the well-being of our fellowmen.[111]

Apart from their objections to the liberal theology of the Social Gospel movement, members of the midwestern Reformed churches were not ready to rally to its urban orientation. Walter Rauschenbusch came to many of his theological social conclusions through his pastoral experience in dealing with the awful living conditions of people in Hell's Kitchen, New York City. Washington Gladden became involved in seeking to bring about reconciliation between management and labor when strikes were threatened during the years he served as pastor in Massachusetts and Ohio.[112] He called for "the redemption of the city" from "poverty and pauperism, idleness and intemperance, bankrupt

---

[108]  Blekkink, "Salvation," *Leader*, January 9, 1924, 1.
[109]  Blekkink, *Fatherhood of God*, 86.
[110]  Blekkink, *Fatherhood of God*, 84.
[111]  Ibid., 85.
[112]  Gladden dealt with labor-management issues in his book, *Working People and Employers* (New York: Funk and Wagnalls, 1885).

households and neglected children, groups of incapables and ne'er-do-wells and criminals, the multitudes on whom Jesus looked with compassion because they were distressed and scattered as sheep not having a shepherd."[113] Gladden's phrase, "applied Christianity," was a call to action when he asserted that "the thing the world needed most was a direct application of the Christian law to the business of life."[114]

From time to time paragraphs about working conditions of laborers and the living conditions of impoverished urban dwellers appeared in the editorial and news pages of *De Hope* and the *Leader*. However, such items were few and far between. Almost all of the Reformed Church in America congregations in the Midwest were located in small towns, villages, and rural areas where large cities were perceived more as a threat than as a call to applied Christianity and redemption.[115] When Christian responsibility for the cities was recognized, it was usually qualified by making reference to other needs. Peter De Pree was sensitive to the needs of slum dwellers in New York City where one in three people were living in squalor, according to a book he had just read, but he then went on to comment that the problem is everywhere, in rural areas as well. He urged his readers not to avoid their social responsibilities.[116]

Two of the major editors of the *Leader*, Gerrit Dubbink and Evert Blekkink, approved of preaching on social themes. In his memorial service address upon the death of Gerrit Dubbink in 1910, Evert Blekkink praised him for preaching on social themes with the Bible in his hand.

> He believed in the regeneration of society as he did of the individual through the transforming power of the gospel. He assailed the evils in social, commercial and political life because they are contrary to the will of God. He believed that Christian civilization consists in bringing all the interest and activities of life under obedience to Christ. When some years ago he preached a sermon on capital and labor, it was criticized by some one who

[113] Washington Gladden, *Social Salvation* (Boston: Houghton, Mifflin, 1902), 3, 203-35.

[114] Quoted in Robert Handy, ed., *The Social Gospel in America, 1870-1920* (New York: Oxford Univ. Press, 1966), 49.

[115] The Dutch who settled in Chicago became the exception when Chicago grew rapidly to become a metropolitan city. However, most of the Dutch in Chicago were antagonistic to American labor unions and strongly opposed to strikes (Robert P. Swierenga, *Dutch Chicago: A History of the Hollanders in the Windy City* (Grand Rapids: Eerdmans, 2002), 640-49.

[116] Peter De Pree, "Wekeljksch Budget," *De Hope*, May 4, 1904.

heard it and said that while the discourse was interesting and excellent he had brought too much Bible into the discussion. No greater compliment could possibly be paid to any preacher.[117]

The most passionate call to sympathy for laboring men had to do with rural coal miners rather than urban laborers. In 1910, the *Leader* pointed out, "The coal miner has never gotten a square deal....And this tragedy is an even more serious indictment of state and church than the economic maladjustments made so conspicuous by labor controversies....There is the call of the coal miner, come down into our darkness and give us the light of the gospel."[118]

In contrast to the Social Gospel movement's call to respond to the plight of the urban slum dwellers and the working class, articles in *De Hope* and the *Leader* were unanimously opposed to unions and strikes and generally favorable to management, while calling for management to exercise Christian benevolence and fairness regarding the needs of their employees. But they remained pessimistic about the possibility of redeeming the cities so long as they were being overrun by the new types of immigrants beginning late in the nineteenth century.

The speech, "The Labor Question," given by the Honorable Gerrit J. Diekema in Overisel, Michigan, July 4, 1886, was consistent with the thinking of the midwestern Reformed leaders in the final decades of the nineteenth century. In his analysis of the situation, the problem of labor unrest was due to the rapid growth of cities such as Chicago and to the type of immigrants arriving there. Large cities became the hiding places of murderers, thieves, and burglars, as well as prostitutes and a mass of other bad characters. They were the locations of saloons and all that went with them. Therefore he urged the young men not to forsake their rural and village homes for the sake of the glamour of the cities. Moreover, he was opposed to the new immigrants arriving in the cities. These newcomers were not like previous generations from northern Europe who had built up the country. They brought with them socialist and anarchist ideas and disregard for the Sabbath that are in contrast to American ideas of freedom and morality.[119]

---

[117] Blekkink, "Memorial Service Address," *Leader*, October 12, 1910, 2.
[118] *Leader*, November 23, 1910, 69.
[119] Gerrit Diekema, "De Arbeidsquestie," *De Hope*, July 21, 1886. Diekema was an immigrant from the Netherlands and served in many local political offices. He was a member of Hope Church in Holland, Michigan, and superintendent of its Sunday school. After serving four terms as a Michigan state legislator, he was elected to the House of Representatives in 1907, having been enthusiastically endorsed by the *Leader*. He served four terms as state chairman of the Republican Party. In congratulating him upon

Those who lived in the Dutch enclaves prior to 1930 were able to avoid many of the issues that were of vital concern to the proponents of the Social Gospel. Their farms, towns and villages prospered and their poor were taken care of in one way or another. Living in a Christian nation where the president was always Protestant, where, after World War I, prohibition was the law of the land, where Sunday laws were still enforced, and where the Ten Commandments still could be found on the wall of the United States Supreme Court, midwestern Reformed Church members saw no reason to advocate for radical social change in the economic, social, or political system. Contrary to some leaders in the Christian Reformed Church, they saw no reason to establish separate Christian social or economic organizations.

## Midwestern Defense of Capitalism and Rejection of Socialism and Communism

Throughout their first century in America, the Dutch immigrants took a firm stand against Socialist and Communist movements in Europe and the United States. However, when the Great Depression arrived in the 1930s, issues of unemployment, dire poverty, and social unrest could no longer be ignored. Socialist movements gained power in America. The capitalistic economic system began to be called into question when national unemployment approached 20 percent of the work force. In 1932 in the depth of the Great Depression, the Reverend Dr. Siebe Nettinga declared that each century has its own burning issue. In the Apostolic Church, the issue was Christian freedom from the Mosaic Law. In the second and third centuries, it was the encounter with paganism. In the fourth and fifth centuries, the theological doctrines of the Trinity and Christology required creedal formulation. In the sixteenth century, it was the Protestant Reformation. The burning question in the twentieth century was now the *social and economic question*. Not the relation of human beings to God, but the relation of human beings to each other now had to occupy center stage.

Nettinga concluded his series, "Our Standpoint Over-against American Christendom," by listing its positive characteristics. In opposition to those Dutch Americans who viewed cooperation with American Christendom as "watering the milk," he called attention to the

---

his being elected to the House of Representatives, the editors wrote, "Our congressman is a *child* of the Emigration of Forty-seven. If William Alden represents the excellent characteristics which the Mayflower and Pilgrim's Rock bequeathed to this country, Gerrit J. represents the virtues and graces with which Van Raalte and his followers enriched this nation" (*Leader*, May 1, 1907), 424.

The Rev. Siebe C. Nettinga, D.D.
(1875-1938)

*Courtesy of Western Theological Seminary*

"President Nettinga's life and my own have been peculiarly parallel. We were boys together in college and seminary. Part of the time we were classmates. His pastorate was near so that we saw each other frequently. His professorate and presidency were almost parallel to my own. It was a joy to talk with him about the seminaries and their policies. Ever since his coming to Holland he lived and thought for the school in which he taught. He was intimately familiar with every detail of its present and its past. He not only knew facts, but he knew how facts were related to each other and what facts might mean for human life. He was convinced that the seminaries exist not for themselves but for the Church, to train ministers able to deal with people and to meet—whatever local conditions they may find in their parishes, not men who can merely recite words. He was training ministers not for work in general but for the particular needs of the Reformed Church he loved so dearly and to whose ideals and standards he remained so loyal."— John W. Beardslee, Jr., President, New Brunswick Theological Seminary, "President Nettinga as Colleague," *Intelligencer-Leader*, September 9, 1938, 4.

wide and voluntary participation in church life in America. American Christians were active and it was good to sing their hymn, "To the work, to the work, we are servants of God." American Christians were generous in their charity. They were engaged in wrestling with the great ethical and social problems of the age. Nettinga reminded his readers that they lived in America and their children were adopting American perspectives and practices. While it was good to renew an emphasis upon the essential principles of the Christian faith, it was crucial that they do so in full participation in American Christendom.[120]

[120]  Nettinga, "Onze Verhouding tegenover Het Amerikaansche Christendom," *De Hope*, June 7, 1932.

In his series, "The Church and the Social Question," Nettinga emphasized that Reformed preaching must deal not only with how the soul can be redeemed from sin, but also how human beings must live in their relationships in the world. Sermons must lay out the great social principles about property in the eighth commandment. Wealth as such is not to be condemned but must be handled responsibly, with mercy and love and charity for the poor.[121]

Nettinga defended capitalism as an economic system and gave credit to Calvin for having pointed the way to the development of responsible capitalism. In contrast to Lutheranism and Pietism, Calvin believed that it was necessary for capital to be brought together on a great scale to meet the economic demands of his age. He taught that charging interest for capital ventures is compatible with the Christian faith. It is not the charging of interest that is wrong, but the misuse of such activity through charging high rates of interest and taking advantage of the poor that must be condemned. He believed that loans to the poor should be given without demanding interest. Moreover, Calvin in Geneva was sensitive to the needs of the poor and recognized the social danger of not responding to their needs.[122]

A series of articles had appeared in 1932 in the liberal Protestant paper, the *Christian Century*, that raised the question of whether socialism or even communism could be the way out of the present crisis in America. Nettinga wrote that it would be wrong to follow that road. Communism in Russia had not brought freedom and prosperity but had served to bring individuals under the yoke of a new tyranny. The same objection had to be brought against fascism as it was being installed by Mussolini in Italy. The individual becomes little more than a piece in the machinery of the state. In contrast, Nettinga wrote that we must stand for the rights of the person. He contended that the right to private property is a basic principle that leads to the highest development of individuals and the society.[123]

He contended also that the Reverend Dr. R.H. Tawney (1880-1962) in his book, *Religion and the Rise of Capitalism*, incorrectly argued that individualism in religion logically leads to individualism in morality and undercuts the development of social morality in comparison to development of personal character.[124] On the contrary,

---

[121]  Nettinga, "De Kerk en Het Sociale Vraagstuk," *De Hope*, August 30, 1932.
[122]  Nettinga, "Calvijn's Beschouwing van Het Economische Vraagstuk," *De Hope*, October 11, 1932.
[123]  Nettinga, "Behoort Het Capitalism te Blijven?" *De Hope*, November 8, 1932.
[124]  Richard Henry Tawney, *Religion and the Rise of Capitalism: A Historical Study* (New York: Harcourt, Brace, 1926), esp. 227-31.

the Christian faith not only recognizes the individual but also teaches that one has a calling to serve one's neighbor. Nettinga recognized that Calvin's followers did not always keep to his ideals; if they had done so, the present criticism of capitalism would not exist. Capitalists must be reminded of their position as stewards and the need to use one's possessions responsibly.[125]

## Where They Stood in the 1930s:
## Faithful to Their Tradition While Open to the Future

At this point in our study of the history of theology in the midwestern Reformed Church in America, 1866-1966, we pause to summarize the stance of the Reformed Church's theological leaders in the Midwest as set forth above. Our summary will take note particularly of the writings of six men who taught at Western Theological Seminary between the two great World Wars. These men and their years at the seminary were Evert Blekkink (1913-1928), John Kuizenga (1915-1930), Seibe Nettinga (1918-1938), Albertus Pieters (1926-1939), and John R. Mulder (1928-1960). Evert Blekkink (died 1948) and Albertus Pieters (died 1956) continued to write for the church until their deaths.

Although these men had quite different personalities and differed from each other in details of theology and social understanding, they were united in their basic understanding of the Reformed faith and the place and mission of the Reformed Church in America. We now take note of six points on which they were in agreement regarding the relation of their Reformed faith to American society.

First, they all held firmly to the Reformed faith as it had been formulated in the Heidelberg Catechism, the Belgic Confession, and the Canons of Dort. They opposed the New Theology and increasing strength of theological modernism in America. In this respect, it could be said to be true of them as it was for Charles Hodge at Princeton, that "no new ideas entered the seminary while they taught there." They would have accepted that charge not as a reproach but as an affirmation of their teaching.

Second, they had a strong sense of the unity of the one church of Jesus Christ. They were open to cooperation with a wide variety of denominations and refused to isolate themselves from other American churches. Within the Reformed family, they were not ambitious to be "distinctively Reformed" from others, even when they were suspicious that other Reformed or Presbyterian denominations were in danger of straying away from one or more of the doctrines of the confessions.

[125] Nettinga, "Capitalism," 2.

Third, they continued to believe that America was still a Christian nation in spite of its increasing pluralism, materialism, and secularism. They accepted the basic thesis of Abraham Kuyper that the principles of Calvin lay behind the American principles of freedom and democracy. They rejected a doctrine of the antithesis that required the forming of separate Christian organizations. Instead, they believed that it was important for Reformed Christians to cooperate with others in the community for the public welfare.

Fourth, while rejecting the liberal theological position of the Social Gospel, they accepted the basic thrust of the movement that the church had to practice compassion toward the poor and marginalized in society. They also agreed that those who had wealth and responsible positions had to use their wealth and power to meet the needs of those who were less fortunate. They rejected a theology of salvation that gave priority to the social over against the personal.

Fifth, they were all opposed to and fearful of the doctrines of socialism and communism. They feared that American labor union leaders were leading the country in the direction of socialism.[126] They feared that those systems led to a new tyranny. They favored the capitalist system as best suited to develop the American nation and meet the needs for the public welfare.

Sixth, although on the pages of *De Hope* and the *Leader* they consistently disclaimed any political affiliation or adherence to any political party, it is difficult to avoid the conclusion that the content of the articles and news reports consistently favored the stance of the Republican party over the Democratic party.[127] Henry Geerlings, the managing editor of the *Leader*, who wrote the weekly column "Current

[126] The editors of *De Hope* agreed that within the capitalist system the laborers had the right to strike when the company did not uphold the provisions of a contract. They also held that under the provisions of the American Constitution capitalists and workers were obligated to work together for the improvement of their own lives as well as for the public welfare. However, those who went on strike were not to be allowed to engage in violence or to interfere with right of others to earn their daily bread ("De Werkstakingen," *De Hope*, July 28, 1885).

[127] In favoring the Republican Party, the midwestern Reformed Church leaders were allied with other Protestants in America. The Republicans were also favored in the Christian Reformed Church (James A. De Jong, *Henry J. Kuiper*, 76-77). George Marsden has traced the support that Republicans inherited from the older Whig party in American political life: "According to this tradition, religious hierarchy and political authoritarianism went hand in hand. So on one side of the ledger were Catholicism, Anglicanism, centralized monarchical power, corruption, and tyranny; on the other side Protestantism, Puritanism, representative government, virtue and freedom.

Events," seldom missed an opportunity to praise those who sought to cut taxes and government expenditures.[128] This was particularly true regarding support of immigration policies when large numbers of Roman Catholics were entering the country, support of the imperialist policies of the McKinley Administration during the time of the Spanish-American War, and support for prohibition. Their constant praise of Republican presidents for their Christian faith also reinforced the favorable view of the Republican Party.[129] Nevertheless, when a Democratic president was elected, they readily gave their support to him, according to what was taught about obedience to civil authorities in the Heidelberg Catechism on the Fifth Commandment, Question and Answer 104.

In spite of the advance of the Great Depression, beginning in 1929, the editors of the *Leader* continued to express confidence in the leadership of Republican president Herbert Hoover. They were unhappy in 1932 when both the Republican and Democratic parties placed planks in their platforms opening the door to the end of prohibition, despite the fact that Hoover himself continued to favor prohibition. Although it was against the policy of the *Leader* to endorse any candidate

---

The American way thus had strong religious and ethical dimensions" George Marsden, *Understanding Fundamentalism and Evangelicals* (Grand Rapids: Eerdmans, 1991), 87. After the Civil War, "the Republican party had a strong Puritan-evangelical component, bent on regulating the society according to Christian principles. Antislavery was the great achievement of this outlook; but anti-alcohol and anti-Catholicism were just as much its trademarks," ibid., 89. The favorable attitude toward the Republican Party and anti-alcohol, anti-Catholic bias remained strong at least through the election of President John F. Kennedy in 1960.

[128] For example, in his October 19, 1921, column, Geerlings praised Republican President Harding for reducing disbursements 33 percent in the first quarter of the year, in contrast to the "reckless spending" of the Democrats during the administration of Democratic President Woodrow Wilson. Three weeks later, he again praised Harding's administration for cutting expenses and called it "hope for the taxpayer" (November 23, 1921, 5). The following week, he urged reducing the number of the Navy's warships as an economy measure (November 30, 1921, 4).

[129] The high point of adulation of a president may have been reached in the memorial by Henry Dosker for William McKinley following his assassination by an anarchist in 1881. McKinley was declared to be "a top American," "the apostle of American welfare," an "apostle of peace" with China and Europe, and an "inspiration for young men." American Christendom and American society had lost much with his death. He died with the hymn "Nearer my God to Thee" on his lips. His last words were "Farewell, may you all fare well. It is God's will; let his will come to pass" (*De Hope*, September 16, 1901).

for national or state office (except for Gerrit J. Diekema in 1906), the longstanding tilt toward the Republican Party had not disappeared.[130] Therefore, the election of Roosevelt was a disappointment.

Nevertheless, in the week after the election, the editors of the *Leader* continued their long tradition of accepting the results of elections and of supporting the president of the United States. They wrote that it is good that "elections are a substitute for revolutions, and we recognize this when we boast that we settle our internal disputes at the polls."[131] They went on:

> This election has given the farmers and the unemployed and other sufferers an opportunity to express themselves. With the victory of their candidate they feel better....The new regime that will assume the responsibilities of power on the fourth day of next March should have the good wishes and the good will of every American. Its road will not be easy, nor will its burdens be light.[132]

Two weeks later, the editors found even more reason to be satisfied with the election. It was a sign that in spite of American individualism, the people continue to be concerned for their neighbors and accept the responsibility to care for each other. "But they realized, also, that no one was isolated from his fellows. All were involved. It was everybody's business. It was a corporate responsibility, a mutual obligation, a common task."[133]

The editors even had a good word for the Socialist Party. They took comfort that in spite of the fact that Mr. Norman Thomas was an able candidate, the Socialists had received less than one million votes rather than the two or three million that some had predicted. Therefore the party now had little future as a political movement. However, the editors noted that the Socialists had some good ideas and that America "frequently approves Socialist measures when they are sponsored by either of the major parties."[134]

*******

[130] All of the Dutch enclaves have favored the Republican Party, with the exception of the one in Pella, Iowa. The district in which Holland and Zeeland, Michigan, are located has never elected a Democrat to the House of Representatives.

[131] *Leader*, November 16, 1932, 11.

[132] Ibid.

[133] Ibid.

[134] Ibid.

At the beginning of this chapter, we recalled Herman Bavinck's criticism of the pietists of the Secession of 1834. Their practice of piety led them to separate themselves literally from everything and leave nation, state, and society to their own devices, to the extent that some even shipped off to America, abandoning their fatherland. However, after reviewing the ways in which they cooperated with other evangelical Protestant churches and voluntary societies in America and showed themselves to be loyal American citizens who constantly and often uncritically supported the presidents of the country, it is clear that they did not seek to withdraw from American life. On the contrary, the real problem may have been that they proved ultimately to be too uncritical of the discrimination and injustice that was present and of the economic system in which they were participating.

# CHAPTER 6

# The Authority of the Bible in the Modern World

## The Authority of the Bible and the Doctrine of Inspiration in the Midwestern Reformed Church

The authority of the Bible was central in the piety of the immigrants who settled in the Dutch enclaves in nineteenth century. They read it daily at mealtimes. They taught it to their children who went to Sunday school and catechism classes. They sang the psalms when they went to church. They insisted that "the Holy Scriptures are the only rule of faith and practice in the Reformed Church in America."[1] They held to the central teaching of the Protestant Reformers who taught that the Bible was the source of the truth and that the Bible as a whole was the only rule for faith and practice. From the Bible flowed the water of life.[2]

For the leaders of the Secession of 1834, it was no mere platitude to affirm the ultimate authority of the scriptures. Affirmation of that ultimate authority went against the tide in the modern world. In 1893,

---

[1] "Preamble," *Book of Church Order*, 1.
[2] Nicholas Steffens, "Bijbelsch Christendom," *De Hope*, April 12, 1893.

Nicholas Steffens set forth a brief history of the question for readers of *De Hope*. He wrote that in the European Enlightenment of the eighteenth century, human reason was given priority over revelation. The Bible has authority only insofar as it is in accord with or not contrary to reason. The result was that the churches became empty. Those Christians who did continue to hold to its authority narrowed their faith to an unhealthy pious mysticism separated from life.[3]

In the nineteenth century, he wrote, there were pastors who sought to rescue people from the dry rationalism that had undermined their faith. Unfortunately, the greatest of those pastors and theologians, Friedrich D.E. Schleiermacher, placed self-consciousness or "feeling," rather than biblical revelation, at the center of his system of thought.[4] Schleiermacher sought to defend the Christian faith against the ridicule of the "despisers of religion" by maintaining that true piety is to be found neither in reason nor in the will, but in "feeling." "Feeling" for Schleiermacher did not simply denote a sentimental emotion or sensitivity, as the word often does today. Rather, "feeling" denoted the very center of what it means to be human. Feeling is "the consciousness of being absolutely dependent, or, which is the same thing, of being in relation with God."[5] This feeling of absolute dependence, expressed as consciousness of God, "is the highest grade of immediate self-consciousness; it is also an essential element of human nature."[6]

Steffens respected Schleiermacher for seeking a way to bring the "despisers of religion" back to faith in Christ and for the warmth of faith that showed through his preaching and writing. However, confidence in "feeling" as central still gave human activity the priority, with the result that a back door was opened for the triumph of reason in a new way.[7] Steffens lodged the same objection against the position of Claus Harms, who made the conscience the crucial authority as the rule for faith and life.[8]

Finally, he had to deal with the charge made against Reformed orthodoxy that it placed the Reformed Standards of Unity above the scriptures as the rule of faith and practice. It did so because the *Constitution* required that every minister sign the declaration that he accepted the doctrines taught in the standards as authoritative.

[3]    Ibid.
[4]    Ibid.
[5]    Schleiermacher, Friedrich D.E., *The Christian Faith*, ed. H.R. Machintosh and J.S. Stewart (Edinburgh: T. & T. Clark), 1928 (first published 1830), 12.
[6]    Ibid., Sec. 6, 26.
[7]    Steffens, "Bijbelsch Christendom."
[8]    Ibid.

Steffens clarified the relation between the scriptures and the Reformed confessions by pointing out that the confessions always function under the authority of scripture. The "symbolic confessions point the finger back to the Bible. They are not added to the Bible; they do not recount everything that is in the Bible, but what they do give us is derived from the Bible."[9]

Steffens opposed the saying of some of the Dutch modernists that "the Bible *contains* the Word of God," while they did not want to say that "the Bible *is* the Word of God."[10] The distinction allowed the advocates of rationalism or of feeling or of conscience to decide what in the Bible is or is not the Word of God. In opposition to them, it is essential to insist that the whole Bible is the Word of God. For Steffens, this meant that one must hold that the Bible is verbally inspired by God and to insist that God gave to the authors of the books of the Bible the very words that God wanted in the Bible. He opposed the idea that God gave the thoughts to the writers who then used their own words to write down the thoughts they had received from God.[11]

When the Holy Spirit inspired men to write, the inspiration was not mechanical in the sense that their personalities were overridden or negated. On the contrary, the personalities of the writers do shine through the various books of the prophets, as is apparent when Isaiah is compared with Jeremiah. Steffens confessed that he did not know just how the Holy Spirit gave the precise words while respecting the personalities and experience of the authors. Nevertheless, it is essential to believe that the words of the Bible are the words that God intended. It is wrong to make a separation between the Word of God and the words of scripture.[12]

---

[9]  Ibid.

[10]  Steffens, "De Woordelijke Ingeving der H. Schriften," *De Hope*, January 27, 1892.

[11]  Ibid.

[12]  Ibid. At the end of the nineteenth century, other Reformed Church theologians agreed with Steffens. For example, Egbert Winter taught that the whole Bible is the Word of God, "Here we are distinctly and clearly taught, that all scripture is theopneustic—that the HOLY SPIRIT dwells in those writings here intended, and animates them, and gave them to men. Now it is quite evident that this can only refer to a definite class of scriptures, that is the recognized scriptures." "The writers were borne along—were made passive by the HOLY GHOST." Inspiration "extends not merely to the matter, but also to the very words of the original autographs" (Egbert Winter, Class notes on *Dogmatics*, I, WTS/JAH, 153; capitalization and underlining are Winters's).

The Rev. John Walter Beardslee,
D. D. (1837-1921)

*Courtesy of Western Theological Seminary*

John Beardslee was professor of biblical languages at Western Theological Seminary from 1888-1917 and New Brunswick Theological Seminary from 1917-1921. Because he seldom wrote for *De Hope* and the *Leader*, his influence on midwestern Reformed Church theology came chiefly through his teaching. "No one who knew Dr. Beardslee could fail to appreciate the quiet force of his gentle yet positive Christian character. The creative work he did for Western Theological Seminary will last through all the years and his life will be prolonged in many theological students who came under the sweet influence of his faith character. His generous gift of a library to the Seminary a few years since as well as many other liberal donations attest to the largeness and usefulness of his labors for the future of the institution and the church it serves." – *Acts and Proceedings*, 1921, 640-41.

Steffens's colleague at the seminary, the Reverend Dr. John Walter Beardslee, provided a more nuanced understanding of the nature of the inspiration of the Bible.[13] Beardslee taught that God used a variety of methods in leading men to compose the books of the Bible. God gave visions and dreams—in an audible voice to Moses and through the

[13]    Beardslee taught at Western Theological Seminary from 1888-1917. Steffens was there from 1884-1895 and 1903-1912. Both were teachers of Albertus Pieters, who was a student at the seminary from 1888-1891. In his approach to theology and biblical studies, Pieters's writings give evidence that he learned much from those two men. Dr. John Walter Beardslee must be distinguished from his son, John Walter Beardslee, Jr., who taught at Western Theological Seminary, 1913-1917, and New Brunswick Theological Seminary, 1917-1949; and also from his grandson, John Walter Beardslee, III, who taught at New Brunswick Theological Seminary, 1964-1984.

individual experiences of the prophets. God did not have to give the writers the precise words to be recorded.

> All that we can say is that when God has a message to deliver to men he will give such evidence of his will as must satisfy both the man whom he sends to deliver it and the people to whom it is to be delivered, that it is God who sends the message.[14]

Beardslee's published writings do not set forth a specific doctrine of inspiration in spite of the fact that there was deep controversy about the nature of biblical inspiration at the turn of the twentieth century.[15] His concern was to defend the Bible as the revelation of the will of God rather than as the record of human beings coming to God consciousness.

> A careful study of the Scriptures teaches us that prophecy is not man's interpretation of life as revealed in history or providence, nor yet an expression of man's personal hope in regard to the future, but God's own declaration of what he has determined to do for the world. The prophets did not first study out the great facts in regard to man's duty and then publish the result of their study; they did not begin as careful historians and astute statesmen by seeking to learn the result of a course of action, and then declare what they thought would happen. They began by listening to the Divine voice, by studying attentively the lesson God gave them, and then they received it. So Amos says, 3:8, "The Lord Jehovah hath spoken; who can but prophesy?"[16]

It would be wrong to accuse any of the professors at Western theological seminary of a "bibliolotry" that would make the Bible itself an object to be worshiped. Nowhere does one discover any statement by

---

14  Beardslee, *The Prophets* (Holland, Mich.: privately printed, located in Beardslee Library, Western Theological Seminary, 1908), 26.

15  Beardslee was a colleague of Egbert Winter at the seminary at the time Winter published his pamphlet, "What is Inspiration?" (privately printed, 1894, located in WTS/JAH), in his vigorous attack on the book by New Brunswick Professor John De Witt, *What is Inspiration?* (New York: Randolph, 1893). There is no record that Beardslee gave support to Winter or to the Classis of Holland in their charges against the views of De Witt. Beardslee's position on biblical criticism was more conservative than that of De Witt, however. See also John W. Beardslee, III, ed., *Vision from the Hill*, Historical Series of the Reformed Church in America, no. 12 (Grand Rapids: Eerdmans, 1984), 61-71, for crucial excerpts from De Witt's book.

16  Beardslee, *The Prophets*, 5-6.

midwestern leaders that implies that the Bible itself may be an object of worship in any sense of the word. Thus, the Reverend Jacob Van Houte pointed out that while the Bible is God's Word and cannot be separated from God's Word, it must be distinguished from Christ as the Word of God. Because there is a distinction, it is possible, he wrote, for a person to carry the Bible around for fifty years and not have the Word of God. Moreover, the Bible as the Word of God needs to be interpreted in the life of the church as the bride of Christ.[17] Thus the Bible as the Word of God is the living Word because the Holy Spirit remains with it in the life of the church.

According to the professors at Western Theological Seminary, biblical revelation is communication of what is in the mind of God and is information about the will of God. Egbert Winter taught, "By revelation we mean that divine agency by which GOD makes known his mind to men, or makes known in some supernatural way what but for such information never would become known to men, or else could not have been known by them at that time."[18] God's will is not revealed all at one time as a great system of doctrine but is progressively revealed in the Old and New Testaments. Recognition of the progressive nature of revelation helps us know how to reconcile some of the differences between the two testaments. For example, when one compares the teachings of the commandments revealed through Moses with the Sermon on the Mount, we see that "there is no real disagreement. It brings to light that the N.T. in accordance with the progress of Divine revelation, teaches truth in a fuller and clearer way. What seems discrepancy is only proof of fuller light and development."[19] Blekkink agreed, "The beauty and significance of the 'Old' is that it is the background and foundation of the 'New'; and of the 'New' is that it

---

[17]   Jacobus Van Houte, "De Bewaring van God's Woord—de Taak der Gemeente," *De Hope*, October 11, 1893. Van Houte (1845-1919) was born in the Netherlands, graduated from Hope College and New Brunswick Theological Seminary, and served congregations in Ohio, Illinois, Michigan, and Iowa.

[18]   Winter, *Dogmatics*, I, 135.

[19]   Ibid., 173. Gerrit Dubbink taught that the progressive nature of revelation in the Bible encourages us to be patient in expectation of how God is with us today, "Indeed, one of the prominent lessons of every book of the Bible is the slow but certain progress of God's purposes. There is a progressive revelation of his will, and a progressive fulfillment of his counsels. God waits, and he makes us wait" ("Sunday School Lesson for 19 May 1907," *Leader*, May 19, 1907, 438.

is the unfolding and application of the fundamental principles of the 'Old' in ever widening circles in times that are new." [20]

As the revelation of God, the Bible informs us about God's actions in the history of the patriarchs and Israel in the Old Testament and especially about God's presence in Jesus Christ in the New Testament. John Beardslee taught that messianic prophecy runs through the whole Old Testament. It records the

> promise that God will set up a kingdom, over which will reign His own Anointed Son, and whose purpose will be to provide for the salvation is his people. It must not therefore be limited to the person of this king whom God will anoint, and who will become the efficient cause of salvation, but must include an account of all those agencies employed by God to advance his kingdom until it reaches its grand consummation. [21]

Biblical revelation therefore is progressive, increasing in clarity as time rolls along. It gives increasing evidence of the immensity of God's work that makes salvation possible, culminating in the picture of Jesus of Nazareth in fulfillment of the messianic prophecies of the whole Old Testament. Therefore, he can be "safely accepted as the divine King enthroned in God's kingdom which has for its end the salvation of sinners."[22] The Bible, therefore, is a sure guide for the great doctrines of the Christian faith. As progressive revelation, Blekkink pointed out that it deals in the first principles of "truth that never grows old. It is eternal in its very nature. Hence we hear Christ say, 'I am the truth.' There is no truth save for Christ: for all things were made by him. He is before all things and in him all things hold together. The laws of the universe find their being in final explanation in him."[23]

The fact that revelation was understood by the midwestern professors and ministers as progressive communication of information about God's actions in history, about God's will for human beings, and about first principles, made it possible for them to find proof texts for the great doctrines of the faith without always giving due regard to context. By such attention to the words of the Bible as the revelation

[20] Evert Blekkink, "Progressive Revelation," *Leader*, June 6, 1923, 2.
[21] Beardslee, *Notes on Messianic Prophecy*, (Holland, Mich.: privately printed, 1908, located in Beardslee Library, Western Theological Seminary, special collections), 3.
[22] Ibid., 4.
[23] Blekkink, "Progressive Revelation," *Leader*, June 6, 1923, 2

of God, and by comparing scripture with scripture, it was possible to develop a coherent and stable system of theology that could serve the church over the centuries.

## Challenges from a New Emphasis in Modern Thought About the Nature of Historical Development

### *(1) Historical and Literary Criticism*

During the nineteenth century the impact of new methods of literary and historical criticism in the study of the Bible was felt only indirectly in the midwestern Reformed Church. However, because of its impact by 1870 in American Christianity on the understanding of essential Christian doctrines and the interpretation of Genesis 1-11, it is important at this point to discuss briefly the early history of the movement and early responses to the challenge by midwestern leaders.

Johann Salamo Semler (1721-1792) "insisted that the importance of biblical writing lay in the insight that it provided human beings rather than any divinely imposed authority."[24] He taught that the Bible must be subjected to the principles of literary and historical analysis just like any other book. In the early nineteenth century, German scholars, including J.G. Eichhorn (1742-1827) and W.M.L. De Wette (1780-1849), worked "to reconstruct the writing of the biblical books, including both the historical setting and the literary styles and methods employed."[25] In doing so, they also sought to gain more insight into the meaning of scripture by comparing and contrasting it with the thought patterns of the surrounding cultures. They began with human reason's ability to trace out the growing understanding of God among the people of Israel, rather than with the Bible as the revelation of God to the people.

The basic objection that teachers at Western Theological Seminary had against nineteenth-century German biblical scholars and theologians was that they traded objective faith in God for a subjective conception of faith.[26] They were well aware that the subjective conception of Schleiermacher had been mediated to the church in the Netherlands through teachers of theology in the University of Groningen and in the University of Leiden. In the years leading up to the Afscheiding of 1834, Hendrik De Cock and Simon Van Velsen felt that influence through

---

[24]    Howard Clark Kee, "Biblical criticism," in *The Dictionary of Bible and Religion*, ed. William H. Gentz (Nashville: Abingdon, 1986), 137.

[25]    Ibid.

[26]    See Henry Dosker, "Wekelijksch Budget: De Moderne Jezus Literatuur," *De Hope*, October 8, 1902.

the Groningen professor of theology, Petrus Hofstede De Grote, who taught that "Jesus was a person who, by virtue of his preexistence, had an advantage over us all and was therefore able to become our example. In virtue of divine generation and his own obedience he was superior to us: the Son of God."[27] Although he still believed that Jesus was the Son of God, he had moved in the direction of the old heresy of Arianism. The Seceders recognized that it severely compromised the old faith. They also knew that the Modernists through their preaching had preached the church empty.

The future leaders of the Secession of 1834, Hendrik Scholte, Simon Van Velzen, and Albertus Van Raalte, were students of the father of Dutch "Modernism," Professor Johannes H. Scholten in the University of Leiden (1843-1881). Scholte, Van Velzen, and Van Raalte were all students at Leiden when he began to teach there. Under the influence of Schleiermacher, he taught that through the message of Jesus, "God intended that through a long process of development the human world would renounce its animal drives, that is, sin; that at the same time it would increasingly follow its true moral-rational nature, that is, the life of God within us, in order thus to arrive at genuine freedom and humanity."[28]

The teachers at Western Theological Seminary objected to literary and historical biblical criticism that accepted the premises of men such as John H. Scholten. They especially opposed scholars who wrote lives of Jesus based on its methodology and their own presuppositions. The Reverend Dr. Henry Dosker pointed out in 1902 that in Otto Holtzmann's book, *Leben Jesu*, Jesus was not God and did no miracles. He did not die in fulfillment of Old Testament prophecies such as are found in Isaiah 53. Jesus was a character full of wisdom and courage. Dosker also criticized the book by W. Wrede, *Das Messias Geheimnis in den Evangelien* ("*The Messianic Secret in the Gospels*"), because it built on the self consciousness of Jesus rather than on the testimony of the Old and New Testament to the messianic calling of Jesus.[29] Dosker's nuanced position was set out in an extended statement:

> We owe a great deal to the thorough textual and historical criticism of the New Testament, and especially of the Gospels on

[27] Hendrikus Berkhof, *Two Hundred Years of Theology* (Grand Rapids: Eerdmans, 1989), 97. Hofstede De Grote was the predecessor of Hendrik De Cock in the congregation at Ulrum in the province of Groningen.

[28] Ibid., 99.

[29] Henry E. Dosker, "Wekelijksch Budget: De Moderne Jezus Literatuur," *De Hope*, October 8, 1902.

which all the modern Christology is built. The person of Christ has been subjected to an acid test which would have destroyed him utterly had mere tinsel covered an underlying base material. But in the applying of this test Modernism has proved that it is not wholly modern. That is, it has been felt how utterly unfair and even unscientific were the methods employed in the effort to reconstruct a new Christ. Where objective truth was demanded, they handed us subjective tests. The true Christ was to be found in a "Source gospel," lying behind our Gospels, but no one had ever seen a trace of it....Whatever men may think or make of Christ, we accept Him as revealed in the Gospels, our King, our Priest, our prophet, our only hope and all sufficient Savior. He must be either that or nothing at all. If He is what modern Liberalism claims Him to be, He has no message for us, the children of the twentieth century.[30]

Dosker's twentieth-century article was consistent with Nicholas Steffens's attack on the Christology of the biblical critics. In 1893 Steffens had complained that in writing lives of Jesus, the critics sought to undermine the doctrine of the deity of Christ and substitute for it the doctrine of a Jesus who had lived a life of God consciousness and who is the perfect ethical example for us. They had probed the gospel sources to develop theories about the nature of his personality as an example of true humanity. Steffens insisted that the divinity of Jesus can never consist in his God consciousness. Jesus' deity rests in his being sent as the Son of God into the world to make atonement for the sins of humankind. Only as such can he be worshiped as fully God rather than as a being a little lower than God such as in the Arian heresy, or as a mixed being, half God and half human.[31] None of the midwestern professors ever retreated an inch on this point from the language of the ancient creeds or the Reformed confessions.

In spite of the firm opposition to higher critics who were undermining the teaching of the creeds of the church, John Beardslee believed that it was the liberal theology of the higher critics rather than the methodology itself that was to be rejected. He wrote in *Outlines of an Introduction to the Old Testament*, which grew out of fifteen years of study and teaching,[32]

---

30    Dosker, "The Christ of Scriptures," *Leader*, May 17, 1922, 2.
31    Steffens, "De Christus Gods," *De Hope*, January 25, 1893.
32    John W. Beardslee, *Outlines of an Introduction to the Old Testament* (New York: Revell, 1903), 7.

If the positions here taken seem conservative, it is not because the writer has ignored the later criticism or underestimates its value, but because the newer ideas do not seem to be sufficiently established to demand the abandonment of the older. Great gain has already come from the learned and laborious investigations of the new school of criticism and we hope for still richer fruitage in the future, but the results thus far secured are too vague to become a satisfactory basis for the interpretation of Scripture.[33]

Beardslee went on to summarize his leading objections to the work then being done under the name of higher criticism:

The primary laws of exegesis are too easily violated, too much importance is attached to minute and unessential details, the integrity of the text is not sufficiently guarded, constant pressure is put upon the text to make it yield a result in harmony with a preconceived theory, and the subjective impulses of the critic have too much influence in determining his conclusions.[34]

Beardslee defended his conservative approach to the results of biblical criticism on the basis of what he saw in the biblical text rather than on the basis of a formal doctrine of biblical inspiration. He continued to hold that Moses was the author of the Pentateuch and that the eighth-century prophet Isaiah had written the entire book of Isaiah. Nevertheless, he recognized that the book of Isaiah in its present form had been modified from what Isaiah had written. "It has doubtless met with some modifications by later editors, as have so many of the Old Testament books, yet they are not of such a character as to deprive Isaiah of the claim to authorship. Until more positive and decisive reasons are presented, the claim for a divided authorship must stand as 'not proven.'"[35]

With regard to Mosaic authorship of the Pentateuch, Beardslee rejected the conclusion of the higher critics that it had been compiled by editors during and following the Exile.[36] He accepted the testimony of Jesus and of Old Testament references to the law of Moses as sound evidence of Mosaic authorship. However, he recognized that Moses had inherited older traditions or documents that were helpful in the composition of the first five books of the Old Testament and that

[33]   Ibid.
[34]   Ibid., 7-8.
[35]   Ibid., 81.
[36]   Ibid., 29.

certain modifications were made after Moses completed his work. His conclusion was that

> Moses was the author of the Pentateuch, that he used either writ-
> ten documents or oral tradition as the historical basis of his work,
> that he received the legal portions directly from God, and that in
> writing it he was constantly guided by the Holy Spirit both in the
> selection and preparation of his material. In thus asserting the
> Mosaic origin of the Pentateuch we do not mean that every word
> of it, in just the form that we now have it, is just as he left it.[37]

Having seen briefly how professors at Western Theological Seminary responded to the challenge of the higher critics, it is important now to take note of two other challenges that were intertwined with the issues raised by the literary and historical criticism of the Bible. These two challenges were the growth of liberal theology in American theological seminaries and the theory of evolution as set forth by Charles Darwin and Herbert Spencer.

### (2) The Challenge of Nineteenth-Century American Liberalism

Modern thought shifted away from mechanical metaphors to organic metaphors in the course of the nineteenth century. At the beginning of the nineteenth century, the watchmaker metaphor enjoyed popularity. According to that metaphor, God was the Great Watchmaker who had created the perfectly working universe, just as a skilled watchmaker could make a watch that would run perfectly without interference after it was wound. According to that metaphor, the universe runs according to the fixed physical laws and mathematical principles and the eternal ideas of God. The extreme Deists who used the watchmaker metaphor discounted reports in the Bible about miracles, on the ground that a good watch does not require interference or adjustment by the watchmaker.

Although Reformed theologians continued to defend the historicity of biblical accounts about miracles, the mechanical metaphor to describe the workings of the universe was attractive to them. It was consistent with the idea that God had created the great variety of species with fixed characteristics. The mountains, seas, and continents had been in place since the beginning of the world. It also was consistent with the idea that human nature has been the same through the whole human history that, according to Bishop Ussher's chronology, began about 4004 B.C.

---

[37]   Ibid., 31.

Beginning in the late eighteenth century, historians and scientists began to favor organic metaphors over mechanical ones. They were joined by nineteenth-century Romantic writers and philosophers who thought of the world and human life developing somewhat as an acorn grows to be an oak tree. Historical processes take place according to the laws of biology and geology rather than the laws of Newtonian physics. Organic metaphors were open to the idea that the species are not fixed once for all, but can change their character and even mutate into new species. The continents can drift and rocks can be formed over a very long process of natural and historical change. Human beings come to new understandings of nature, of human nature, and even of God over the long process of human history.

The use of organic metaphors encouraged modern thinkers in the nineteenth century to be alert everywhere to ways in which human culture and religion had developed over the millennia and centuries. The shift of metaphor or paradigm represented a challenge to American Protestantism in general, as well as to Reformed Church theologians and pastors. During the last half of the nineteenth century, the members of the midwestern Reformed Church remained relatively isolated from the shift that was taking place, due to the fact that most of them were located in Dutch enclaves using the Dutch language and for the most part were in local control of education through the high school level.

The leading ministers in the Dutch enclaves were aware of the modernistic trend of theological thought in the Netherlands they had left behind. However, in their relative isolation from developments in American Protestant thought, it was not necessary for those who wrote articles in *De Hope* to spend much energy countering modern ideas in America until after about 1875, especially because American evangelical Protestantism continued to work on the basis of the old paradigm throughout the nineteenth century.

When the Reverend Dr. Philip Schaff came from Germany to America to teach at the Mercersburg Pennsylvania Theological Seminary of the German Reformed Church in America in 1844, he had introduced the idea that there is historical progress in the understanding of church doctrine. He along with his colleague John W. Nevin claimed that "the principle of Protestantism" makes room for something more glorious in the nature of theological thought in the future.[38] This opened the possibility that Reformed confessional

---

[38]   See the account of events around Schaff's 1844 inaugural lecture, "The Principle of Protestantism," in George H. Schriver, *American Religious Thought* (Nashville: Abingdon, 1966), 34-35. For a concise introduction to

statements could be opened to revision in the direction of Protestant liberalism, although Schaff himself was not an American liberal. He was officially charged with heresy by a minister in the German Reformed Church, Joseph F. Berg, who later was invited to teach at New Brunswick Theological Seminary.[39] Although Schaff was cleared of the charge against him, suspicion of the orthodoxy of what became known as the "Mercersburg Theology" of Schaff and Nevin continued for decades.[40] The eastern Reformed Church in America paper, the *Christian Intelligencer*, remained suspicious of Schaff and the orthodoxy of the German Reformed Church.[41]

Reformed Church ministers Nicholas Steffens and Egbert Winter became concerned in 1874 that accepting Schaff's "Protestant principle" could lead to a compromise with the liberal spirit of the modern age. The immediate occasion for their anxiety was that charges of heresy had been brought against the pastor Raymond Swing of the Fourth Presbyterian Church in Chicago. Swing had insisted that "all religious expressions are dependent upon the culture within which they are formulated, and they cannot be understood apart from that

---

the role of Philip Schaff and John Nevin in the development of nineteenth-century Protestant theology, see James H. Nichol, ed., *The Mercersburg Theology* (New York: Oxford Univ. Press, 1966), 4-10. For a full evaluation of the contribution of Schaff and Nevin at Mercerburg to the life of the American church, a reading of the whole book is important. The Reformed Church in America's liturgy for the Lord's Supper now shows the influence of Nevin. Although Schaff was theologically suspect in nineteenth-century Reformed Church in America, by 1958 his history of the Christian church was republished by William B. Eerdmans Publishing Company and well accepted in conservative circles.

[39]  John Karsten and Egbert Winter were students at New Brunswick Theological Seminary when Berg arrived there. In spite of Berg's objection to Mercersburg Theology, both of them proved to be supportive of the efforts in 1893 to unite the Reformed Church in America and the German Reformed Church in the United States.

[40]  Protestants became especially fearful of the idea that there could be new developments in church dogma after December 8, 1854, when Pope Pius IX proclaimed as dogma the immaculate conception of the Virgin Mary, by virtue of which she was kept free from all original sin. As church dogma, it became mandatory for Roman Catholics to accept the teaching. In the middle of the 1840s, many suspected for a time that John Nevin was going to become a Roman Catholic. He remained Reformed to the end of his life.

[41]  See *Christian Intelligencer*, July 9, 1846; July 16, 1846, 2; July 23, 1846, 6; July 30, 1846, 10.

culture."[42] This meant that the scriptures, confessions, and doctrines of the church are all time bound and that with time we can expect some to become outmoded and others in need of serious revision. Swing admitted that the Bible contains many terrible things, such as the psalmist's plea to destroy the enemies' babies.[43] He also used ambiguous language that could be interpreted as orthodox but could also be understood quite differently.

Egbert Winter, who was pastor of the First Reformed Church in Pella, Iowa, at the time, pointed out that the actions of the Chicago Presbytery had to be taken into account by the Reformed Church in America because the denomination was having preliminary discussions in the early 1870s about entering into an organic union with the Presbyterian Church. Although the Presbytery did vote to condemn Swing by a margin of 48 to 13, Swing had enjoyed considerable support, and the matter had been more in doubt than the vote indicated. Winter opposed moves that would allow the Reformed Church to be sucked into such a "monstrous body" that was powerless to deal with those who taught that the confessions are little more than a relic of previous centuries. No classis of the Reformed Church in America, he declared, would act so irresponsibly. The Chicago Presbytery's action alerts us that we are threatened, not so much from within as from without. The slogan of the age, "more freedom," that had been sounded by Swing's supporters, is a siren song that can enchant the heart but is in principle the self-deification that now surrounds us.[44]

One week later, De Hope included a subsequent article by Winter that suggested what could be learned from the case. (1) Watch out for an overdriven wrestling with theological language that is rationalistic or speculative in nature. (2) Watch out for ambiguous language from the pulpit that contains orthodox vocabulary but can be interpreted in several different ways. (3) Watch out for so-called "practical" preaching that is in essence not biblical. (4) Let us emphasize nourishing the members of the congregation in the clear truth of the confessions. Winter wrote that Swing was able to attract multitudes because they had little knowledge, but that there were also many who were educated in the truth and would not be lead astray by every wind of doctrine. Winter therefore urged his readers to be faithful in catechizing the

[42]  William R. Hutchison, *The Modernist Impulse in American Protestantism* (Cambridge: Harvard Univ. Press, 1976), 52.
[43]  Ibid., 53. Swing resigned from the Presbyterian ministry rather than appeal to a higher judiciary for reversal of the presbytery's decision.
[44]  Egbert Winter, "Het Patton-Swing Onderzoek," *De Hope*, July 1, 1874.

youth in the basic doctrines of the faith. So long as we catechize our youth, "none of our Dutch congregations would follow Swing." [45]

The following year *De Hope* included an article by the Reverend Nicholas H. Dosker, the father of Henry Dosker, that set forth a list of the articles of faith that the nineteenth-century Modernists were denying. The Modernists, he said, denied the doctrine of the Trinity, the deity of Christ, the supernatural enlightening by the Holy Spirit, the divine authority of the Bible, redemption through the blood of Christ, and the historicity of miracles. We know from our Dutch experience what modernism does, he wrote. Dosker pointed out that the theological faculty of the University of Leiden, with its modernism, in his day had few students and that the liberal churches were left without pastors, while the more orthodox faculty in the University of Utrecht had many students.[46]

Beginning in the late 1870s, Nicholas Steffens wrote a number of articles attacking the "New Theology" that was entering the American scene through the Congregationalist Andover Theological Seminary.[47] One of the purposes in founding that seminary in 1808 was to defend Calvinism against the inroads of Unitarianism in Massachusetts.[48] However, with regard to the doctrine of total depravity, Andover emphasized that responsibility for depravity belonged to the individual rather than the depravity inherited from Adam. Therefore, it included in the seminary's creedal statement the clause, "man is personally depraved, destitute of holiness, unlike and opposed to God...."[49] With regard to regeneration, they gave more prominence to what the sinner must do in coming to conversion. In holding that a human being "has understanding and corporeal strength to do all that God requires of

45  Ibid., 97.
46  Nicholas H. Dosker, "Eenige Opmerkingen," *De Hope*, June 16, 1875. The orthodoxy of the Presbyterian Church in Chicago was important to the midwestern Reformed Church because several Reformed Church theological students enrolled in the Presbyterian McCormick Theological Seminary in Chicago. Nicholas Dosker's son, Henry Elias Dosker, studied at McComick in 1878-79.
47  The historical development of what came to be known as "New Theology" at Andover Theological Seminary has been traced in detail by Daniel Day Williams, *The Andover Liberals* (New York: Octagon Books, 1970). A briefer exposition is given in Hutchison, *Modernist Impulse*, 76-110.
48  George M. Marsden, *The Evangelical Mind and the New School Presbyterian Experience* (New Haven: Yale Univ. Press, 1970), 43. Nearly half of Andover's graduates had entered Presbyterian churches.
49  Williams, *Andover Liberals*, 5.

him,"[50] the door had been opened to the use by evangelists such as Charles Finney of "means" such as the "anxious bench" and extended emotional prayer meetings designed to bring about the conversions of sinners.[51]

The Andover New Theology liberals taught that "Salvation is a process and admits of degrees."[52] They used the idea of evolution as support for their theory that the history of humankind is not one of human failure but is one of increasing achievement of moral worth.[53] The change of life that God brings about is not instantaneous, "but is rather that slow accumulation of variations which according to Darwin finally produced a new species."[54]

They sought to develop a Christology that emphasized the ethical rather than the metaphysical significance of his Christ's life and death. They focused attention on Jesus' personal piety in his relationship to God. His sinlessness and his unique personality made such an impression upon human beings that "he gave them such a revelation of truth and such an inspiration as no other man has ever given."[55] Through his life we can have a new relationship with God, even though his exact words may not have been preserved, the disciples may have idealized his life, and miracles may not have occurred in the sense that the biblical writers reported them.[56]

Although most of the members of the midwestern Reformed Church had little knowledge of the New Theology, Steffens and other writers believed it necessary to attack it in the pages of *De Hope*. His first charge against the new "Modern Theology" is that it is ambiguous in its use of theological language, and also that it is not really new at all. It is in essence the old heresy of Arianism in a new form. He said that we who came from the Netherlands had heard this already from Petrus Hofstede de Groot in Groningen and Johannes W. Scholten in Leiden.

---

[50]  Ibid., 6.
[51]  Although the midwestern leaders, during the course of the nineteenth century, developed much closer relationships with the Old School Presbyterians at Princeton Theological Seminary than with the more revival-oriented New School Presbyterians, the midwestern Reformed Church was favorably disposed to the revivalism of evangelists who appeared in their colonies, as well as to nationally renowned evangelists such as Dwight L. Moody and Billy Sunday.
[52]  Williams, *Andover Liberals*, 73.
[53]  Ibid.,74.
[54]  Ibid.
[55]  Ibid.,105.
[56]  Ibid.

The New Theology is but a siren song that tempts us to forsake the truth. It is always in an evolving process, but never really settles down anywhere. [57]

Steffens warned his readers that the New Theology was coming into America from Germany and was under the influence of Schleiermacher. It continued Schleiermacher's error in making the God consciousness of a Christian the basic principle for theology. Objective knowledge of God was replaced by a subjective principle.[58] Given the basic principle of their theology, Steffens charged that they would finally end up in some sort of idealistic rationalism that denied the historicity of the revelation in the Bible. He saw such reliance on human reason already emerging when liberal biblical scholars taught that Isaiah 40-66 was the prophecy of a second Isaiah. To deny that the primary reference of Isaiah 40-66 is to the coming of Jesus Christ is to reject the way God used revelation in scripture to point to Christ. He also saw surrender to subjectivism and rationalism in their denial of the virgin birth of Jesus. When matters such as the virgin birth are turned into legend, there is nothing higher than our own God consciousness.[59] In light of the way the New Theology uses the Bible, it is clear that the question about the Bible has shifted. The old question among the Lutherans, Arminians, Calvinists, and Baptists was, "How are we to understand the Word of God?" Now the question is, "Is the Bible the infallible Word of God?"[60] In the face of the challenge of the developing nineteenth-century American liberalism, the midwestern leaders insisted adamantly on maintaining the language of the ancient creeds and the Reformed confessions.

---

[57]  Nicholas Steffens, "De Nieuwere Theologie," *De Hope*, February 2, 1887. The midwestern leaders constantly made this charge that the New Theology and Modernism used ambiguous language and were always shifting positions. Sixty years after Steffens registered this complaint, Siebe Nettinga maintained that however much it changes, the heart of modernism is its naturalism and antagonism to supernaturalism. The Bible is only man's religious experience, not a supernatural revelation. He also wrote that modernism is not new, but finds its origins in the fifteenth and sixteenth centuries. In its eighteenth-century forms, it emptied the church and led to the French Revolution, which that in turn led to anarchy and socialism (S. Nettinga, "Wekelijksch Budget," *De Hope*, April 15, 1930; "Het Modernisme in de Nederlandse Hervormde Kerk," April 7, 1931.)

[58]  Ibid.

[59]  Ibid.

[60]  Ibid., 3, esp. footnote 11.

## (3) The Challenge of the Theory of Evolution to Biblical Faith

Progress in history and evolutionary change were of great interest to Americans in the first half of the nineteenth century. New inventions such as the cotton gin, the telegraph, the McCormick Reaper, the steamboat, and railroads made people aware of rapid changes in manufacturing, transportation, and communications. Education was becoming more widespread. Geologists were publishing the results of their study of rock formations, which led to the conclusion that the surface of the earth had gone through gradual changes during long geological ages. Thus, when Darwin's *Origin of the Species* was published in 1859, it had an immediate impact on the church's doctrine about creation, the origin of the species and human beings, and the doctrine of scripture.

The midwestern leaders in the nineteenth century, like Protestants in general, were for the most part ready to await the conclusions of scientists on matters of scientific investigation. They did not oppose Darwin immediately for teaching "natural selection" as an evolutionary process, but they objected when his findings were used to propagate sociological and philosophical theories inconsistent with their Christian faith. Thus, Jacob Van Der Meulen in 1878 distinguished between the writings of Charles Darwin and Herbert Spencer. Darwin, he wrote, is not an atheist; he is a pure natural scientist.[61] However, Herbert Spencer, in *Principles of Sociology*, is an atheist who has changed Darwin's "natural selection" into "the survival of the fittest" and turned it into an atheistic sociological and racial theory. Spencer turns human beings into a race of murderers. Men eat their bread with their swords in their hands. Even so, Spencer has changed Darwin's idea of evolutionary change into a philosophy of upward progress.[62]

---

[61] Charles Hodge of Princeton Theological Seminary agreed that Darwin himself may not have been an atheist but insisted that Darwinism is atheistic: "What is Darwinism? It is atheism. This does not mean, as said before, that Mr. Darwin himself and all who adopt his views are atheists; but it means that his theory is atheistic; that the exclusion of design from nature is...tantamount to atheism" (Charles Hodge, "What is Darwinism?' in *Princeton Theology, 1812-1921*, ed. Mark A. Noll (Grand Rapids: Baker, 1983), 152.

[62] Jacob Van Der Meulen Sr., "Hebben de Beginselen des Ongeloofs eene menschlievende Strekking?" *De Hope*, August 21, 1878. Jacob Van Der Meulen was a son of Cornelius Van Der Meulen, the leader of the colony in Zeeland, Michigan. He was the first pastor of the Third Reformed Church in Holland, Michigan, 1868-1871.

Nicholas Steffens agreed that we do not know how long the six days of creation lasted (Genesis 1),[63] but he insisted that the theory of evolution must not be allowed to rule out several basic Christian doctrines. A theory of evolution must not be allowed to rule out the fact that the world had a beginning. Pantheism, which teaches an essential oneness between God and the universe, must be rejected. Evolution must not rule out the fact that God has a purpose for the creation. Creation is a work that was completed when human beings were created in the image of God. God continues to rule over the universe and bring it to its goal by his providential and redemptive activity. Therefore, wrote Steffens, we must oppose modern positivists, agnostics, evolutionists; we can excuse the ancient philosophers for their speculations because they did not have the revelation of God in the Bible, but these modern men cannot be excused. Their opposition is not due to ignorance; they are enemies of the gospel.[64]

Steffens maintained that in spite of the objections of the evolutionists, a clear line must be drawn between God, humankind, and the animals. Human beings, he taught, did not evolve from animals, but came into being by a special act of God. Natural evolutionary processes could not rise to the level of the image of God. [65] Furthermore, if the line between God and human beings as the image of God disappears, then the line between human beings as the image of God and the animals that do not bear that image will be erased.[66]

In the first half of the twentieth century, professors at Western Theological Seminary remained cautious in their statements about evolution. The theory of evolution had no impact on the way systematic theology was taught prior to World War II. Egbert Winter was typical when he wrote in class notes for his course in dogmatic theology that the theory of evolution "may have some basis of fact as applied to vegetable life, but it can never be made to answer for the origination of matter."[67] Evert Blekkink even in 1945 thought that the theory of

---

63  Steffens, "De Scheppingsdagen," *De Hope*, November 28, 1911.
64  Steffens, "In den Beginne schiep God Hemel en Aarde" *De Hope*, September 25, 1883.
65  Steffens, "De Mensch," *De Hope*, January 30, 1912.
66  Steffens, "God en Mensch," September 7, 1909.
67  Egbert Winter, *Dogmatic Theology*, III, 67 (on file at WTS/JAH). The course notes are undated. Other teachers of systematic theology at the seminary apparently paid little attention to the theory of evolution; Gerrit Dubbink and John R. Mulder mention it only in passing. One can surmise that they basically accepted the position of Steffens that the investigations

evolution in the Darwinian sense was losing its hold. Missing links had not been found. Even among scientific men there was

> a turning away from the materialistic and mechanical conception of the origin of things to a spiritual one....We anticipate that a day is not far off when Christian thinkers, scientific men of every type, will abandon evolution as a finality and emphasize the fact of God as the Creator of all, and that He has marvelously stored nature with residential forces for development within fixed limits—the vegetable, the animal, and the human "after their kind."[68]

Blekkink had not always been so sanguine about the prospects of the theory of evolution. In 1909 he had opposed vigorously the philosophical doctrine of evolution as articulated by Herbert Spencer and others. He believed that its foundation principle of the struggle for existence and the survival of the fittest can only lead to justification of violence in international relations and to oppression in domestic affairs. It replaces the command to love with the thesis that might makes right. He wrote,

> This exceedingly popular philosophy, when carried to its logical conclusions, reverses the golden rule; regards the sermon on the mount as an expression of weakness and helplessness, harmful counsel in a world where one must learn first of all that place is dependent on power; and thus has for its fundamental commandment, on which hang all the law and the prophets of this system, "Thou shalt love thyself with all thy heart, and with all thy soul, and with all they strength, and with all thy mind, and thy neighbor when it is for thine own advantage." It would make might right, and would have for its heroes, instead of the meek and lowly Jesus and those who are most like him, as already suggested by a recent German philosopher, whose writings have during the last decade grown amazingly in popularity, the Neros, the Borgias and the Napoleons of human history, men of boundless energy, self-assertion and self-seeking.[69]

of scientists were not to be opposed; they were confident that ultimately God's book of nature and God's book of scripture would harmonize with each other. Christian anthropology, with its doctrine of the fall and redemption as they taught it, was not affected in its essence by the question of the length of the days or the natural selection of the species apart from humankind.

[68] Blekkink, *The Fatherhood of God*, 1942, 70.
[69] Blekkink, "Intellectual Tyranny," *Leader*, June 2, 1909, 497.

Professor John Kuizenga wrote a series of editorial articles on evolution in the *Leader* during 1922-23, when the issue of teaching the theory of evolution in the public schools was under debate. Like his predecessors, he held that science has the right to independent research into the facts. Science, even in the hands of unregenerate people, can be very useful and gather an enormous number of facts that can serve not only to improve

> conditions under which we must live in the world, but which can help us to larger and better conceptions of God and man that we must take up into our theology.... Truths that science discovers in nature and human nature will be seen in their true meaning only when interpreted in the light of God's revelation, and by the insight of regenerate men under the illumination of the divine spirit.[70]

In his series of editorials, Kuizenga left the door open to the possibility that human beings were descended from animals, but he found it strange that evolutionists in the same breath asserted that "man is descended from a monkey and that man is really God."[71] He wrote that theism tells us that man is something other than a monkey because man has a moral, spiritual, rational nature that has come as a direct gift from God. If we hold that this nature of man has come as a special act of God, then we must say that even though God may have acted through natural law, God in creating man in the divine image has accomplished what the natural process could never do. "With Theism, miracles supervene on the natural process. And of course this is utterly unacceptable to modernistic thinking. Hence Modernism faces the dilemma, either Materialism or Pantheism." [72]

The Reverend Dr. Albertus Pieters, professor of English Bible and missions at the seminary, was the first to publish a careful study of the relation of Genesis 1-2 to the theory of evolution. He taught that the six

---

[70]  John Kuizenga, "Evolution: III:b Scientific Evolution," *Leader*, September 6, 1922, 9. The year 1922 was also when Harry Emerson Fosdick gave the Cole Lectures at Vanderbilt University on the subject, "Christianity and Progress." Fosdick linked the concept of progress with that of evolution. He said that in the nineteenth century evolution became a credible truth and a "comprehensive philosophy of life." "Growth became recognized as the fundamental law of life." (*Christianity and Progress*, New York: Revell, 1922), 31.

[71]  "The Divinity of Man, I," *Leader*, March 28, 1923, 9.

[72]  Ibid.

days of creation were long geological and biological ages.[73] The language of Genesis 1-2, he wrote, is "phenomenal" or popular language, not the language of science. "By this we mean that the facts are stated as they appeared to the eye, without any intention to express a judgment as to whether they were in reality what they appeared to be."[74] Pieters used the interpretive metaphor of the "phenomenal observer" to deal with other reports in the Pentateuch. Thus when Genesis reports that the waters of Noah's flood covered "all the high mountains that were under the whole heaven," it means only that "the observer could not see any that were not covered." When it said that the sun stood still or that the hare chews the cud, it means only that the sun appeared to stand still and that the hare appears to chew the cud.[75]

Pieters taught that the wording of Genesis 1:11-13 must be understood to refer to the processes of life as involving a continuous process of birth, growth, and death. "God did not call into existence permanent things; He started a continuous process. He takes nature, so to speak, into partnership with Himself, and lays upon it the duty of continuing what He has begun."[76] Although the fall of man brought much misery to the whole earth, it did not affect the basic life cycle of vegetation or of animal life. The fossil record shows that the process of life and death went on long before human beings appeared on earth. The existence of carnivorous birds and beasts was necessary to preserve the "balance of nature" through long ages.[77] The world through the long ages was "good" because it was "perfectly adapted to the end to which it was designed, that is, to be a home and training school for a self-conscious, reasoning, but fallen human being. Man's thought life results primarily from the reactions produced in him by his environment."[78]

Pieters was inclined to believe that God created human beings "from the dust of the earth" by a special act of creation, but he was open to the possibility that God "took one of the man-like brutes" that

---

[73]  Albertus Pieters, *Notes on Genesis for Ministers and Serious Bible Students* (Grand Rapids: Eerdmans, 1943), 29-33. Pieters's *Notes* were developed during his teaching career and were published only after he retired. For a brief sketch of Pieters's contribution to midwestern Reformed Church theology, see Eugene Heideman, "Dr. Albertus Pieters, V.D.M: Biblical Theologian," in *A Goodly Heritage*, Jacob Nyenhuis, ed., 65-84.

[74]  Pieters, *Notes on Genesis*, 12.

[75]  Ibid.

[76]  Ibid., 39.

[77]  Ibid., 55-59.

[78]  Ibid., 60.

The Rev. Albertus Pieters, D.D.
(1869-1955)

*Courtesy of Western Theological Seminary*

"Dr. Pieters was eminently qualified, both by temperament and by experience, to be professor in this newly established chair [named Dosker-Hulswit Chair of English Bible and Missions]. Temperamentally, he is a philosopher and a logician, so that he could easily discover the problems that arose in connection with the study of the English Bible. His experience as a missionary in the Far East enabled him immeasurably to vitalize statements of the Scripture whose orientalisms made them almost meaningless to the occidental mind. Oftentimes the students would leave Dr. Pieters' classroom with the words of the disciples upon their lips, 'Did not our hearts burn within us while he opened to us the Scripture?'" –John R. Mulder, "Our Tribute to Albertus Pieters," *Western Theological Seminary Bulletin*, II/3 (1948), 2.

the process of evolution had produced and "made him the first human being, by endowing him with a human soul and a morally responsible human nature."[79] Pieters believed that there were still many "missing links" in the chain of evolution, especially in the leap from animal to mankind. He found support for his position in the writings of many scientists, including eight from whom he supplied quotations.[80]

Because the teachers at Western Theological Seminary respected scientists even when they did not agree with them, they enabled the midwestern Reformed Church to avoid the deep chasm between those who became zealous advocates of the theory of evolution and those who condemned it. They remained theologically conservative in their firm maintenance of the line between human beings and the animals and in insisting that the first chapters of Genesis were historical in the

[79]    Ibid., 52.
[80]    Ibid., 52-54.

sense that Adam, Eve, and their descendants named in Genesis were living participants in human history, not mythological or legendary characters. Yet they were open to long geological ages and biological evolution of the species. They held firmly to the idea that God has a providential and purposive design for the creation. They believed that ultimately there can be no real conflict between science and religion, in spite of the fact that at any given time it may be impossible to reconcile them. Under the guidance of the teachers at Western and New Brunswick seminaries and the Reformed Church colleges, the Reformed Church has escaped the severe battles about evolution that have scarred the lives of many American churches.

## The Credibility and Authority of the Bible in the Modern World

At the end of the nineteenth century, the conflict over the possibility that doctrine had developed in an evolutionary manner and that ideas about God had evolved among the people of Israel became more intense. Many American liberals and modernists favored such ideas while American conservatives opposed them. The midwestern theologians in the Reformed Church drew the line against the encroaching American modernism's suggestion that "Christianity is itself a progressive movement instead of a static finality."[81] Harry Emerson Fosdick, in his Cole Lectures delivered at Vanderbilt University in 1922, articulated clearly some of the ideas about progress that had long been left ambivalent by the nineteenth century New Theology. He stated that

> The most crucial problem which we face in our religious thinking is created by the fact that Christianity thus statically conceived now goes out into a generation where no other aspect of life is conceived in static terms at all. The earth itself on which we live, not by fiat suddenly enacted, but by long and gradual processes, became habitable, and man upon it through uncounted ages grew out of an unknown past into his present estate.[82]

[81] Fosdick, *Christianity and Progress*, 136.
[82] Ibid., 138. Harry Emerson Fosdick was the most articulate and widely known liberal of the 1920s, especially after he as a Baptist minister preached the most famous sermon of his career in the First Presbyterian Church in New York City, entitled "Shall the Fundamentalists Win?" [For accounts of Fosdick's role in the controversy, see Bradley J. Longfield, *The Presbyterian Controversy: Fundamentalists, Modernists, and Moderates* (New York: Oxford Univ. Press, 1991), 9-27; see also Hutchison, *Modernist Impulse*, 258-59, 280-86.]. Fosdick became the whipping-boy for the fundamentalists.

Fosdick was opposed vigorously because he included in his concept of progress the idea that the revelation in the Bible is not final. "The revelation is progressive....We are continually running upon passages like this: 'It was said to them of old time,...but I say unto you;'...but finality in the Bible is *ahead*. We are moving toward it. It is too great for us yet to apprehend."[83] John Kuizenga objected to Fosdick's "pragmatism" whereby he taught that "truth is relative, instrumental, and in the making. Truth is not yet."[84]

A second major objection to modernism was that its methodology of higher criticism in the study of the Bible undermined the authority of scripture. Steffens reminded the readers of *De Hope* in 1893 that Protestant churches since the Reformation have insisted that the Bible, rather than the Pope in Rome or my feeling of God-consciousness or human reason, is the only rule of faith and practice for the Christian.[85] Writers in *De Hope* agreed that the Bible is the inspired Word of God, as Article 5 in the Belgic Confessions states clearly. Steffens's exposition of the doctrine of inspiration in *De Hope* in 1892 is typical of what was taught consistently in Western Theological Seminary. The scriptures not only contain God's Word, but they are as a whole entirely inspired by God. Moreover, it is not only that the writers were inspired to write

---

The midwestern leaders, however, usually spoke of him with a measure of respect because they believed that he stated unambiguously where he stood, in contrast to the New Theology churchmen who, in their opinion, used ambiguous language constantly.

[83]   Fosdick, *Christianity*, 215. Fosdick did not teach that progress was inevitable; destructive forces are manifold as well. "This world needs something more than a soft gospel of inevitable progress. It needs salvation from its ignorance, its inefficiency, its apathy, its silly optimisms and its appalling carelessness" (ibid., 40).

[84]   Kuizenga, "Fosdickism" *Leader*, September 13, 1922, 8.

[85]   Steffens, "Bijbelsch Christendom," *De Hope*, April 13, 1893. *De Hope* printed a number of articles on the authority and inspiration of the Bible in 1893 in relation to a bitter dispute that was raging in the Presbyterian Church. The dispute concerned the position of the Rev. Dr. Charles Augustus Briggs at the Presbyterian Union Theological Seminary in New York City. Briggs used higher criticism of the Bible in his teaching and rejected the doctrine of the *verbal* inspiration of the Bible. Briggs was supported by Philip Schaff, who had left Mercersburg Theological Seminary to teach at Union. The Reformed Church in the Midwest was following the controversy not only because of the doctrinal issues involved, but also because the denomination was in that year voting on whether to merge with the German Reformed Church in the United States as well as being involved in discussions of Federal Union with the Presbyterian Church, the Congregational Church, and the Reformed Church in the United States.

the thoughts of God, but the words themselves are the very words of God. This does not mean that the words of the Bible were dictated mechanically by God. God used the experience and personalities of the writers he had prepared to write the words in such a way that the words of God have come to us in the individual styles of prophets such as Isaiah and Jeremiah.[86]

In their defense of the inspiration and authority of the Bible, midwestern leaders often relied on the doctrine as taught at Princeton Theological Seminary in the last quarter of the nineteenth century. Under the leadership of Charles Hodge and Benjamin Warfield, there was strong opposition to the idea that the teachings of the Bible are the product of a long evolutionary development in human consciousness or in the religion of Israel. On the contrary, Hodge taught that just as the fossil record in rocks is the storehouse of facts for the geologist, so the Bible is the storehouse of facts for the theologian.[87] Biblical scholars must not begin by finding their own first principles in their own reason or God consciousness and make those principles the source

---

[86]  Steffens, "De Woordelijke Ingeving der H. Schriften," *De Hope*, January 27, 1892.

[87]  Midwestern Reformed Church theologians followed Hodge in their understanding of the word "facts." Some nineteenth- and twentieth-century historians held that the facts varied with the time, the place, and the perspective of the historians. "To set forth historical facts was not like 'dumping a load of bricks'" (George M. Marsden, *Understanding Fundamentalism and Evangelicalism*), 190. In contrast, John Gresham Machen, who was teaching at Princeton Theological Seminary in 1925, wrote, "The facts of the Christian religion remain facts no matter whether we cherish them or not: they are facts for God; they are facts both for angels and for demons; they are facts now, and they will remain facts beyond the end of time" (Machen, *What is Faith?* 1925, 249, quoted in Marsden, *Understanding*, 191).

Nicholas Steffens and Albertus Pieters agreed with Hodge and Machen in their use of the word "facts." Both had respect for natural scientists and archeologists in their diligent search for the facts. Pieters wrote, "The scientific spirit of our age has great respect for facts; it sets little store by anything that is mere speculation, without a firm basis in observation and experiment. This is right. The Christian religion, by virtue of its origin and nature, meets this demand for facts" (*The Facts and Mysteries of the Christian Faith*, 11). "We must not take them on faith, we must demand evidence, and good evidence of their truth," (ibid., 9). In contrast, mysteries "must be given us by revelation; things that can indeed be proved to have come from well-accredited organs of revelations, but that can not independently of such revelation, be supported by sufficient proof—many of them by any kind of proof," ibid., 9.

or test of Christian doctrines. Rather, the Christian theologian must first ascertain, collect, and combine all the facts that God has revealed concerning himself and our relation to him. "These facts are all in the Bible. This is true, because everything revealed in nature, and in the constitution of man concerning God and our relation to Him, is contained and authenticated in Scripture."[88]

Hodge's declaration that the Bible constitutes a storehouse of facts meant that the Bible has a timeless quality about it in that it is always and everywhere true. Because it was written by people under the direct inspiration of God and is internally coherent and without contradiction in what it intends to teach, it is incumbent upon the systematic theologian to assemble and collect the facts and organize them into a coherent system. Benjamin Warfield went on to teach that systematic theology is not a historical discipline that seeks to discover what has been held to be true by previous theologians. On the contrary, it sets forth "what is ideally true; in other words, it is to declare that it deals with absolute truth and aims at organizing into a concatenated system all the truth in its sphere....it is at all events one, inclusive of all theological truth and exclusive of all else as false or not germane to the subject."[89] In contrast with Schleiermacher, who understood systematic theology to be grounded in the feeling of absolute dependence on God, the Princeton theologians taught that theology as a science,

> presupposes the objective reality of the subject-matter with which it deals; the subjective capacity of the human mind so far to understand this subject matter as to be able to subsume it under the forms of thinking and to rationalize it into not only a comprehensive, but also a comprehensible whole; and the existence of trustworthy media of communication by which the subject-matter is brought to the mind and presented before it for perception and understanding.[90]

This view of theology does not rule out the character of systematic theology as a progressive discipline. As the knowledge of the scriptures grows and as the church grows in its understanding of the faith, there is progress in theological articulation of the faith as well. But such progressive movement will not be such as to move beyond

---

[88]  Ibid.
[89]  Benjamin Warfield, "The Idea of Systematic Theology," in Noll, *Princeton Theology*, 244.
[90]  Ibid., 245.

the revelation that has already been given in the canon of scripture. We no longer have to lay new foundations for theology. That work has been done in previous centuries. We "must rather give our best efforts to rounding the arches, carving the capitals, and fitting in the fretted roof."[91]

Following Hodge and Warfield, midwestern Reformed Church ministers prior to World War II opposed vigorously the higher critical method of studying the Bible. They could not understand how it was possible to accept the Bible as the Word of God if the Pentateuch had been formed by a "pious fraud," as some German higher critics were teaching. Wilhelm M.L. De Wette had argued that Deuteronomy was the law book found in the Temple during King Josiah's Reform of 624 B.C. According to De Wette, the law book "found" in the Temple was not the old inspired book written by Moses, but it was a new book of Deuteronomy produced by priests in a pious fraud designed to centralize the worship of God in the Temple and to consolidate the priests' position in Israel. De Wette's theory required a complete revision of the history of Israel, its religion, and of the way the Old Testament had come into existence.[92] The midwestern leaders were especially critical of the work of Julius Wellhausen, who proposed the "documentary hypothesis" that there are four strands of material, JDEP (Yahwist, Deuteronomist, Elohist, and Priestly), that were brought together by editors to form the Pentateuch. Wellhausen ruled out Mosaic authorship. Since Jesus had spoken of the Pentateuch as being written by Moses, this raised questions not only about the historicity of the first five books of the Bible, but also about the extent of Jesus' knowledge as the Son of God. In their theory of priestly fraud, the Old Testament was to be understood as a record of the development of the religion of Israel rather than as a book verbally inspired by God. Midwestern Reformed Church ministers were appalled that certain New Testament scholars had questioned even the historical existence of Jesus.

Steffens charged that higher criticism was opposed to the supernatural and was evolutionary in its philosophy of history.[93] He charged that the critics read the Bible like any other book, as if it had

---

[91]  Ibid., 258.
[92]  For a very brief introduction, see John Sandy-Wunsch, *What have They Done to the Bible: A History of Modern Biblical Interpretation* (Collegeville, Minn.: Liturgical Press, 2005), 307.
[93]  Steffens, "Is het niet Zelfbedrog," *De Hope*, November 3, 1897.

no supernatural origin as a revelation from God. He was disappointed to know that the *Congregationalist*, a church paper, had shifted into the critics' camp. Steffens wrote that as a teacher of the church, it was his professional responsibility to read the critics from time to time because he must know what is taught elsewhere, but that it unsettled him.[94]

Although midwestern Reformed Church leaders warned constantly against the higher critics, Henry Dosker at Western Theological Seminary in 1885 distinguished between the radical and the conservative higher critics and thereby opened the door to a more nuanced way to deal with the issues.[95] Several Reformed contemporaries of Dosker, including Philip J. Hoedemaker and Geerhardus Vos, showed that there is a way that a critical study of the scriptures can be carried out without undermining the credibility of the Bible as the inspired Word of God. In his four hundred-page book on the Mosaic origin of the laws in the Books of Exodus, Leviticus, and Numbers, Hoedemaker, who was teaching at the Free University in Amsterdam, defended the Mosaic authorship of the Pentateuch.[96] Dosker wrote that Hoedemaker's very readable book would be useful to Sunday school teachers as well as to those who are theologically trained. Gerhardus Vos, the outstanding biblical scholar in the Christian Reformed Church, had left Calvin Theological Seminary in 1893 to teach biblical studies at Princeton Theological Seminary. His book, *Biblical Theology*, was praised by conservative scholars.[97]

[94]  Ibid.
[95]  Henry Dosker, "Het Hogere Critiek," *De Hope*, March 27, 1895.
[96]  Dosker, "Het Hogere Critiek"; Ph. J. Hoedemaker, *De Mosaische Oorsprong van de wetten in de boeken Exodus, Leviticus en Numeri* (Leiden: D.A Daamen, 1895). Hoedemaker was an associate of Abraham Kuyper in the founding of the Free University. However, he continued to hold to the idea that the Nederlandse Hervormde Kerk was the "Volkskerk." Therefore he refused to give up his membership in it; instead he continued to work within that church for its reform. When the Nederlandse Hervormde Kerk in 1947 adopted its new church order, Hoedemaker was regarded as one of the heroes in the 125-year struggle to restore the General Synod to its proper role and free the church from the old Directorate.
[97]  (Grand Rapids: Eerdmans, 1948). A writer in the Christian Reformed Church paper *De Wachter* questioned whether it was theologically correct for a Christian Reformed scholar to accept a position in a Presbyterian seminary, since the Presbyterian Church, like the Reformed Church in America, was viewed as a "false church," lacking the mark of discipline. On the other hand, for one of their scholars to receive the honor of becoming a professor at Princeton was a mark of distinction. The editors of *De Hope* reported with a measure of satisfaction the Christian Reformed Church's dilemma on this matter (*De Hope*, Sept. 13, 1893, 4). Two Reformed

Albertus Pieters, who began to teach at Western Theological Seminary in 1926, agreed with Dosker that it was not necessary to reject higher criticism as a method for studying the Bible. He wrote,

> the first step is to ask what kind of Book it is, who wrote the various documents that compose it, and when. This inquiry is what we call "Higher Criticism," a term that has come into bad odor with many people, but that in itself carries no implication contrary to the Christian faith. The man who studies this subject and writes upon it with a believing heart is as truly a "Higher Critic" as the unbeliever who does the same."[98]

"Criticism," he pointed out, "does not mean to criticize in the sense of finding fault, but merely to exercise a judgment about the matters studied." [99]

As a "higher critic," Pieters did not fit into the radical or conservative camp as classified by Dosker but was a kindred spirit to Hoedemaker and Gerhardus Vos. As a biblical scholar and theologian, he was conservative by nature. Pieters also remained conservative in matters such as infant baptism, biblical inspiration and interpretation, opposition to revision of the Reformed Church confessional statements, and defense of miracles in the Bible.[100] Thus Pieters remained a man of the old era in his basic orientation to theology. It was this conservatism that made it possible for the church to continue to trust him even when some of the positions he took were upsetting to them.

Nevertheless, Pieters brought a new spirit into the theological tradition of the midwestern Reformed Church in America. He and his wife, Emma Kollen Pieters, had served as missionaries in Japan for thirty-two years (1891-1923). They had to return to the United States

---

Church in America professors left Western Theological Seminary to teach at Presbyterian seminaries in that era; Nicholas Steffens went to the Presbyterian Dubuque Theological Seminary in 1893 and Henry Dosker went to the Presbyterian Louisville Theological Seminary in 1903.

[98] *Can We Trust Bible History?* (Grand Rapids: Society for Reformed Publications, 1954), 10. The dates of publications by Pieters should not be taken as an indication of when he first wrote the material. A number of the books were published only a few years before his death, when there was a demand in the church for works by him, but the basis for the published material was laid decades earlier during his teaching and writing career in Japan as well as at Hope College and Western Theological Seminary.

[99] Pieters, *Can We Trust*, 10.

[100] D. Ivan Dykstra, "His Theological Contribution," *Western Theological Seminary Bulletin*, 2 (December 1948), 2-4.

on account of the health of two of their daughters. He taught for three years at Hope College prior to his appointment to the chair of English Bible and missions at the seminary. While in Japan he had been a pioneer in newspaper evangelism, which involved writing short articles on the Christian faith for publication in secular newspapers. Not only did that require him to write clear, concise articles for the general public, but it also meant that he was writing biblical and theological exposition for an audience that did not yet accept the Bible as the Word of God or as an inspired book.[101]

Pieters held the "plenary" theory of the inspiration of the Bible. By plenary inspiration he meant that the Bible in all its parts is the word of God.[102] It did not mean, however, that every word in the Bible has been given directly to the authors by the Holy Spirit.[103]

Although Pieters often set forth a vigorous defense of the doctrine of the plenary inspiration of the Bible, he seldom if ever used the doctrine as the basis for defending a biblical position or a theological point. He maintained that the doctrine of plenary inspiration functions more as a conclusion that comes after long study and meditation on the Bible. When he states at the beginning of one of his books that he holds "plenary inspiration" to be his position, he does so in order to "make full disclosure" of where he stands rather than to make an argument.

Pieters never ceased to be an evangelist in spirit. He wrote to bring his readers to faith, to strengthen their faith, or to defend themselves against wrong interpretations of the faith. Therefore, without insisting that his readers accept any theory about biblical inspiration, he called upon them consistently to have confidence in the *trustworthiness* of the Bible.[104] He stated, "Such confidence in the trustworthiness of the Old

---

[101] Albertus Pieters, *Seven Years of Newspaper Evangelism in Japan* (Kyobunkwan, Japan: Published under auspices of the Association for the Promotion of Newspaper Evangelization, 1919); "Newspaper Evangelism: Present Status and Prospects," read at Evangelical Committee, January 28, 1921; and "The Daily Paper as an Evangelist," a report written for *CMS Quarterly*, both on file at WTS/JAH.

[102] *The Inspiration of the Holy Scriptures*, 19. After the publication of Herman Bavinck's *Dogmatic Theology*, teachers at Western Theological Seminary usually defended the "plenary" taught by Bavinck rather than the "verbal" inspiration of the Bible proposed by Warfield and Hodge. "Plenary" can be interpreted as "full, entire, complete," without insisting that God has actually given to the writers the exact words.

[103] Ibid., 18.

[104] The trustworthiness of the Bible is the theme that runs throughout *Can We Trust Bible History?* Pieters argued for the trustworthiness of the Bible in his major work, *The Facts and Mysteries of the Christian Faith*, 29-43.

Testament record rests primarily upon faith in Jesus Christ and the holy apostles as founders and authoritative teachers of the Christian church."[105]

Pieters held that the four gospels were written by the men whose names were attached to them by the early church. In his mind, Matthew and John were disciples of Jesus. Mark as a close associate of Peter had composed the second gospel and Luke, a careful historian and companion of Paul, had written Luke. All were sober and reliable eyewitnesses to what they had seen and heard.

> The church believed the things narrated in the Gospels and Acts to be true on the evidence of reliable witnesses, before the books themselves were written. When the books appeared they were accepted as true because the Christian people already knew the facts to be as therein stated, and knew the authors to be trustworthy men. Later still the belief arose that the books were inspired, that is, were to be given the same rank as those which Christ and the apostles had endorsed as such. Belief in the history thus preceded...belief in the inspiration of the books in which said history was recorded.[106]

Pieters taught that the situation is reversed in the case of the Old Testament, where belief in inspiration precedes belief in historical truth and the trustworthiness of the eyewitnesses. The inspiration of the Old Testament is accepted on the basis of the testimony of Jesus and the apostles that it is the Word of God, rather than upon historical evidence.[107] Nevertheless, Pieters does not simply insist that his readers accept that the Old Testament is true because it is inspired. On the contrary, he continually argues for its credibility on the basis of the trustworthiness of Jesus and the apostles and on archeological and other historical evidence that the Old Testament record is consistent with what is known from other sources. He recognized, however, that all evidences for the truth of the Bible fall short of certainty. "Such acceptance is an act of faith. It is reasonable on the part of those who trust in Jesus Christ, but we can not expect it from others. It is not based on historical evidence."[108]

---

[105]  Pieters, *Notes on Genesis*, 11.

[106]  Ibid., 12; See also Pieters, *Divine Lord and Savior* (New York: Revell, 1949), 69-74.

[107]  Pieters, *Notes on Genesis*, 12.

[108]  Ibid.

Pieters did not teach that the Bible is without errors in the original manuscripts.[109] He wrote that we cannot say anything about the original manuscripts because they are not available. When it comes to statistics, dates, and similar matters, there certainly are errors in the Bible as we now have it. The fact that there are some errors in the Bible as we have it does not render it untrustworthy. "A document can be a trustworthy source of information even though minor errors exist in it; and therefore it is not inconsistent with the position here assumed to believe that some such minor errors may have existed even in the original documents."[110]

The Christian faith is not based on legends, fictions, or even our feeling of absolute dependence on God. It is grounded in history. Pieters accepted the commonsense philosophy that was taught at Princeton in his understanding of science and historical evidence. "Beyond every other system of religion or philosophy, it [the Christian religion] is rooted first of all in the soil of facts, by which we mean externally observable and historically provable events, things that have really happened, and can be shown to have happened."[111] There are "mysteries" that can be known to us only by revelation. These include such things as the creation of the world out of nothing, the pre-existence of Jesus as the Son of God, the regeneration of the soul, the second coming of Christ, and the resurrection of the body.[112] "The facts are the external, earthly, natural part of the Christian religion; the mysteries are the heavenly and spiritual part."[113]

However, the heavenly mysteries are not divorced from the facts. With our knowledge of the mysteries, we must demand evidence of their truth. The central event in the mysteries is that Jesus Christ who died on the cross was resurrected on the third day. We can use methods of historical research to search out evidence that Jesus truly was resurrected. In *Facts and Mysteries*, six chapters are devoted to searching the evidence and the nature of the resurrection. Pieters says that the nature of the eye-witnesses, the number of eye-witnesses, and

---

[109] Benjamin Warfield and other Princeton theologians had taught that the Bible is without error in the original manuscripts; see Benjamin B. Warfield, "The Inerrancy of the Original Autographs," in Mark A. Noll, *Princeton Theology*, 269-74. Warfield agreed that there are errors of transmission and copying in the manuscripts that we have today but claimed that these are minor.

[110] *Notes on Genesis*, 13.

[111] *Facts and Mysteries*, 8.

[112] Ibid., 9.

[113] Ibid., 11.

the evidence for the empty tomb all serve to confirm the witness of the Holy Spirit in our hearts and in the history of the church. These all bear testimony to the fact that Jesus did come out of the tomb on Easter morning.[114] Having strong evidence that the greatest miracle of all, the resurrection, was credible, it is not incredible to believe that Jesus' miracles as reported in the gospels are reports of actual events in history. It is not necessary to believe that they all happened exactly as reported or to harmonize every discrepancy between the accounts in the gospels.[115]

The writings and classroom teaching of Albertus Pieters between 1923 and 1956 were major factors enabling the midwestern Reformed Church in America to accept new perspectives on the teachings of scripture, the role of Reformed confessions, and the nature of Reformed piety. While remaining true to the heritage that Van Raalte and the other Dutch immigrants had brought with them, he opened doors for a new generation to remain faithful in its encounter with a rapidly changing world.

## Premillenialism and the Interpretation of Scripture

Midwestern Reformed Church theologians defended their traditional theology successfully against the inroads of American liberalism and modernism. During the first half of the twentieth century, however, they faced a more serious threat to their traditional Reformed theology from the premillenialists and dispensationalists. Throughout the nineteenth century, many of the leaders in the Reformed Church had been postmillenialists who believed that under the powerful activity of the Holy Spirit the kingdom of God was being realized on the earth. In the not too distant future, perhaps around 2000 A.D., Christ would return to earth and rule his kingdom of peace for a thousand years. On the other hand, premillenialists gave a more pessimistic interpretation of the Bible. They taught that the world was getting worse, not better. They taught that at an unknown date in the future, Christ would break in to overthrow wickedness, to judge the world and then rule for a thousand years.

Prior to 1920 premillenialists, postmillennialists, and amillennialists lived together peacefully in the Reformed Church in America. They all expected the personal and visible return of Christ. They agreed that the present age will not come to a close with the peacefulness of an October evening. It will instead have a cataclysmic

[114] Ibid., 114-37.
[115] Ibid., 86-92.

ending when the heavens will pass away with a great noise and the elements will be dissolved with fire. They all looked for a new heaven and a new earth in which righteousness will be complete.[116]

Evert Blekkink delineated the points on which there was disagreement. The postmillennialists believed that the regular means of grace—the preaching of the Word, the celebration of the sacraments, and prayer—are made effective through the power of the Holy Spirit and therefore are adequate instruments by which the kingdom of God is to come. On the other hand, the premillennialists held that Christ will come in person and rule from Jerusalem for a thousand years prior to the final judgment. Those who believe will arise in the first resurrection at the beginning of his reign and rule with him as Christ directs the affairs of the kingdom and the world through a period of incomparable blessedness.[117]

Few of the midwestern Reformed Church leaders gave careful attention to the study of the book of Revelation and the apocalyptic passages. Gerrit Dubbink was typical of other leaders when he taught his students that passages such as Revelation 20:1-6 about the millennial kingdom and the mark of the beast should not be allowed to overwhelm other teachings in the Bible.[118] On the other hand, Egbert Winter wrote a very long series of articles for *De Hope* in 1877 in defense of the premillenial position. The most forceful proponent of premillenialism was the Reverend Gerrit Hendrik Hospers, who sent letters and articles constantly on the subject to the editors of *De Hope*. He opposed the optimistic worldview of the postmillennialists, who were so confident that the world is improving. As a defender of high Calvinism, he declared that American postmillennialists were Arminians. Among their evils were a lack of solid preaching and a lack of solid doctrine.[119]

In spite of the nineteenth-century agreement to disagree about differences of interpretation of the Bible on the matter of millennial

---

[116] Evert Blekkink, "Brotherly Love and the Second Coming of Christ," *Leader*, March 9, 1921.

[117] Ibid.

[118] Gerrit Dubbink, *Systematics*, 103.

[119] Gerrit H. Hospers, "De Gereformeerde Wereldbeschouwing," *De Hope*, January 5, 1909. Hospers served as pastor of congregations in New York and Michigan and was the principal of the academy in Cedar Grove, Wisconsin, from 1905-1908. He was born in 1864. During the years of his youth, he lived in Pella and Orange City, Iowa. Egbert Winter served as pastor in Pella, 1866-1884.

expectations, midwestern Reformed Church leaders could not avoid dealing with controversies that came to the fore in the first half of the twentieth century and continued to play an important role in American religious and political life into the twenty-first century. Many Christians were encouraged to become premillenialists by three developments in the first two decades of the twentieth century. One was the rise of the Zionist movement under the leader Theodore Herzl, beginning in 1894. The second was World War I, which undercut the optimism of the nineteenth century. The third was the publication and wide sale of the Scofield Reference Bible in 1908.

Under the impact of those developments, as well as suspicion of modernism in American churches, three major issues were (1) principles of biblical interpretation; (2) the church as inheritor of Old Testament promises; (3) the role of the Jews and the significance of their return to the Holy Land.

### (1) Principles of Biblical Interpretation

The Scofield Reference Bible, published in 1909 and revised in 1917, may have been the most important factor leading members of the Reformed Church in the Midwest to come under the influence of a premillennialist interpretation of the Bible.[120] Cyrus Ingerson Scofield (1843-1921) was a lawyer turned Bible teacher. When he was converted he came under the influence of the dispensationalist and premillennial views of John Nelson Darby (1800-1882), who was the founder of the Plymouth Brethren.[121] Darby taught that the Book of Revelation in conjunction with the prophecies of Daniel contained the key to

---

[120]  C.I. Scofield, The Scofield Reference Bible, rev. ed. (New York: Oxford Univ. Press, 1917). The New Scofield Reference Bible was published in a new edition in 1987. A number of the notes of the first edition were revised significantly, but the basic tenets of Scofield have remained in place. Since our purpose is to gain an understanding of what has been the midwestern Reformed Church's theology in relation to dispensationalism prior to 1966, it is not necessary to examine how dispensationalists themselves may have changed their views since the original edition of the Scofield Reference Bible was published. For an excellent brief exposition of contemporary dispensationalism, see Vern S. Poythress, Understanding Dispensationalists (Grand Rapids: Academie Books, Zondervan, 1987).

[121]  Dr. Hendirk P. Scholte in Pella was a friend of Darby and had exchanged correspondence with him. After Scholte's death, his second wife, Mareah, married a Darbyite, Robert Beard, and attended Darbyite worship. Leonora R. Scholte, A Stranger in a Strange Land (Grand Rapids: Eerdmans, 1946), 108-110.

revelation of future events in world history prior to the return of Christ and the Last Judgment. He also taught that at the end of the "church age" the "Rapture" would take place, and the believers would be taken up into the clouds to reign with Christ for a thousand years.

Scofield saw the need for a Bible with reference notes to help people without formal biblical training obtain historical background information, to receive brief exposition of key doctrines, and to understand difficult passages. His King James Version reference Bible with footnotes was an innovation and immediate success. There was no other such reference Bible available in the first decades of the twentieth century.[122] It provided clear definitions for many of the basic doctrines of the faith, such as the Trinity, the Atonement, faith, justification, and regeneration. Many people carried the Scofield Reference Bible along when they went to church and Bible study groups. It also became a major resource at Bible conferences.

A basic principle of interpretation in the Scofield Reference Bible is that one must recognize the differences between the dispensations. This includes the understanding that all biblical prophecy must be fulfilled literally. A "dispensation" was defined as "a period of time during which man is tested in respect of obedience to some *specific* revelation of the will of God."[123] According to the Scofield Reference Bible, there is but one overarching dispensation, redemption in Christ.

> There is also a sevenfold series of dispensations: (1) Innocence (Gen. 1:28) to the loss of Eden; (2) Conscience or moral responsibility (Gen. 3:7) up to the Great Flood; (3) Human Government (Gen. 8:15) up to the call of Abraham; (4) Promise, the rest of Israel's response to God (Gen. 12:1) down to the covenant at Sinai; (5) Law, to the death of Christ (Ex. 19:1); (6) the church, the dispensation of the Holy Spirit (Acts 2:1) to Christ's

---

[122]  The American Bible Society's policy was to publish Bibles without any notes. Thereby it was able to avoid being drawn into theological controversies among the denominations about the interpretation of biblical texts and to keep their support for its work of promoting the publication and distribution of the scriptures.

[123]  Scofield Reference Bible, 5. The word "dispensation" was the translation in the King James Version of the Greek word *oikonomia*, 1 Cor. 9:17; Eph. 1:10, 3:2; Col. 1:25. The translators of the New International Version, the New Revised Standard Version, and other modern speech versions do not translate *oikonomia* as "dispensation" because the meaning of the word has shifted since the sixteenth century.

return (Second Coming); and (7) the millennial kingdom to Eternity (Rev. 20:4).[124]

The midwestern Reformed theologians agreed that premillennialism is compatible with the teaching of the scriptures and the Reformed confessions, but they soon concluded that dispensationalism is not compatible.[125] Albertus Pieters led the attack on dispensationalism in many of his writings. He rejected the teaching that the seven dispensations proposed by Darby each has its own test of obedience according to some specific revelation of the will of God. Instead, Pieters insisted that the covenant made with Abraham continues through the covenant made at Sinai and in the redemptive work of Jesus Christ, "thus continuing the Abrahamic relation through the New Covenant into the Visible Church, composed of all those who profess the name of Christ, together with their children."[126]

The dispensationalists taught that Christ established his church in the interim before the Second Advent. The church is not in any way a fulfillment of the Old Testament promises. It is something that was unknown to the prophets and, as something wholly new, is not a part of the continuing life of Israel. "It is a 'parenthesis in history,'"[127] that will come to an end in the "Rapture," when all the true believers are taken

---

[124] John Charles Cooper, "Dispensationalism," in Gentz, *Dictionary of Bible and Religion*, 274. Dispensationalists emphasize the need to "rightly divide the word of truth" (2 Tim. 2:15). "That is, they carefully separate the parts of the Bible that address the different dispensations. People following this route learn that the Sermon on the Mount is 'legal ground' (cf. Scofield's note on Matt. 6:12). It is kingdom ethics, not ethics for the Christian. Christians are not supposed to pray the Lord's Prayer (Matt. 6:9-13), or use it as a model, because of the supposed antithesis to grace in 6:12. These dispensationalists might be called 'hardline' dispensationalists." "Softline" dispensationalists do make some applications of the Old Testament dispensations to Christians. (Vern S. Poythress, *Understanding Dispensationalists*, Grand Rapids: Academie Books, Zondervan Publishing House, 1937, 31).

[125] The controversy about premillenialism and dispensationalism became especially sharp in the Christian Reformed Church after the Rev. Harry Bultema published his book, *Maranatha!*, in 1917. For the events and trial that led to his deposition from the ministry, see Michael G. Borgert, "Harry Bultema and the *Maranatha* Controversy in the Christian Reformed Church," *Calvin Theological Journal*, 42 (April 2007) 101-109. Bultema and his followers went on to form the Berean Reformed Church.

[126] Pieters, *Seed of Abraham*, 85.

[127] Albertus Pieters, *The Lamb, the Woman, and the Dragon: An Exposition of the Revelation of St. John* (Grand Rapids: Zondervan, 1937), 57.

up to meet Christ in the air. It will be visible to believers but not to the world at large. The Rapture is the first stage in the Second Advent. The public, visible stage will take place seven years later; it is called by some "The Revelation." The seven years corresponds to the seventieth week of the prophecy in the ninth chapter of Daniel. "The sixty-nine weeks ran out at the first coming of Christ, but with the rejection of Christ by the Jews and the postponement of the kingdom, prophetic time ceased to run. As Harry Ironside puts it: "The prophetic clock stopped at Calvary. Not one tick has been heard since."[128]

Ironside's comment reflected the Scofield Bible's second basic principle of biblical interpretation, which is that all Old Testament prophecy must be fulfilled literally. Since many of the prophecies of the Old Testament were not fulfilled literally during Jesus' time on earth, it must be anticipated that they will be fulfilled at the end of the church time. Included in those prophecies that must yet be fulfilled are the restoration of the Jews to Palestine, the rebuilding of the Temple in Jerusalem, the restoration of the sacrificial system, and the regathering of the Lost Ten Tribes of Israel. During the last seven years the Antichrist will rule. These years will be the years of the "Great Tribulation," during which time a few of those unbelievers left behind by the Rapture will come to faith and experience terrible persecution. At the end of the seven years the second stage of the Second Advent will take place, the Antichrist will be destroyed, and Christ will establish his earthly kingdom and rule for a thousand years.[129]

[128] Ibid., 58. The Rev. Dr. Harry Ironside was the pastor at Moody Church in Chicago. He was a very popular preacher on the Moody Bible Institute radio station, WMBI. He had a strong influence among Reformed Church members who lived within 150 miles of Chicago.

[129] Ibid., 58. Dispensationalists differ from each other in their understanding of the details of the chronology of the end times and have developed complex charts setting forth the sequence of events. Such charts can be purchased in Christian bookstores that carry dispensationalist literature. In 1970 Hal Lindsey's *The Late Great Planet Earth* (Grand Rapids: Zondervan) stimulated broad public debate about the end times. More recently, the series of books written by Timothy La Haye and Jerry B. Jenkins in the "Left Behind" series published by Tyndale Press in Wheaton, Illinois, has sold more than forty-two million copies and has been made into a popular movie. Tim Lahaye wrote a commentary in 1973, *Revelation: Illustrated and Made Plain* (Grand Rapids: Zondervan, 1973). La Haye related prophecies in the Book of Revelation directly to contemporary world events. Soon the United Nations headquarters will move from New York to Babylon in Iraq. "By that time the Babylonian religion under the leadership of Rome will have consumed the World Council of Churches and its ecumenical movement

Albertus Pieters opposed both principles of interpretation found in the Scofield Reference Bible. Because Pieters was so effective in his teaching and writing, only a very small percentage of the members in the Reformed Church in the Midwest became dispensationalists, although the percentage who continued to accept a premillenial, but not dispensational, position was probably somewhat larger. Because of the broad influence of dispensationalism in right-wing American Protestantism today, it is helpful to summarize very briefly Pieters's interpretation of the Book of Revelation.

Albertus Pieters agreed with dispensationalists that the Bible must be interpreted literally. He wrote that ordinarily all passages of scripture "must be understood in their plain and natural sense, unless there is reason to take them figuratively. The presumption is always in favor of the literal sense: if any man takes it otherwise, he must show cause."[130] In the case of Revelation, Pieters taught that there were strong reasons for holding that the "symbolical, not the literal, interpretation has the right of way."[131] The Book of Revelation, he wrote, is a "divine picture book, a book of spiritual cartoons, a pictorial presentation, through symbols, of certain forces which underlie the historical development of the Christian church and its unceasing conflict."[132]

Pieters rejected the "historical interpretation" of Revelation that holds that the book was a prophecy of the course of history from the end of the first century moving through the fall of the Roman Empire, the coming of the eastern barbarians, the Muslims, and the Turks to the Reformation with the pope as anti-Christ, and then to the end of the age. This interpretation, favored by some ancient writers, by men such as John Wycliffe and Martin Luther, as well as some modern expositors, is too focused on the history of western civilization and the place of the papacy, and "has been shown by history to be a 'will-o'-the-wisp,' leading only into a bog of endless and profitless speculation."[133] Pieters also rejected the dispensationalist "futurist interpretation,"[134]

---

and will be rapidly moving toward amalgamating the major religions of the world under the headship of one who bears the title "Pontifex Maximus. The world bankers will be more than happy to finance the rebuilding of Babylon as the greatest city in the world to accommodate the headquarters of this one-world government and one-world religion" (*Revelation*, 242).

[130] Pieters, *The Lamb, the Woman, and the Dragon*, 69-70.
[131] Ibid.
[132] Ibid., 69.
[133] Ibid., 54, 45-54.
[134] Pieters distinguished between futurists such as Abraham Kuyper (who was not even premillenialist) and Theodor Zahn, on the one hand, and the

which holds that in the Book of Revelation "nothing of that which is prophesied from the beginning of chapter four on has yet taken place, nor can take place until just before the end."[135] The futurists are literalists who do not see the symbolical character of the book. Readers of the Scofield Bible pointed to Revelation 1:3, "Blessed is the one who reads aloud the words of the prophecy, and blessed are those who hear and who keep what is written in it, for the time is near" ( KJV reads "is at hand"). The Scofield Bible understands the phrase "is near" or "at hand" to refer to the fulfillment of prophecy in the end times. Its position is based on its teaching that prophetic time is reckoned only to Israel and not to the church. The period of the church is the "parenthesis" in history following the Jewish rejection of Jesus as the Messiah. The dispensationalist teaching rules out the historical interpretation of the book of Revelation.[136] However, Pieters taught that there is no evidence in the Bible that John the Baptist's and Jesus' proclamation that the kingdom is "at hand" (Matt. 3:2; Mark 1:14) is to be fulfilled only after the Jews return to Palestine.[137]

Pieters's understanding of the nature of biblical prophecy led him to adopt the "preterist" interpretation of Revelation. The preterist interpretion holds that almost everything, but not everything, in the book was fulfilled in the first three centuries. It is called "preterist" because that word means "the past."[138] The preterists believe that "it is one of the great basic principles of prophecy that it takes its start with the generation to which it is addressed, and has primarily its origin in the need of that generation for comfort, warning, instruction, etc."[139] Pieters pointed out that one of the great gains in understanding the Old Testament prophets in the previous fifty years came about because it was recognized that those prophets proceeded according to the principle, *"Prophecy begins with its own generation."*[140]

---

dispensationalists, on the other. His criticisms do not apply to Kuyper and Zahn (ibid., 60). Pieters mentioned Zahn because conservative pastors had high regard for the German New Testament scholar Theodor Zahn (1838-1933), whose three-volume *Introduction to the New Testament* (Edinburgh: T. & T. Clark) had been translated into English in 1909 by a group of fellows and scholars of Hartford Theological Seminary; see vol. 3, 436-49. For a recent brief review of Zahn's life and work, see Erich H. Kiehl, "Theodor Zahn," in *Bible Interpreters in the Twentieth Century*, Walter A. Elwell and J.D. Weaver, eds. (Grand Rapids: Baker, 1999), 50-58.
[135]  Pieters, *The Lamb, the Woman, and the Dragon*, 55.
[136]  Ibid., 62-63.
[137]  Ibid., 62.
[138]  Ibid., 40.
[139]  Ibid., 63.
[140]  Ibid., 64; (italics are Pieters's).

In his chapter, "A Bird's-Eye View of Revelation," Pieters summarized his interpretation of the book. He followed the seventeenth-century expositor, Joseph Mede (died 1638), who took the contrast between the Great Book, Sealed (5:1), and the Little Book, Open (10:2), to be the major divisions. "The Great Book is God's secret counsel with regard to judging a sinful world; the Little Book is His revealed counsel with regard to the Christian church and her conflict with her foes."[141] In the second section, pertaining to the Little Book,

> the thing in the foreground is no longer what is determined in heaven and sent down from heaven upon the earth; everything is viewed from the standpoint of the church militant, her glory, her foes, her sufferings, her conflicts, and her eventual triumph.... That the church is to have such experiences must not be kept secret from God's people, lest they faint in the midst of the trial; therefore the book is not only open, but the seer is expressly told to eat it, that is, to thoroughly familiarize himself with it, that he may tell it to his brethren.[142]

### (2) The Church as Inheritor of Old Testament Promises

Pieters insisted that the church is the continuation of Israel as the people of God, in contrast to the dispensationalist doctrine of the church as a "parenthesis" in history. Moreover, the church that is the "new Israel" is a visible church with preachers of the Word, administration of the sacraments, and the exercise of spiritual discipline all visible.[143] Those who have been baptized are members of the church. Pieters never accepted the radical distinction that some of the seventeenth-century Dutch pietists had made between the elect believers in the invisible church and the many baptized who were members of the visible church. For those pietists, the preaching of the Word and sacrament of baptism were only external; it was the internal word that the Holy Spirit applied to the heart. It was the regenerating work of the Holy Spirit that placed one in the invisible church. In the minds of the most extreme pietists, there was a radical discontinuity between those who had plumbed the depths of their own sinfulness and come to know the majesty of God's gracious redemption, on the one hand, and those gathered in church on Sunday morning to hear the external word and externally receive the sacraments, on the other hand. The internal word was the seed; the external word was the husk.

---

[141]  Ibid., 77.
[142]  Ibid., 78.
[143]  Pieters, *The Seed of Abraham*, 76.

The dispensationalists had a view of the relation of the invisible church and the visible church something like that of the earlier pietists. The visible church is dominated by the "nominal Christians" who may be going through the spiritual exercises and living ethical lives, but who do not really know the Lord. In the last times, it will come under the anti-Christ and submit to wearing the mark of the Beast.[144] Pieters, like his predecessors in the Midwest, refused to entertain such a sharp distinction between the visible and the invisible church. He taught that the preaching of the Word and the celebration of the sacraments are not mere externals, but are the means of grace by which the Holy Spirit leads people to faith and assurance of salvation.

The visible church then is the church of the new covenant, the continuation of Israel of the Old Testament. Pieters rejected the position of dispensationalists who spoke of the church as the "gentile church." In the New Testament church there is neither Jew nor Greek. "There is no such thing as 'The Gentile Church' and can not be. It is a contradiction in terms. When a Gentile becomes a Christian he by that very act ceases to be a Gentile and becomes a member of the commonwealth of Israel, the household of God."[145]

That this New Covenant Israel, the church, is a visible community is shown by the fact that little children of members are also members of it, even before they exercise faith, as Paul wrote, "Else were your children unclean, but now they are holy (1 Cor. 7:14)."[146] When Paul called children of believers "holy," he did not mean "holy in personal character" or faith, for they had been born in sin. That "they can be quite as naughty as others every Christian father and mother knows very well. In what sense, then, are they 'holy'? There is no sense conceivable except that they are by birth members of the holy covenant group, the Christian church, the New Covenant Israel."[147]

[144] In the twentieth century, it was not unusual for dispensationalist preachers to suggest that agencies such as the Federal Council of Churches, the National Council of Churches, and the United Nations were in alliance with the Beast. The Left Behind series of books points in that direction. "Nominal Christians" are called "apostates" in the Scofield Reference Bible. "Apostasy, 'falling away,' is the act of professed Christians who deliberately reject revealed truth (a) as to the deity of Jesus Christ, and (b) redemption through his atoning and redeeming sacrifice....The apostate is perfectly described in 2:Tim.4:3,4. Apostates depart from the faith but not from the outward profession of Christianity....Apostasy in the church, as in Israel...is irremedial, and awaits judgment...."(Scofield Reference Bible, 1280-81).
[145] Albertus Pieters, *The Seed of Abraham*, 77.
[146] Ibid.
[147] Ibid.

*(3) The Continuing Role of the Jews and the Significance of their Return to Palestine*

Nineteenth-century midwestern Reformed Church leaders were uncertain about the theological significance of the return of Jews to the "Holy Land." Midwestern Reformed Church leaders speculated in the last quarter of the nineteenth century about the return of the Jews to Palestine. The Reverend Henry Utterwick in 1869 believed that according to Deuteronomy 30:1-14, Zachariah 12-14, and Romans 11, the Jews continued to have a role in God's plan of salvation for the world. He also predicted that the Jews will soon once again have a national state in Palestine.[148] The Reverend John Van Der Meulen in 1875 was anticipating not only that the Jews would return to Jerusalem, but that gentiles would also be there to reign with the returned Messiah in a rebuilt temple and an Aaronic priesthood. He also believed that the Sabbath as a day of rest would again be celebrated on Saturday instead of Sunday.[149] Some Jews had already begun to return to Palestine from Russia in 1882. Another writer in *De Hope*, E. Kropveld, believed that that event marked the beginning of the fulfillment of biblical prophecy.[150]

Premillennialist thought heightened interest in the question of how to interpret the return of Jews to Palestine. However, postmillennialists were interested in the possibility that their return was also a sign of the coming of the end of the age. Prior to 1920, midwestern pastors and theologians agreed that the Jews still had a role in God's plan of redemption, but they were not in agreement about what attitude one should take toward the Jews or how to interpret their return to Palestine. Nicholas Steffens withheld judgment. In 1911 he wrote that we must still wait and see whether the Jewish movement to Palestine was a fulfillment of prophecy. He was glad, however, that the Zionist movement had given up suggestions that the new land for the Jews be in Turkey or Uganda. He agreed that the establishment of

---

[148] Henry Utterwick, "De Hope Israels," *De Hope*, November 24, 1869. Utterwick (1841-1928) was a pastor in Vriesland, Michigan, at the time he wrote the article. Between 1872-1880 he was pastor of the Third Reformed Church in Holland, Michigan, after which he accepted a call to a Congregational church.

[149] John Van Der Meulen, "De aanstaande Besnijdenis der Heidenen," *De Hope*, August 4, 1875.

[150] E. Kropveld, "De Treurtochte der Joden naar het land hunner Vaderen," *De Hope*, July 12, 1882.

Jewish colonies in Palestine was the best solution to providing a land in which they could live.[151] However, fulfillment of prophecy would require the Jews to adopt the Hebrew language, something that had not yet happened.[152]

Steffens hoped for the day when the Jews would again take their place among the nations of the world.[153] He believed that Hosea 3:4-5 tells us that the future of the Jews has not come to an end. In 1910, they were still dispersed around the world and despised because of their rejection of Christ. Moreover, in Steffens judgment the God being taught to the Jews by the rabbis was not the God of Israel who has been revealed in Jesus Christ. Steffens was confident, however, that a time would come when the Jews would turn to Jesus as their Messiah. Therefore, he encouraged support for Jewish mission because such mission had a future.[154]

In opposition to the twentieth-century dispensationalists, Albertus Pieters taught that, following the rejection of Jesus by the Jews, they were replaced by the church as the seed of Abraham. "Their national existence had come to an end with the destruction of Jerusalem."[155] The rabbis meeting at the Council of Jamnia (90 A.D.) acted without authority from God by exalting "above measure all the provisions of the Mosaic law that could serve their purpose...."[156] "No prophetic voice directed them to set themselves up as the heads of the Jewish people. They did it of their own mind and on their own authority absolutely. It was a movement not of God but of men."[157]

The way for the Jews to be restored to the community of Abraham is now the same as for the rest of humankind. It is the way of faith in Christ. It is faith as an individual act, not a corporate act.[158]

Pieters taught that the Jews as a nation through their disobedience have forfeited their right to any future fulfillment of the promises in the Old Testament. Therefore, the question about the establishment

---

[151] Gerhard De Jonge in 1921 called attention to the fact that those who support the return of Jews to Palestine must not forget that large numbers of Arabs have been and are living there. The Arabs were likely to suffer on account of Jewish colonization of the land ("Wekelijksch Budget," *De Hope*, April 26, 1921).

[152] Nicholas Steffens, "De Zionisten in Palestina," *De Hope*, October 31, 1911.

[153] Steffens, "Wekelijksch Budget," *De Hope*, May 20, 1891.

[154] Steffens, "De Toekomst der Joden," *De Hope*, August 16, 1910.

[155] Pieters, *The Seed of Abraham*, 136.

[156] Ibid., 134.

[157] Ibid., 135.

[158] Ibid., 148.

of the state of Israel is a political question, not one of the fulfillment of prophecy. Pieters as a biblical scholar could make no forecast about whether such a state should or would be formed. He concluded,

> No doubt God has His plans for this new development, as for the whole course of affairs in the world, but as students of prophecy it is our task to determine what He has revealed concerning such plans; and whether this new state become permanent or not, we are still sure that no such thing is to be found in the scriptures.[159]

Pieters's exposition of the apocalyptic biblical material was developed almost entirely in reaction to the aggressive presence of dispensationalist Christian preachers and teachers who based their exposition on the Scofield Reference Bible, 1917 edition. In his firm conviction that the Jews as a nation after their rejection of Christ no longer had any place in God's plan of salvation, he was moving in a direction few of his predecessors had taken. Most of them had followed Steffens in leaving open the question about the continuing role of the Jews. In one way or another, they were ready to wait and see. However, the reputation of Pieters among his students as a teacher and scholar and the clarity of his writings for the members of the church carried the day in the Reformed Church in America for decades.

[159] Ibid.

# CHAPTER 7

# New Perspectives on the Old Faith

The year 1966 marks the end of this study of the history of theology in the midwestern theology of the Reformed Church in America. The date has been selected not only because it rounds off one hundred years of theological thought, but especially because it is not possible to discuss the theology of the midwestern Reformed Church after 1966 in relative isolation from the theology of the Reformed Church in the eastern states or Canada.[1]

[1]  For the past two decades, Donald Luidens and Roger Nemeth have been publishing results of their research in demographic and attitudinal changes in the Reformed Church in America. Their period of study covers the years from 1966 to the present. For their latest book, published jointly with two representatives of the Christian Reformed Church, see Corwin Smidt, Donald Luidens, James Penning, and Roger Nemeth, *Divided by a Common Heritage: The Christian Reformed Church and the Reformed Church in America at the Beginning of the New Millennium,* Historical Series of the Reformed Church in America, no. 54 (Grand Rapids: Eerdmans, 2006). Their social profile of the Reformed Church in America records that in the year 2000, 59 percent of Reformed Church members resided in the Midwest and 29 percent in the East, with the remainder living in the rest of the United States and

After 1966 the Reformed Church in America had to wrestle with a whole series of issues that were just becoming apparent. Among these issues were the rise of the charismatic movement, the ordination of women, the impact of Supreme Court decisions regarding human sexuality and abortion, and concern for the physical environment. Conscientious objection by young men during the Viet Nam War forced the General Synod to wrestle with the extent to which the denomination should stand behind such young men. While in 1966 most of those issues were in the background, during the period 1947-1966 new perspectives on the old faith were emerging that would help the denomination wrestle creatively with the new issues for faith and theology.

During the period 1947-1966, the only journal that remained specifically midwestern in the Reformed Church was the *Western Theological Seminary Bulletin*, which was renamed *Reformed Review* in 1955. Because of the decline in the use of the Dutch language, wider community contacts on the part of those who grew up in the Dutch enclaves, and lack of money during the Great Depression, there was no longer adequate support for the continuation of *De Hope* and the *Leader*. They were both united with the eastern Reformed Church paper, the *Christian Intelligencer*, in 1934 to become the *Intelligencer-Leader*. In 1943 the name of the paper was changed to the *Church Herald* with the mandate to serve the entire denomination. It is significant that when economic conditions improved after World War II there was no interest in again publishing a paper that would meet the specific needs of the midwestern Reformed Church.[2] Apart from the *Western Theological Seminary Bulletin*, which was first published in 1947, the midwestern Reformed Church no longer had any publications that provided a unifying forum for midwestern life and thought.

---

Canada (47). In that year, 50 percent of the church's membership had a heritage of Dutch ethnicity and 15 percent German (48). They conclude that older differences between the East and the Midwest have not entirely disappeared, but that on the whole Reformed Church lay people are much less Reformed in their doctrinal positions than their Christian Reformed Church counterparts.

Whereas 74 percent of Christian Reformed parishioners can be classified as subscribing to Reformed doctrine based on their level of agreement to the three questions relating to Reformed theology in Table 3.4, less than half that number (44 percent) of the Reformed Church in America laity fall within that grouping, with only 24 percent of RCA laity in the East being so classified (70).

[2]    The Dutch language paper, *De Volkvriend*, continued publication in Orange City, Iowa, until 1951.

## Three Responses to New Challenges after World War II

In the years immediately following the end of World War II, the premillenialist expectation that human history would soon reach its end with the Second Coming of Christ took a secular turn in the nation at large. During the period 1947-1966, the atomic bomb had the capacity to bring civilization to an end. Those who were in elementary school in the early 1960s still remember how civil defense drills taught them to crawl under their desks to find a safe place from a bomb attack. In 1962 the Roman Catholic writer, John A. O'Brien, opened his book with the observation:

> We are a "shook up" generation living in an anxious age. We have the unenviable distinction of living in a day when, for the first time in history, it is possible to destroy civilization and annihilate the human race within a few weeks. Faced with the threat of multi-megaton hydrogen bombs, intercontinental missiles and radioactive fallout, we are tense, jittery and scared stiff.[3]

The midwestern Reformed Church in America shared the anxieties of the "shook up" generation. Louis Benes, editor of the *Church Herald*, reflected the anxieties of many in the Reformed Church when he wrote a review of Dr. Wilbur M. Smith's book, *This Atomic Age and the Word of God*.[4] Benes urged his readers to heed the call of Smith to reflect more upon the existence of the atomic bomb as a sign that the return of the Lord is imminent. Smith pointed out how many passages in the Word of God were pointing to what was now on the horizon.

> Dr. Smith describes the seemingly inevitable trend toward "one World," toward internationalism, and World Government....It

---

[3]  John A. O'Brien, *Eternal Answers for an Anxious Age* (Englewood Cliffs, N.J.: Prentice-Hall, 1962), 1.

[4]  The 363-page book published by Moody Press was available at Reformed bookstores. Wilbur M. Smith had moved to the newly established Fuller Theological Seminary from Moody Bible Institute in Chicago in 1947. He was highly respected in the midwestern Reformed Church as the writer of *Peloubet's Select Notes on the International Sunday School Lessons*. The annual editions were given a paragraph review in the *Church Herald* each year and always recommended by the reviewer. The notes were "conservative, comprehensive, constructive, full of information" (Clarence P. Dame, *Church Herald*, January 19, 1945, 27). Smith was a dispensationalist as well as a premillenialist. For more information on Wilbur M. Smith, see George M. Marsden, *Reforming Fundamentalism: Fuller Seminary and the New Evangelicalism* (Grand Rapids: Eerdmans, 1987), 69-75.

The Rev. Louis H. Benes, D.D.
(1906-1978)

*Courtesy of JoAnn Benes*

"When I arrived on the scene twenty-nine years ago the Reformed Church did not have much *esprit de corps*. It was ashamed of its size, unaware of its heritage and uncertain about its future. In many places, in fact, it was considered fashionable to bury the word *Reformed* just as in other places it was considered best to conceal all traces of a Dutch background. Slowly, sometimes painfully, that has all changed and in my opinion the *Church Herald* has had much to do with the change....We have begun to see that none of these things hinders our possible contribution to the life of the ecumenical church"—Howard Hageman, "The Old Order Changeth," *Church Herald*, January, 10, 1975

would mean loss of national sovereignty, a world police force, a world economic authority, world education, and ultimately, some believe and hope, a world religion. Such world education is frightening, for it is certainly not going to make Christ preeminent.[5]

Paradoxically, the period 1947-1966 was a time of optimism in the country. Employment was usually high. People were able to purchase appliances, cars, and houses that were not available during the war years. The birth rate led to the phenomenon of the baby boom generation. Young families flocked to the new suburbs. The

[5]    Benes, "God's Word and our Age," *Church Herald*, July 23, 1948, 4. The Rev. Dr. Louis Benes, Jr. (1906-1978) was a graduate of Hope College and Western Theological Seminary. After serving as pastor of Reformed Church in America congregations in New York, Michigan, and California, he was editor of the *Church Herald* from 1945-1974.

membership of churches grew and Sunday schools enrolled a record number of children.

Three major responses arose simultaneously in the Reformed Church in America to the challenges of the era. In one response, it appointed a minister of evangelism to assist the denomination in calling for a revival of faith in America. In a second response, it linked the doctrine of election to its doctrine of mission and encouraged renewed dedication to church extension in America. In a third response, an eschatological perspective permeated the Reformed doctrine of election.

### (1) The Call for Revival in America

It was not the threat of the atomic bomb that attracted the most attention of writers in the *Church Herald*. There were three other dangers that called forth many editorials, news reports, articles, and letters to the editor. These were the growing power of the Roman Catholic Church in America, the international threat of communism, and the erosion of the faith and the Christian character of America. The third was perceived to be the greatest danger.[6] During the four-year period, 1947-1950, the *Church Herald* included more than six major articles and editorials annually about the threats of Rome and communism, in addition to innumerable brief new notes and comments in articles not related directly to the subject at hand.[7] Benes feared that within one or two decades Roman Catholicism would replace Protestantism as the dominant religion in America. Particular threats included Roman Catholic political pressure on governments to give aid to education in its parochial schools[8] and to appoint an American envoy to the Vatican.[9]

---

[6]    Benes, "No Longer a Protestant Country," *Church Herald*, March 25, 1955, 6-7.

[7]    Fear of the growing power of Rome had been fueled by the books written by Paul Blanshard. The first edition of his book, *American Freedom and Catholic Power*, published in 1949, went into twenty-six printings and sold a total of 240,000 copies [2nd ed. (Boston: Beacon Press, 1958), facing title page]. Titles of articles and news reports in the *Church Herald* included "Mexican Protestants ask Tolerance" (October 31, 1947, 3), "What about Protestant-Catholic Marriages" (October 10, 1947, 7), "Freedom of Religion" (July 16, 1948, 4), "What does Rome Want?" (September 9, 1949, 6), "Intolerance of Rome in Quebec 'Everywhere the Same'" (September 8, 1950, 4).

[8]    Editorials and "Religion in the News" notes October 17, 1947, 6-7; October 31, 1947, 3; March 25, 1949, 3; April 29, 1949, 6.

[9]    See for examples, "Warn Vatican Envoy May Cause National Disunity," November 10, 1950, 12; "No Vatican Ambassador," November 2, 1951, 6-7.

Immediately after World War II, Louis Benes was somewhat favorable toward maintaining a positive relationship with the Soviet Union. In "Comments on the News" he wrote that he was pleased that Henry Wallace had spoken out against war hysteria about Russia. He took note of Wallace's "religiously rooted social idealism" and commented that it is the soundest realism that we must live in the same world with Russia.[10] When the Cold War broke out, writers in the *Church Herald* were strong supporters of a "get tough" policy with communism and called it a "menace."[11]

Benes believed that the House of Representatives' Un-American Activities Committee was on the right track when it required loyalty oaths from teachers and others, because he feared the subversive forces of Communists.[12] He wrote that Wheaton College president V. Raymond Edman had acted correctly when he supported the requirement that faculty members sign the loyalty oath as well as students who were obtaining college loans.[13]

Benes believed that positive steps should be taken in response to communism. A more just social and economic order must be established everywhere. Wherever possible, democratic systems that illustrate the precious heritage of freedom must be built up. It was also important to develop the protective force against communism that was envisioned in the Atlantic Pact of the free nations of America and Europe. Benes criticized the Foreign Missions Conference (in which the RCA Board of Foreign Missions participated) that had undertaken to speak for Protestantism in its opposition to the pact.[14]

Benes was opposed to those Protestants who argued that the Roman Catholic Church was the bulwark against communism. He agreed that some Protestant groups had drifted so far away from the New Testament gospel that they had become primarily proponents of social reform and economic change and were ready to travel with Communists. Nevertheless, he thought that the Roman Catholic

[10]  *Church Herald*, October 4, 1946, 3. Henry Wallace had been vice-president under Franklin D. Roosevelt, 1941-1945, and then secretary of commerce in Harry Truman's cabinet. He resigned from that position in 1946 because he opposed Truman's "get tough" policy toward Russia. Born in Adair County, Iowa, in 1888, Wallace was popular in the rural Midwest because of his support for favorable farm policies while serving on the staff of *Wallace's Farmer* (1910-1928) and *Wallace's Farmer and Iowa Homestead* (1928-1933).
[11]  Benes, "The Communist Menace," *Church Herald*, July 29, 1949, 6-7.
[12]  Benes, "Loyalty Oaths," *Church Herald*, July 18, 1952, 6.
[13]  Benes, "Editorial," *Church Herald*, January 1, 1960, 7.
[14]  Benes, "Communism—A World Threat," *Church Herald*, September 2, 1949, 4.

Church was actually more vulnerable to communism than were such Protestants. Because of its papal system, Rome's totalitarian structure created the preconditions for communism.

> Rome's grasp for political power makes very obvious that it is not solely a religious institution, and its use of that political power through the centuries has frequently crushed both the souls and bodies of men....Rome has never allowed people to think for themselves, but has instead taught and developed a slavish obedience to her own decrees. Communism has capitalized on this pre-conditioning.[15]

The third and perhaps greatest danger facing the church was the erosion of the faith and the Christian character of America. The signs of decay were all around. Prohibition had been repealed in 1933. Sunday was being taken away from the churches and given to commercial and recreational interests. Sexual immorality was increasing, as was the frequency of divorce. Bible reading and prayer in the public schools were being abolished. Benes perceived it to be a time of great danger to the Christian faith in America. Harold Englund, in his *Church Herald* column, declared that those who were afraid were not simply victims of paranoia; the peril was real. These were times that sounded like Armageddon. It was time to emphasize a ministry of prayer.[16] The old postmillenial confidence that history was moving toward the arrival of Christ's kingdom on earth was in disarray.

Even though many new church buildings were being erected and the number of church members was growing after World War II, there was great anxiety about the moral state of the country and its churches. Louis Benes wrote that there could be no argument about whether America needed a revival. If a revival did not come soon, he wrote,

---

[15]  Benes, "Our Bulwark Against Communism," *Church Herald*, April 1, 1949, 6. During the 1950s some of the most intense debate on the floor of the annual meetings of the Reformed Church General Synod were occasioned by the constant repetition in editorials and articles in the *Church Herald* of the dangers of communism, especially in the years when McCarthyism was dominant in American political life. There was also considerable opposition to the magazine's continuing crusade against the power of the Roman Catholic Church, especially in eastern congregations where former Roman Catholics had become members of the Reformed Church following marriage to a Protestant.

[16]  Harold Englund, "Focus on the World: Community of Fear," *Church Herald*, March 10, 1961, 8, 23. Englund (1923- ) was acting president of Western Theological Seminary from 1960-1962.

we will inevitably travel down the road of spiritual degeneration and moral decay, to the end that befell Sodom and Gomorrah. The love of pleasure, the love of this present evil world, and the "lust of the flesh, the lust of the eyes, and the pride of life" are rotting away our moral and spiritual foundation....Unless, in the gracious providence of God, some mighty counter-action is set in motion, America is doomed.[17]

Not only America as a nation, but its churches needed revival, Benes wrote. Too many had lost their passion for Christ and the gospel. Too many were contented and complacent and did not care about the millions of the lost who were living and dying without Christ. "We are satisfied to be religious on Sunday, for a few hours, in the Church building. But the battle for Christ and His Truth and Righteousness must be brought out into the open, into the street and market place, to claim every sphere of life for God."[18]

In recognition of the need for revival in America, the Reverend Dr. Jacob Prins, a highly respected midwestern pastor, was called to be the denomination's first minister of evangelism in 1945.[19] He was a graduate of Hope College and Western Theological Seminary. He was an excellent preacher and spoke the spiritual language of the Midwest, yet he was broad enough in outlook to be acceptable to the churches in the East as well.

In their prayers for a great revival in America, midwestern Reformed Church members were in tune with evangelical Protestants in the country. They listened to radio evangelists and supported Christian youth rallies. During World War II, the "Old Fashioned Revival Hour" led by evangelist Charles Fuller was heard by twenty million people each Sunday evening. A high percentage of them were not members of any church.[20] Inter-Varsity Christian Fellowship came from Britain to begin its Christian ministry to college and university students in 1941. Youth for Christ began holding its impressive youth rallies in cities during

[17]  Benes, "Are We Ready for Revival?" *Church Herald*, April 21, 1950, 6.
[18]  Ibid.
[19]  Jacob Prins (1898-1975) served as minister of evangelism from 1945-1959, with a short break when he served Hope College in church relations. He had served previously as pastor of Reformed churches in Michigan and Iowa.
[20]  George Marsden, *Reforming Fundamentalism*, 14-15. Many enthusiastic articles were published in the *Church Herald* in support of the evangelistic campaigns of Billy Graham; see for example, Benes, "Billy Graham in New York," March 15, 1957, 6-7. Many Reformed churches in New York cooperated in sponsoring the campaign there.

The Rev. Jacob Prins, D.D.
(1888-1975)

*Courtesy of Joint Archives of Holland*

"Dr. Prins was called to the position of Minister of Evangelism by his denomination as a result of his deep devotional life, his knowledge of the Bible, and his marked preaching ability. The common testimony has been from those who have heard him that there is something about his personality and spirit that leads one into the very presence of God and a deep experience of the meaning of Jesus Christ." —Doris Kipp, ed. "First Reformed Church News," monthly newsletter of the First Reformed Church in Hudson, New York, in JAH files.

World War II.[21] One of its leaders, Jack Wyrtzen, preached on the radio in New York City and several times drew more than twenty thousand young people to rallies in Madison Square Garden. Another radio evangelist, Percy Crawford, preached to seventy thousand at Soldier Field in Chicago on Memorial Day, 1945. Youth for Christ had hired a young man, Billy Graham, to be its first full-time evangelist.[22]

While supporting evangelistic efforts under the leading of such men as Charles Fuller, Jack Wyrtzen, and Billy Graham, Prins chose to promote "Through-the-Year Evangelism" that had strong roots in the life of a congregation. He believed that evangelism does not mean whipping up enthusiasm periodically but instead requires

---

[21] Youth for Christ was welcomed by many midwestern Reformed churches. The Rev. Spencer C. De Jong resigned as pastor of Emmanuel Reformed Church to carry out a Youth for Christ ministry in the Netherlands after leading a successful Youth for Christ tour there. He reported following the tour, "The Team is back in the United States now with a thrilling story of the outpouring of the Holy Spirit. Never in our Christian experience have we seen God move with such tremendous sweeping power. It was like Pentecost come down" (Spencer C. De Jong, "Youth for Christ Team Reports on Holland Tour," *Church Herald*, January 31, 1947, 4).

[22] Marsden, *Reforming Fundamentalism*, 51.

sustained effort by people who have a real, vital faith. Through-the-Year Evangelism was consistent with Reformed doctrine, which maintains that individual believers must be united in the visible body of Christ, where the preaching of the Word and celebration of the sacraments are carried on regularly.[23]

Prins taught that evangelism involved calling people to repent and yield themselves to Christ. Each individual must open his or her heart to the Lord. "The new world for which we long and pray, calls for new men and women, regenerated by the Holy Spirit. If God's Kingdom is to come, it must first come into individual hearts. Unless His Kingdom comes into individual hearts and lives, it will never come. Am I willing to have Him rule in my heart?"[24] Revitalized members were invited to sign a pledge to be more faithful in the study of God's Word and more faithful as doers of the Word. They pledged to be loyal to their church with their prayers, their presence at worship, their financial gifts (preferably a tithe), and with their service in one or more organizations of the church. They also pledged to seek to win at least one person to Christ and his church during the year, to be willing to teach in the Bible school, to sing in the choir, and to serve as a church visitor to those outside the church.[25]

The call for revival in America was a constant theme of writers in the *Church Herald*. However, the idea that a revitalized organized church should become directly involved in the social issues of the day was rejected firmly by the magazine's editor. In the spirit of his statement that the battle for Christ and his truth must be brought into the open, into the street and into the marketplace, Benes was adamant that it was not the role of the church to become involved in "secondary matters" concerning labor relationships, economic programs, and social betterment. "The Church must be the Church!...For when an organized church ceases to be the Church of the living God, believing and obeying His Word, she becomes something else, a social club, an economic forum, or a religious society."[26] It is not the responsibility of the church to intervene as an ecclesiastical organization in labor issues.

23    Jacob Prins, "Toward the Evangelization of America," *Church Herald*, November 14, 1952.
24    Jacob Prins, "Revitalized Lives in Me and through Me," *Church Herald*, April 23, 1948, 7.
25    Ibid. Each of the Reformed Church ministers who succeeded Jacob Prins in the office of evangelism developed a distinctive program to stimulate evangelistic efforts. The unifying theme that ran through the following decades was evangelism based in the life of a witnessing congregation.
26    "The Church in the Economic Order," *Church Herald*, September 1, 1950, 4.

"It is rather to bring the laboring man to Jesus Christ, and to produce and mold under God, such laboring men as will effectively influence their environment for Christ and His Church."[27] The Christian member of the labor union can give his testimony by opposing the use of the Sabbath for labor union meetings, all day outings and important elections.[28]

With regard to the relation of the church to social policy, Benes insisted that the primary aim of the church is to reach individuals with the gospel of Jesus Christ and to bring them into the church. The secondary task is to build each other up in the faith. Included in the building up is the doing of good individually and socially.[29] Because Benes spoke for many in the midwestern Reformed Church, believers were left pretty much on their own to deal with the larger Christian ethical and social issues. At a time when many contended that the Protestant faith was eroding rapidly in America, the only hope offered was that God would somehow bring about a remarkable revival in the land through converted individuals.[30]

One can question how it came about that during the 1950s there was such an emphasis among American evangelicals on the erosion of faith and the need for revival, while it was also the decade when the percentage of Americans who were church members reached an all-time high. One answer might be that it was the liberal, mainline denominations that were experiencing especially rapid gains in membership. Evangelicals were suspicious that much of the religiosity

[27]  Ibid.
[28]  Ibid.
[29]  Ibid. Benes's position reflected his agreement with other American evangelicals such as Harold Lindsell, who was teaching at Fuller Theological Seminary at the time. See Marsden, *Reforming Fundamentalism*, 84-85.
[30]  The evaluation of Benes's stance on social issues applies chiefly to his position prior to 1963. Benes's stance on the matter of involvement of the church and individual believers on matters of public policy and action in issues such as race, civil rights, and war, is discussed later in this chapter. In 1975, when Benes retired as editor of the *Church Herald*, Howard Hageman assessed his contribution much more positively. Hageman wrote:

> The Reformed Church today is more alive to the outstanding social issues of the world in which in it lives and ministers. I think this is a result, to a large degree, of the leadership of the [*Church*] *Herald*. I am thinking of strong editorial stands that were taken on such questions as civil rights, South Africa, the situation in our cities, to name only a few. Of course, the General Synod made pronouncements on all of them, but in all honesty how many people read the minutes of the General Synod? (*Church Herald*, January 10, 1975, 26).

was "nominal" rather than real.[31] In advocating greater efforts to bring about revival, it was also useful to emphasize any signs of the erosion of religion in America.

### (2) The Link between Election and the Missionary Calling of the Church in America

In his book, *The Road Ahead*, the Reverend Dr. John Piet,[32] professor of English Bible and missions at Western Theological Seminary, called attention to the need for linking the doctrine of election to the missionary calling of the church. Election must not only look back to a decree of election of individuals, but also look forward to God's ultimate purpose for the world. He called attention to God's call of Abraham (Gen. 12:1-3) and commented, "In order to have meaning, however, election must have a forward as well as a backward look. It must result in purpose, and this purpose must encompass a circle wider than the elected one."[33] The election of Israel had mission as its purpose. "Israel believed that God chose her in order to be His people, living His way in the world, and thus to be a blessing to other nations."[34] Turning to the New Testament, Piet taught that individual election takes place

31  It was not only evangelicals who were suspicious. In 1960, Gabriel Vahanian, who was in the neo-orthodox tradition following Karl Barth, was critical of the rapid increase in church membership and American religiosity during the 1950s. He wrote in the forward to his book, "Presenting, then, the case for a new Christian culture which is made by certain contemporary Christian thinkers, I try to show how and why our civilization contradicts this case, its imperiousness to Christianity, its cultural incapacity for, as well as disavowal of, God. From this point of view the so-called religious revival of the preceding decade marks the transition from the Christian to the post-Christian era..." [Gabriel Vahanian, *The Death of God: The Culture of our Post-Christian Era* (New York: George Braziller, 1961], xxxiii.

32  John H. Piet (1914-1992) was born in Grand Rapids, Michigan. He graduated from Hope College and Western Theological Seminary. He taught at Western Theological Seminary from 1960 to 1984, after serving as a missionary in India from 1940-1960. In India, he adopted the newspaper evangelism technique pioneered by Albertus Pieters. He emphasized Bible distribution combined with correspondence course lessons on the gospels, designed for Hindu and Muslim students. He was also active in establishing new congregations.

33  John Piet, *The Road Ahead: A Theology for the Church in Mission* (Grand Rapids: Eerdmans, 1970), 40. Although *The Road Ahead* was published in 1970, its themes were present in his classroom teaching much earlier. His book also resonated in the life of the church because it gave articulation to what leaders in the church extension and mission programs of the Reformed Church had already been promoting since World War II.

34  Ibid., 44.

The Rev. John H. Piet, Ph. D.
(1914-1992)

*Courtesy of Western Theological Seminary*

John Piet's ministerial career began as a missionary in India (1940-1960) and then continued as professor of English Bible and missions at Western Theological Seminary (1960-1984), after which he served as a pastor of congregations in Nepal and Japan until 1989. With his incisive mind and sound theological judgment, he was an inspiring teacher who never lost his missionary zeal. "Convinced that in India, where ninety-seven percent of the population is non-Christian, evangelism should have top priority in the church, he extended himself in that area of service....He taught future catechists and evangelists in the Arcot Theological Seminary in Vellore and guided pastors, teachers and others in spreading the good news of Jesus Christ....By character Dr. Piet has always been straightforward and honest in his dealings with others, never hesitating to express what he believes to be right."—J. Sam Ponniah, Bishop in Vellore, India, *Reformed Review*, 37/3 (Spring, 1984) 113.

in the wider covenantal context of the Old Testament. "And in Romans 8:28-31, Paul teaches that God calls individuals to salvation. Individual election, however, is not an isolated thing. It takes place within the context of God's people, and its purpose is to implement the intention of God for His people."[35]

Unfortunately, according to Piet, in the age of the Protestant Reformation the reformers discovered that they had to defend their claim to be the true church by showing why they believed the Roman Catholic Church to be a false church. "Secessionist parties must, therefore, establish that *they*, not the main body, preach the Word rightly, administer the sacraments purely, and exercise discipline for punishing sins."[36] Piet charged that the need of Protestants to draw a clear line between the "true church" and the papal Roman Catholic that was the "false church" created an introverted mentality. It also

[35]    Ibid., 45.
[36]    Ibid., 26.

encouraged each Protestant church to give priority to defending its own creed and polity against those of other churches. This intense interest in their own church tradition against the claims of other churches encouraged competition and defensive attitudes that stand in contrast to "what New Testament writers say. Their concern was mission, which means that it is mission primarily and not Christian differences which govern what New Testament writers say about the body of Christ."[37]

Piet pointed out that because the writers of the three Standards of Unity all found it necessary to define the church over against other churches, they do not deal seriously with the missionary purpose of the church. They have a static view of the church, according to which some particular doctrine is applicable among Christians but not operable in the world. However, in the context of the pluralistic nature of the modern world, "the stance of the church must change. The church must look to God and to the world and find its reason for being as God's people in God's world."[38]

Piet reflected the growing consciousness of the midwestern churches that it was crucial to reach out to people outside their traditional ethnic community.[39] In the second half of the twentieth century, the midwestern Reformed Church caught up with the eastern region's recognition of its responsibility to preach the gospel and establish congregations among the broader American population, rather than confine itself to ethnic Dutch communities. The eastern Reformed Church in America had begun as early as 1788 to carry out church planting activities in New York, Kentucky, Pennsylvania, and Canada. In the first half of the nineteenth century, it had planted new congregations in Illinois, Michigan, and Iowa.[40]

---

[37]    Ibid., 28.

[38]    Ibid., 29. For a call to reinterpret the "introverted" position of the Heidelberg Catechism and Church Order so that "the biblical concept of evangelism and mission as being essential to the ministry of the Spirit and the life of the church" is no longer absent, see Eugene Heideman, "God the Holy Spirit," in Donald J. Bruggink, ed., *Guilt, Grace, and Gratitude,* 112-15.

[39]    John Piet had advocated planting new congregations in America already when he was a seminary student in 1934 and 1935, when he and other students supported the Rev. Clarence P. Dame's call for more churches in his address given in Chicago March 25, 1935; see Eugene Heideman, *A People in Mission: Their Expanding Dream* (New York: Reformed Church Press, 1984), 46-47.

[40]    Ibid., 11-26. For a list of the congregations organized prior to 1851, see Russell L. Gasero, *Historical Directory of the Reformed Church in America,* Historical Series of the Reformed Church in America, no. 37 (Grand Rapids: Eerdmans, 2001), 669-74.

As late as 1910, the policy of the midwestern Reformed classes had been to "follow the Hollander" in organizing new congregations.[41] For that reason, the first congregation was organized among Reformed Hollanders in Monarch, Alberta, Canada, in 1908; in Washington State, beginning in 1917; in California, beginning in 1924; and in Florida, beginning in 1955. It also followed Dutch immigrants into Canada after World War II, beginning in Edmonton, Alberta, in 1944.[42]

When the denomination began organizing congregations in the new suburbs that were being built after World War II, the midwestern as well as the eastern classes soon recognized that denominational identity could not always be given first priority. As early as 1924, the Reverend Klaas J. Dykema, classical missionary of the Classis of East Sioux, recognized that in ministering to the people in southern Minnesota, "denominationalism must be discarded. Loyalty to one's 'own church' is not always a virtue, and may be a sin. People should be told that any church is better than none....To save the country churchism must die."[43] After 1947, the church extension movement among those who were not ethnically Dutch gained momentum. The president of the General Synod in 1949 pointed out the urgency of the task in saving the country from paganism. "Either America is going to be drawn into paganism and finally be dominated by pagan forces, or the church of Christ must arise and commit herself to a nobler and more sacrificial program than heretofore...."[44] He went on to urge the denomination to accept its responsibility to plant churches in new communities: "We should not be negligent in any quarter that is assigned to us. America has hundreds of unchurched communities."[45]

[41]  Heideman, *People in Mission*, 40, 46.
[42]  Gasero, *Historical Directory*.
[43]  Klaas L. Dykema, "The Situation as I find it—A Survey in Southern Minnesota," *Christian Intelligencer and Mission Field*, December 3, 1924, 772, quoted in Heideman, *People in Mission*, 46. Klaas Dykema (1866-1940) was born in the Netherlands and graduated from Hope College and New Brunswick Theological Seminary. He served congregations in North Dakota, Kansas, Iowa, New Jersey, New York, Michigan, and South Dakota. For a very brief survey of the work of Reformed Church extension, 1924-1960, see Heideman, *People in Mission*, 46-49.
[44]  The Rev. Henry Beltman, "Report on the State of Religion, R.C.A.," *Church Herald*, May 20, 1949, 8. Henry Beltman (1893-1984) served as a missionary in China, 1920-1928, and was pastor of congregations in Michigan, California, and Arizona. He was secretary of the Board of Domestic Missions, 1938-1942. He served as organizing pastor of several congregations and was one of the leading advocates in the denomination for planting new churches.
[45]  Ibid.

Although the number of new congregations being planted has varied from decade to decade, the denomination has continued to believe that its doctrine of election includes calling people to gather in the church to hear the gospel preached, to join in the celebration of the sacraments, and to submit themselves to mutual admonition and discipline. Presently in 2009, this calling to organize new congregations and revitalize old ones enjoys the highest priority.[46]

*(3) An Eschatological Perspective on the Old Doctrine of Election*

While the midwestern church was focused on revival and the planting of new congregations in new suburbs in America, professors at Western Theological Seminary and others, including eastern pastors Howard Hageman[47] and Isaac C. Rottenburg,[48] resisted both the pietistic individualism in the National Association of Evangelicals and the American liberal strand in the Federal Council of Churches.[49] They turned to the theological and liturgical works of the Reformation leaders, including especially John Calvin and Martin Bucer, and to developments in the churches in the Netherlands. The renewal of Reformed theology in the Netherlands Reformed Church (NHK) and the Reformed Churches in the Netherlands (GKN) gave an eschatological perspective to the old theology of the Synod of Dort.[50]

---

[46]  *Acts and Proceedings*, 2006, 178-82.

[47]  The Rev. Dr. Howard G. Hageman (1921-1992) was perhaps the most influential Reformed Church leader in the last half of the twentieth century and equally respected in the eastern and midwestern regions of the church. His entire ministry was spent in the eastern region. He served two terms as president of the General Synod and was president of New Brunswick Theological Seminary from 1973-1985.

[48]  The Rev. Isaac C. Rottenberg (1925- ) was born in the Netherlands and studied at Hope College, Western Theological Seminary, and New Brunswick Theological Seminary. He was well read in Dutch and European theology and played a crucial role in helping the Reformed Church gain an appreciation for theological developments in the Netherlands Reformed Church during and after World War II.

[49]  The "liberal strand" was only one thread within the National Council of Churches. A number of denominations in the council, including the Reformed Church in America, would have been more likely to call themselves "evangelical" rather than "liberal."

[50]  The Synod of Dort set forth an understanding of the faith from the perspective of the decrees of God and predestination as described in chapter four of this book. It moved from God's act of creation to the end of the world with a strong emphasis upon God's providence determining all events.

The eschatological perspective grew out of renewal in biblical studies and led the Reformed Church in America by 1966 to revise its church order and liturgy and to consider writing a new confession of faith.

In 1957 M. Eugene Osterhaven, professor of systematic theology at Western Theological Seminary, wrote an article in the seminary's journal, the *Reformed Review,* to remind the church of an old Reformed slogan, *ecclesia reformata quia semper reformanda est* (the church reforming because it always needs reformation).[51] He called attention to the efforts of five ministers and professors in the Christian Reformed Church who had established the *Reformed Journal* in 1951. One of them, James Daane, maintained that the older works in theology were written for another day and do not confront present theological issues. Such older works when used in the present are "largely commonplace and repetitious, more defensive than offensive, more negative than positive."[52]

The Reformed theological understanding set forth in Louis Berkhof's *Systematic Theology* was consistent with what had been taught at Western Theological Seminary prior to World War II. That formulation was helpful in the Dutch Reformed immigrant enclaves in the nineteenth century, when ethnic immigrants from the nations of Europe were living in separate enclaves next to each other in the Midwest. When Dutch immigrants settled down and were establishing roots in America, their type of systematic theology with its clear definitions and defense of the status quo against outside temptations, such as the New Theology of Andover, could provide spiritual assurance and communal stability. However, that theology did not have adequate resources to deal with the rapidity of change in the contemporary world.

It is probable that after World War II no one in the Reformed Church in America was more knowledgeable about traditional Dutch Reformed theology than Eugene Osterhaven. There probably was no one who loved it more. But Osterhaven knew that love of that theology could be real love only so long as the church remained ready to recognize its own weaknesses. Love of the tradition could not allow the triumph of traditionalism. Osterhaven agreed with the editors of the *Reformed Journal* that the theology of the midwestern churches suffered

[51]  M. Eugene Osterhaven, "Quia Semper Reformanda est," *Reformed Review,* 11/1, (1957), 1.

[52]  Ibid., 4. The charge was made by James Daane, one of the editors of the *Reformed Journal,* in its first year, I, 7, 11. It is very possible that Daane had the book *Systematic Theology,* by Calvin Theological Seminary professor Louis Berkhof in mind. Berkhof's textbook followed the *Loci* structure and traditional definitions in theology that were discussed in chapter four.

The Rev. M. Eugene Osterhaven,
Th. D., (1915-2005)

*Courtesy of Western Theological Seminary*

"It is this 'living for God,' or 'doing everything out of a profound sense of the presence of God and the consecration of life to him' which is not only the 'central concept' for [M. Eugene] Osterhaven's understanding of the Reformed tradition (*The Spirit of the Reformed Tradition*, 7-80); it is also the hall-mark of his life-style which cannot be separated from his theology. Not only in the classroom and in the church, but also in the public arena—the schools, the community, and the Boy Scouts, to name only three areas where he has made special contributions—he has been active in seeking to do the will of the Lord."—I John Hesselink, "M. Eugene Osterhaven, Reformed Theologian," *Reformed Review*, 39/3 (1976).

from arrested development when they became either traditionalistic or pietistic. He wrote:

> Traditionalism viewed the theological enterprise as having been accomplished by previous generations of scholars. Its future lay behind it and it had lost the spirit of the Reformation. Pietism retained the Reformers' interest in renewal and reformation, but applied it only to the Church's practical religious life. All effort was concentrated on personal holiness and intensive concern with theology was considered detrimental to true piety. Traditionalism denied theology a living present; pietism divorced the mind of the church from its faith.[53]

Osterhaven pleaded for development of a Reformed theology that escaped the defensiveness of traditionalism and the inward focus of a truncated pietism.

> A preoccupation with our own homes, schools and churches so that we have little concern and no love for those outside our own circle may save us from considerable agony of spirit but is poor

[53]    Osterhaven, Ibid., 3-4.

Christianity and the exact opposite of *Reformed* Christianity with its famed social concern, magnanimity and responsibility.[54]

Between 1939 and 1952, the faculty at Western Theological Seminary underwent a generational change that gave to the seminary the kind of new perspective on the old faith and theology that Osterhaven had in mind. In 1939 Albertus Pieters retired. He was the last professor at the seminary who had learned Dutch before he learned English. Pieters was essentially a bridge between the generations. In his systematic theology and church history courses he continued to teach the old theology that the editors of the *Reformed Journal* thought was suffering from arrested development. However, he was not an uncritical traditionalist; he was a constant foe of legalistic pietism. In his major teaching areas of English Bible and world mission he did not allow traditional theological definitions to overwhelm careful biblical interpretation, especially in his rejection of the covenant of works in the Federal Theology of the Westminster Confession.

Lester J. Kuyper (1904-1986) became professor of Old Testament in 1939 [55] and Richard C. Oudersluys (1906- ) became professor of New Testament in 1942.[56] Their training in leading theological graduate schools made them aware of the importance of rigorous and detailed attention to the biblical text without allowing traditional theological language to overwhelm biblical language. Elton M. Eenigenberg (1915-1987) became professor of church history and ethics in 1952.[57] Eight years later, following the retirement of George Mennenga, John H. Piet was called from his ministry as a Reformed Church missionary in India to become professor of English Bible and missions, the same chair that had been held by Albertus Pieters. Osterhaven, Kuyper, Oudersluys, Eenigenberg, and Piet belonged to the same generation. They had

[54]  Osterhaven, *Quia Semper...*, 12.
[55]  Lester Kuyper was born in Rock Valley, Iowa, and graduated from Hope College and Western Theological Seminary. He earned his Th.D. Degree at Union Theological Seminary in New York. He was Old Testament professor from 1939-1974.
[56]  Richard Oudersluys was born in Grand Rapids, Michigan, and graduated from Calvin College and Western Theological Seminary. His Ph.D studies were carried out at the University of Chicago Divinity School. He was New Testament professor from 1942-1977.
[57]  Elton Eenigenberg was born in Chicago, Illinois, and graduated from Rutgers College and Western Theological Seminary. He earned his Ph.D. at Columbia University in New York City when Paul Tillich and Reinhold Niebuhr were teaching there. He taught at Western Theological Seminary from 1952-1985.

The Rev. Elton M. Eenigenberg,
Ph. D. (1915-1987)

*Courtesy of Western Theological Seminary*

Elton M. Eenigenberg's major field of teaching was Christian ethics and philosophy of religion (1952-1986). He served as academic dean of Western Theological Seminary for seventeen years. He served as a member of the General Synod's Committee on Revision of the Constitution from 1960-1969. "By virtue of continuity, competence and experience, as well as a mind trained in theology and ethics, Elton brought to the areas of parliamentary procedures and constitutional government an insistence that the work of the church should always be done 'decently and in order'....The Reformed Church in America has benefited in many and specific ways from his leadership and good judgment, enhancing the ordering of its life and the conduct of its business."—Dr. Marion De Velder, general secretary, Reformed Church in America, in "Elton Marshall Eenigenberg: General Synod: Parliamentarian and Constitutionalist," *Reformed Review*, 38/3 (1985), 188

been born between 1904 and 1915, prior to American involvement in World War I. They had graduated from Western Theological Seminary between 1928 and 1940. They shared the common experience of having lived through the Great Depression and World War II. With the exception of John Piet, they all served together on the faculty for more than twenty-five years.

Although there is no evidence that they made any conscious attempt to come to a common new perspective, by 1966 they had incorporated into their teaching an eschatological[58] perspective that represented a shift away from Reformed scholastic theology with its emphasis on the immutability of God and infralapsarian decrees of election and reprobation. An eschatological perspective means that one understands theology in terms of God's encounter with the world

---

[58]    In theology, the word eschatology is derived from the Greek word, "eschaton," which refers to "the last things." Traditionally, eschatology dealt with the return of Christ, the last judgment, and the ultimate destiny of souls and God's creation.

from the perspective of God's future purposes, rather than from the perspective of God's eternal and immutable decree before creation. Eugene Osterhaven wrote, "Eschatological theology means rather that God is coming to us out of his own predetermined future. If we are to understand him and his saving activity, we shall have to begin with the end."[59] It is from the Word of God rather than an analysis of providential human progress in history that we learn the nature of the kingdom of God. Osterhaven developed his definition more fully by quoting Professor A.A. Van Ruler, who taught theology at the National University of Utrecht in the Netherlands after World War II.

> In the light of the Word of God everything is directed towards his determined end; it is ordered and formed therefrom and can only be understood from it. Therefore in dogmatic [theology] thinking we must begin with the end and look backwards from there. Rather, we must *walk* backwards—to the cross, and—yet further back—to the beginning of creation and the fall. We move in the action of God which can only be understood from out of the end.[60]

The Reverend Dr. Richard C. Oudersluys taught his New Testament courses with an eschatological perspective.[61] He stated that all serious theological writing today is "based on the conviction that in the Old and New Testaments, all history and all life are to be understood with reference to an ultimate, divine redemptive-historical event."[62] According to the Old Testament, God's redemptive acts

---

[59]    Osterhaven, *The Faith of the Church: A Reformed Perspective on its Historical Development* (Grand Rapids: Eerdmans, 1982), 207.

[60]    Ibid., quoted from Arnold A. Van Ruler, *Theologie van het Apostolaat* (Nijkerk, Netherlands: Callenbach, 1948), 68.

[61]    For an evaluation of his life and ministry, see I. John Hesselink, "Richard C. Oudersluys: Biblical Scholar for a New Age," in *Saved by Hope*, ed. James I. Cook (Grand Rapids: Eerdmans, 1978), 1-14.

[62]    Oudersluys, "Eschatology and the New Testament" (lecture presented at Calvin Theological Seminary, September 25, 1963, on file in WT/JAH), 3. The "divine redemptive-historical event" was given the technical term, "*Heilsgeschichte*," by German scholars. Isaac Rottenberg pointed out that the nineteenth-century professors Crispell, Winter, and especially Steffens included a *Heilsgeschichte* element in their teaching. In his lecture, "Sacred Hisory, a Bulwark of our Christian Worldview," "The concept of redemptive history was important also in his polemics against a mechanistic-evolutionistic worldview..." Isaac Rottenberg, "Tendencies and Trends in a Century of Theological Education at Western Theological Seminary," *Reformed Review*, 20/2 (1966), 47.

The Rev. Richard C. Oudersluys,
D. D. (1906- )

*Courtesy of Western Theological Seminary*

"In the case of Richard Oudersluys there has been an ideal blending of solid scholarship, superior classroom performance, and a steady, significant contribution to the life and work of the church....He made major contributions during the 1960s to the Reformed Church's Commission on Liturgy, and during the 1970s to its Theological Commission. Another area of extended concern and involvement was the former Board of Domestic Missions. In particular he was interested in the work of the new immigrant churches in Canada and for several years was chairman of the Committee for Canadian Work. Thus there has never been a period when he was not actively involved in some phase of congregational as well as denominational church life."—I. John Hesselink, "Richard C. Oudersluys: Biblical Scholar for a New Age," in *Saved by Grace*, James I. Cook, ed., 1978, 9, 10.

did not evolve in the general course of events in ancient near eastern history. On the contrary, God broke into the course of human history by electing Abraham to be the father of many nations, by calling Moses to lead God's people out of Egypt, and finally by coming in Jesus Christ in fulfillment of Old Testament prophecies, "even more importantly, [by the] the fulfillment of God's saving purposes for his people and the world."[63]

Oudersluys pointed out that the eschatological perspective in biblical studies impelled scholars to interpret afresh every biblical event and every biblical doctrine.[64] This was particularly true for the doctrine

---

[63]    Hesselink, "Richard C. Oudersluys," 6.

[64]    In the WTS/JAH archives, Oudersluys attached a note to the manuscripts of his eschatology lectures. He wrote that he found a central organizing perspective for teaching New Testament theology. "I found it in eschatology with the help of Oscar Cullmann's 'Salvation-history theme' and Geerhardos Vos, *Pauline Eschatology.*" For a brief synopsis of Vos's approach to biblical theology, see James T. Dennison, Jr., *The Letters of Geerhardus Vos* (Phillipsburg, N.J.: P & R Publishing, 2005), 49-59.

of the kingdom of God. Modernist theology in the United States had emphasized the role of people of good will in bringing about the kingdom, but the traumatic events in Europe between 1914 and 1945 had led Europeans to a renewed grasp of the depth of human sin and depravity. Theologians such as Karl Barth and Emil Brunner interpreted the Bible to say that the kingdom would not come gradually by human action, but would break in by the action of God. Jesus himself was the kingdom. "But as Jesus Christ himself was God's gift, so the kingdom is a gift."[65] The kingdom of God is not some future Utopia; it is present in the world as yeast working in the dough. The kingdom is known by the signs of its presence. Jesus spoke of the kingdom by means of parables that set forth the nature, character, and coming of the kingdom. "It was the effective power of his kingship that came into view in his miracles as he forgave sins, healed the sick, raised the dead, drove back the demonic forces of darkness, and even subdued the destructive forces of nature."[66]

The eschatological perspective on the kingdom of God was especially important in devastated Europe, where many were tempted to despair and to wonder whether God was really sovereign in this world. Whereas the Reformation had emphasized faith and the nineteenth-century liberals had made love central, the eschatological perspective renewed study of the nature of Christian hope. The emphasis upon the need to be alert to the signs that God was still active and present among the ruins of the cities and the devastation of the countryside encouraged people to recognize the signs and to hope in God. After World War II, it was crucial to call attention to Christian hope in the face of an aggressive communism that was claiming to offer hope to the suffering millions on the continent.

The eschatological perspective had gained prominence in theological reflection after the appearance of Karl Barth's commentary on Romans in 1919, immediately following the devastation of World War I. Prior to that, however, he had already made an attack on theological liberalism in a lecture in 1916 entitled, "The Strange New World within the Bible." It is true, said Barth, that the Bible contains much history and some moral codes and religion, but if we go to it to fulfill our own historical, moral, or religious quests we will find it flat and unsatisfactory. Optimistic talk by liberals about the progress of the kingdom of God brought about by human activity seemed empty in the era of World War I. The Bible unveiled a strange new world because

---

[65]    Oudersluys, see note 64 above, 5.
[66]    Ibid.

there is revelation in the Bible and not human religion only. We find "in the Bible a new world, God, God's sovereignty, God's glory, God's incomprehensible love. Not the history of man, but the history of God!...Not human standpoints but the standpoint of God!"[67]

> It is not the right human thoughts about God which form the content of the Bible, but the right divine thoughts about men. The Bible tells us not how we should talk with God but what he says to us; not how we find the way to him, but how he has sought and found the way to us; not the right relation in which we must place ourselves to him, but the covenant which he had made with all who are Abraham's spiritual children and which he has sealed once and for all in Jesus Christ. It is this which is within the Bible. The word of God is within the Bible.[68]

As Karl Barth was becoming influential in Europe in the 1920s and 1930s, midwestern Reformed Church leaders were cautiously appreciative of his writings. In 1929 Siebe Nettinga called attention to Karl Barth and what was at that time called the "theology of crisis." He welcomed the movement as a turning away from the old optimism and for its protest against the "zeitgeist" and humanism of the age.[69]

John R. Mulder remained cautious about Barth and other German theologians. In 1941 he told his middler class at the seminary that Barth had made theology live again. Mulder especially welcomed Barth's strong criticism of theological liberalism. However, he was uncomfortable with Barth's and Emil Brunner's separation of revelation and history[70] and their finding the Word of God in the Bible while holding that the Bible itself is witness to revelation but not revelation itself. Mulder also objected to their emphasis on the transcendence of God at the expense of immanence and on the emphasis on divinity at the expense of humanity.[71]

Mulder wrote a broad survey of trends in modern theology for the *Western Seminary Bulletin* in May 1941. Following his criticism of the

---

[67] Karl Barth, *The Word of God and the Word of Man*, trans. Douglas Horton (Pilgrim Press, 1928), 44.

[68] Ibid., 43.

[69] Siebe Nettinga, "Wekelijksch Budget," *De Hope*, March 5, 1929, 6.

[70] For a brief exposition of Brunner's concept of history, see Eugene Heideman, *The Relation of Revelation and Reason in Herman Bavinck and Emil Brunner* (Assen, Netherlands: Van Gorcum, 1959), 69-79.

[71] John R. Mulder, Notes on Church History, Middler Class, 1941, in WTS/JAH.

liberal theologies of the nineteenth and twentieth centuries, he reflected on contemporary British and American theologians in relationship to Barth and the continental theologians. He observed that the time of progressive theological optimism was over. He listed the major English theologians in the 1940s—William Temple, Dean Inge, A. E. Taylor, and John Oman—and the major American theologians—Reinhold Niebuhr, Douglas Horton, John Bennet, and Edwin Lewis—and stated, "All these men believe sin to be a reality from which men must be saved, and that salvation is offered men in Christ the Savior." [72]

Mulder was critical of Barth for his total rejection of natural theology and strong eschatological perspective. Mulder preferred the work of Archbishop William Temple, who "speaks about God as revealing himself in Nature as well as in the Word. Temple concedes that Nature lies under the curse of sin, but he argues that, even while under that curse, Nature still speaks of God." [73] Mulder concluded his article by calling for a return to John Calvin, who "was not a transcendentalist, nor was he an immanentalist; he was both. Thus he could take the natural into his calculations as well as the supernatural." [74]

M. Eugene Osterhaven combined his admiration for the theology of John Calvin with a growing appreciation for the eschatological perspective that emerged in Europe after World War II. He turned to biblical language rather than the technical vocabulary of Reformed scholastics for his interpretation of the Belgic Confession. In his discussion of the list of the attributes of God in the Belgic Confession, he said that it is "beside our purpose" to comment on the volumes that have been written by theologians. He provided a biblical and pastoral interpretation of the attributes of God. God's infinity is "His limitlessness, the confession of which reminds us that we cannot flee from his presence (Psalm 139:7)." His immutability "means that He

---

[72] "Trends in Modern Theology," *Western Theological Seminary Bulletin*, I/1, (1947), 6.

[73] Ibid., 6.

[74] Ibid., 7. Mulder's preference for Temple over Barth represents a typical American response to neo-orthodox theology at the end of the 1940s. At that time American writers were still puzzled by the eschatological framework of neo-orthodox theology. For purposes of this book it is not necessary to enter into a discussion of the extent to which Mulder's criticism of Barth is accurate. It is sufficient to note that between 1929 and 1947 professors at Western Theological Seminary appreciated as well as criticized the new theological developments on the Continent. The leading American theologian of the 1930s through the 1950s, Reinhold Niebuhr, apparently had little impact upon the midwestern theologians and ministers.

is 'the same yesterday, today, and forever' (Heb.13:8)...and that He will remember His covenant forever." His justice is "His maintenance of the right and is best exhibited when He remains just and justifies those who believe in Jesus (Rom. 3:26)."[75]

Osterhaven agreed with Calvin that living in the presence of God (*coram Deo*) is fundamental in the life of the Christian. "As the doctrine of the Christian's union with Christ is central to Calvin's teaching on the application of salvation, this conception that man's whole *existence* is lived before the Lord forms the foundation of all his work."[76] For Osterhaven, doctrinal and biblical instruction had a crucial instrumental function. The doctrine of union with Christ was not an end in itself, but it was "a means to holy living before the face of God....The end is living in fellowship with God."[77] He admired a Puritanism that bears witness "to its concern for a daily walk with the Lord and the creation of a holy community."[78]

With his emphases upon living to the glory of God, living in the presence of God, and living in union with Christ, Osterhaven maintained a balance between the perspective of predestination that traces the course of salvation from the beginning to the end of the world, on the one hand, and the perspective of eschatology with its focus on God's reign breaking into the present order from out of God's own future, on the other hand.[79] He usually spoke of the way of salvation from the first perspective. He defended the Canons of Dort with their decree of election for their clear teaching that "Man's salvation is no afterthought with God, or an idea which He originates when He sees this man, or that one dying in sin. Instead, it is the execution of a predetermined plan made before the foundation of the

---

[75]   *Our Confession of Faith* (Grand Rapids: Baker, 1964), 26-27. Compare Osterhaven's pastoral definitions of the attributes of God with the more static definitions given by his predecessors, as included in chapter four above.

[76]   Osterhaven, *The Spirit of the Reformed Tradition* (Grand Rapids: Eerdmans, 1971), 91.

[77]   Ibid., 141.

[78]   Ibid.

[79]   For example, I [eph] studied the doctrine of God under Dr. Osterhaven in the fall term of 1951, when he used Herman Bavinck, *The Doctrine of God*, trans. William Hendrikson (Grand Rapids: Eerdmans, 1951), with a predestinarian perspective. Then in 1952-53 he used Emil Brunner, *Man in Revolt*, trans. Olive Wyon (Philadelphia: Westminster, 1947), for the course on anthropology and Brunner's *The Mediator* for the course on Christology. Brunner's books reflect the eschatological perspective.

world (Eph. 1:4ff)."[80] The history of salvation takes place according to God's plan. "The revelation of God [is] given first in the Garden and afterwards proclaimed through the patriarchs and the prophets, and finally fulfilled in the Son. That is to say, the gospel is no human achievement but altogether from God."[81]

The teachers at Western Theological Seminary believed that it was important to hold the doctrine of the corporate election of Israel and of the church to carry out God's redemptive mission in the world together with the Reformed emphasis on the election of the individual. It is important to recall John Piet's comment, "Individual election, however, is not an isolated thing. It takes place within the context of God's people, and its purpose is to implement the intention of God for His people."[82] The election of the individual is not only for the salvation of that person, but its purpose is fulfilled only when the one elected serves with and in the church through participation in God's mission for the salvation of the world. Richard Oudersluys confirmed Piet's conclusion in his article on eschatology and the Holy Spirit when he wrote:

> According to the Scripture, the first and primary associations of the Spirit are with Christ and his church. The *ordo salutis* is Christ, church, and then the Christian believer. Only when the Spirit's work in the individual is set in the light of these larger and primary relationships will we be enabled to see what is right and what is wrong with the individualism and Pentecostalism of our day.[83]

When the doctrines of predestination, election, and the *ordo salutis* are understood properly in their relationships to each other, it becomes clear that God's redemption of creation is not secondary to the salvation of the individual. The church in mission must be engaged

---

[80]  Osterhaven, *Our Confession of Faith*, 103.
[81]  Osterhaven, "Man's Deliverance," in *Guilt, Grace, and Gratitude*, ed. Donald J. Bruggink, 54. For Osterhaven's understanding of the doctrines of predestination, election, and reprobation, see also *The Faith of the Church*, 77-83; and *Our Confession of Faith*, 100-103. In *The Spirit of the Reformed Tradition*, he gave a definition of predestination: "Simply stated this doctrine means that God is sovereign Lord, who has determined whatever comes to pass, yet not so as to destroy the reality of man's free agency and responsibility," 101.
[82]  See note 35 above.
[83]  Oudersluys, "Eschatology and the Holy Spirit," *Reformed Review*, 4/2, (1965), 11.

in the task of evangelism and not neglect its calling to bear witness to the cultures of the world in their social, economic, psychological, recreational, and artistic activities. Isaac Rottenberg formulated this point in language heavy with the terminology of systematic theology:

> In the terminology of dogmatic theology we would say that the core of God's redemptive activity is to be found in the atonement, justification and reconciliation. They form the ground of redemption. In sanctification, however, and the transformation of existence we find the ultimate intentions of God with the world; namely, the expression of redemption in existence, the establishment of God's kingdom in the world. In other words, from the perspective of the kingdom of God and the renewal of all things, the converted heart is not more important than the "Christianized" culture.[84]

### Biblical Theology and the Inspiration of Scripture

The doctrine of the authority and infallibility of the Bible was one of the most sensitive issues facing the midwestern Reformed Church in the decades after World War II. Many ministers and lay members of the church believed that the doctrine of the infallibility of the Bible had to include the doctrine that the Bible was inerrant in historical and scientific detail as well as in its religious teachings.

Lester Kuyper, professor of Old Testament at Western Theological Seminary, taught that the Old Testament must be interpreted against the background of the customs and thought patterns of the ancient Middle East. Archeological research was making it clear that the "Hebrews were in vital contact with the customs, laws and worship forms of the neighboring peoples."[85] In their encounter with the religious, social, and moral life of the nations around them they were faced with the need to live as "a special people entirely dedicated to the Lord her Redeemer. The people were holy to the Lord and the Lord was the Holy One of Israel."[86] In contrast to the German higher critics who

[84]   Isaac C. Rottenberg, "The Christian Gospel and its Cultural Fruits," *Reformed Review*, 12/4 (1959), 27.

[85]   Kuyper, "Israel and Her Neighbors," *Reformed Review*, 10/3 (1957), 11. For an evaluation of the life and work of Lester Kuyper, see I. John Hesselink, "Lester J. Kuyper: Truth and Fidelity," in James I. Cook, ed., *Grace upon Grace* (Grand Rapids: Eerdmans, 1975), 9-17.

[86]   Kuyper, "Israel and her Neighbors," 19.

read the Old Testament as the religious history of a people coming to monotheistic ethical God consciousness, Kuyper maintained that the Old Testament is the account of God's revelation to a people who had to live in contradiction to their environment. He wrote:

> Under the aegis of the God-established purpose of redemption the prophets of Israel critically examined the so-called *Sitz im Leben* to proclaim the need for repentance and reform or to offer comfort and salvation. They demanded that Israel, a holy people, live responsibly before the Holy One of Israel in that moment— every moment—of holy, redemptive history.[87]

Kuyper then pointed out the moral for our own day;

> One need not labor the obvious application for the Church of Christ which now stands as Israel stood in the world. All one would ask and pray for is that we, as Israel's prophets may realistically and courageously grapple with our *Sitz im Leben*. We too must live responsibly in this world in the presence of Jesus Christ, our Lord and the Lord of history.[88]

Kuyper insisted that the Bible does not provide a philosophical statement or propositional truths about God. If we demand that the Bible help us "develop a rational description of God, then we are requesting the Bible to give us help contrary to its purpose."[89] The Bible is not a theology textbook. It is the sacred record of "God's activity in history." In it we see the "patterns of God's sovereign freedom and of his redemptive grace that rightly illumines the divine-human encounter."[90]

In December 1959 and March 1960, his two-article series, "Interpretation of Genesis Two-Three," was published in the *Reformed Review*. He concluded that in these two chapters the Bible shows that it is aware of the pagan beliefs and practices in the ancient Middle East and gives its witness against them. "The Sacred writer under the inspiration of the Holy Spirit uses language and symbol well-known to the people of that day to depict God's relationship of beneficent

---

[87]   Ibid., 20.
[88]   Ibid.
[89]   Ibid., 471.
[90]   Ibid.

The Rev. Lester J. Kuyper, Th. D.
(1904-1986)

*Courtesy of Western Theological Seminary*

"He is a man who possesses a big heart as well as a big frame, a man with a broad outlook and a great vision. On occasion he became involved in acrimonious, emotional conflicts that racked the community, seminary, or church, for he was too honest and courageous to remain silent where he felt an important issue was at stake. But he fought for issues—freedom, truth, unity, and justice—as he understood them, and did not attack people. Nor did he become involved in petty, personal feuds. He is too big for that. During such debates and conflicts he was occasionally misunderstood and maligned, but he rarely, if ever, retaliated in kind. As a result, most of the people who were his foes in debate continue to be his friends."—I. John Hesselink, "Lester J. Kuyper: Faith and Fidelity" in James I. Cook, ed., *Grace upon Grace*, 1975, 9-10.

grace to man in his creation."[91] The author of Genesis depicted the disobedience of human beings and its consequences thoughout the whole Old Testament and history of the human race. The author also pointed forward to the redemptive acts of God in Israel and ultimately in Jesus Christ.[92]

Because the literary form of the two chapters was common to people of the ancient world, we cannot demand historical accuracy of detail or scientific information that meets the criteria of modern research. Kuyper agreed with biblical scholars who had concluded that there are two accounts of creation in the first chapters of Genesis, the first by the priestly writer and the second by the Jahwist historian. The first account "presents the order of creation which consummates in the Sabbath day, the day by which Israel demonstrates her distinctiveness in the ancient world. The second creation narrative has as its primary

---

[91] Kuyper, "Interpretation of Genesis Two-Three," *Reformed Review*, 13/3 (1960), 29.
[92] Ibid.

purpose the place of man in creation and the break-in of sin into mankind."[93]

Kuyper called this "the pre-history from which the historians narrate the redeeming acts of God in Israel's history."[94] By using the word "pre-history" he was indicating that the first eleven chapters of Genesis are not history in the ordinary sense of the word. The description of the rivers that flowed out of Eden (2:10-14) cannot be located on any map; there is no archeological evidence for their existence. Kuyper wrote:

> For me the account appears here and throughout to combine the real with the symbolical; in this case the combination is between the factual geography and the figurative. The intention of the author may be to set the background of the Genesis story in a definite locale which also becomes the figurative center of the world.[95]

In his articles on Genesis 2-3, Lester Kuyper moved one step farther away from a literal-historical interpretation than had his teacher, Albertus Pieters, in the 1930s. Pieters had sought to reconcile the order of creation in Genesis 1 with the long geological ages that were recognized by the science of his day. For Pieters, the days of Genesis 1 were not twenty-four-hour days, but long ages. He did not insist upon literal accuracy of detail in Genesis 2-3, although he did defend the literal historical presence of the first human pair in the Garden of Eden. Kuyper had concluded that attempts to defend the first chapters of Genesis as providing literal-historical information only led to fruitless debate about such matters as to whether an actual snake spoke in the Garden of Eden.

No one in the Reformed Church in America wrote to challenge his exegesis of Genesis 2-3 specifically, but there was widespread disquiet in the Midwest on the part of those who defended the Bible as inerrant in every detail. It was also feared that by avoiding questions of historicity Kuyper had followed those biblical critics who had consigned the Genesis accounts to the realm of "myth." In his use of the word, pre-history, however, it could remain the case that the fall of humankind took place at the very beginning of human history and continues in the course of human history, even if it is not a dateable event. Whatever Kuyper may have meant by "pre-history," it was clear that he wanted to

---

[93]  Ibid., 13/2 (1959), 5.
[94]  Ibid.
[95]  Ibid., 10-11.

understand Genesis 2-3 as a theological account of God's redemptive history rather than literal human history.

The matter of the doctrine of inspiration of scripture was already on the agenda of the General Synod at the time Kuyper's articles were published. The Classis of Paramus had overtured the 1959 General Synod to refer the matter to the Theological Commission for study and future report to the General Synod.[96] The Theological Commission presented its report in June 1961. The synod encouraged wide distribution of the report for study and comments. The "Revised Declaration on Holy Scripture" was adopted by the General Synod in 1963.[97]

The "Revised Declaration" relied heavily upon the language of the Belgic Confession,[98] Several points were made in the declaration in regard to the affirmation in the Belgic Confession. It reaffirmed (1) that the Bible has been transmitted faithfully to us and is of divine authority as the Word of God. (2) "The central message of Scripture is the redeeming activity of God in Jesus Christ and the coming of His Kingdom in the world...." (3) It affirmed that it is important in

---

[96]  *Acts and Proceedings*, 1959, 124-25. In May 1958 the Classis of Passaic had refused to license or ordain to the office of the minister of the word a student at New Brunswick Theological Seminary, William Coventry, on the ground that he held a doctrine of inspiration of scripture that was at variance with the teaching of the Reformed Church in America. The action of the Classis of Passaic was overturned by the Particular Synod of New Jersey. The Classis of Passaic then appealed to the General Synod, but the action of the Particular Synod of New Jersey was sustained, ibid., 130ff. Overtures from the Classis of South Grand Rapids and the Classis of Paramus led the General Synod to order the Theological Commission to write a report on biblical inspiration. Willam Coventry (1930-1994) was ordained in 1959 and served as a pastor of Reformed Church congregations until his death.

[97]  *Acts and Proceedings*, 1963, 264-67. The "Revised Declaration on Holy Scripture" is included in James I. Cook ed., *The Church Speaks*, Historical Series of the Reformed Church in America, no.15 (Grand Rapids: Eerdmans, 1985), 6-10.

[98]  Article 5 states, "These books [that is, the thirty-nine Old Testament and twenty-seven New Testament books—eph] alone we receive as holy and canonical for regulating, grounding and confirming our faith. We believe without any doubt all that is contained in them, not so much because the Church receives and approves them as holy and canonical, but especially because the Holy Spirit witnesses in our hearts that they are from God; and because they have the evidence of this in themselves, seeing that the very blind can perceive that the things foretold in them are happening."

interpretation to pay attention to the way in which the "Holy Spirit used the language, literary forms, thought-world and vocabulary of the human authors." (4) The Holy Spirit is the primary author of scripture.[99]

Point (5) in the report is the crucial point in the controversy about the inspiration and authority of the Bible. It states, "The authority of Scripture is to be found in God himself who speaks to us in Christ through the Holy Spirit, and therefore in that sense we hold the Scriptures of the Old and New Testaments to be infallible." It (6) then goes on to teach that "Scripture as the word of the faithful God *is infallible and inerrant in all that it intends to teach and accomplish concerning faith and life*" [italics mine]. Because the Bible is written by human authors in human language, it is subject to certain human limitations but these limitations "do not detract from the infallibility of the message."[100]

Regarding inspiration, the declaration holds that any worthy view of inspiration must hold that scripture is inspired "in the whole and all its parts," but since (7) there is no fully detailed and articulated theory either in scripture or in the confessions, the Reformed Church does not require any particular theory. It is sufficient that a minister of the gospel "who confesses the Holy Scripture to be the inspired Word of God, *infallible and inerrant in all that it intends to teach*," discharges his or her obedience to the scriptures, the confession, and the ministerial vows. (8) In the interpretation of scripture, careful attention to the words of scripture requires the use of all the available tools of critical study.

In adopting the revised declaration, the General Synod provided a set of guidelines for use by classes in their assessment of whether to ordain a minister or to accept the minister into the membership of the classis. It allowed for differing interpretations of the early chapters of Genesis on matters such as literary forms and the extent to which Genesis 1-11 is to be understood to be a source of historical and scientific information. The declaration has set the official policy of the denomination without revision since it was adopted in 1964.

However, many in the Midwest and some in the eastern region disagreed with the conclusions in the report. They objected especially to the phrase, "infallible and inerrant in all that it intends to teach," because it limited "what it intends to teach" to the central message

[99]   Cook, *The Church Speaks.*
[100]   Ibid.

of scripture as stated in number 2, and "what it intends to teach" was precisely the point of dispute in matters of inerrancy about historical and scientific accuracy.[101] Therefore the nature of the inspiration of the Bible has remained a matter of dispute in the Reformed Church to the present day.

## Living in Expectation of the Reign of God

During the 1950s, Reformed Church in America classes in the midwestern and eastern regions began to send overtures to the General Synod urging the denomination to make major revisions in the church order and the official liturgy. They asked for a revision of its confessional language to be more contemporary, clear, and concise.[102] They also approved the General Synod's action of appointing a Christian Action Commission to study and advise the church on matters of political, economic, and social concern. Although there was no one dominating concern behind these calls for changes in the life of the denomination, the result was that the official language and action of the denomination shifted from being introverted to being extroverted. The eschatological perspective gained priority, while the older perspective of the Synod of Dort faded into the background.

Overtures from classes to revise the liturgy and the constitution and to develop a more contemporary confession of faith had come before the General Synod from time to time in the decades after World War I. Enthusiasm for revision grew when a number of leaders in the

---

[101] The Rev. John J. Arnold, pastor of the Trinity Reformed Church in Grand Rapids, Michigan, pointed out that a declaration of the General Synod does not have the same force as does a constitutional amendment. He wrote, "Perhaps it would be good for us to remind ourselves that grave theological issues are not finally resolved by what the General Synod of any year has said, but by a continuing effort to say to the world only those things that God has said to us in His Holy Word." John Arnold, "About That Ruling of General Synod," *Church Herald*, March 12, 1965, 7.

[102] A number of churches in America and the Netherlands were thinking about developing new confessional statements after World War II. The Netherlands Reformed Church was considering a confessional statement entitled, "Foundations and Perspectives of Confession" [English translation of title]. The matter came to the attention of the General Synod in 1958, and the Theological Commission began work on a draft in 1964. In 1965 a provisional document was distributed to the classes for comment. In 1967 the Theological Commission reported to the General Synod that it believed it to be unwise to proceed further in the matter. For a symposium on the subject in the *Church Herald*, see "Confessing Church or Creedal Church," May 19, 1961, 12-13, 25, 31.

Reformed Church in America became acquainted with the dynamic developments in the Netherlands Reformed Church during and immediately after World War II. For one hundred years the midwestern Reformed Church had remembered its history from the perspective of the conflict with the Netherlands Reformed Church that had led to the Secession of 1834. As Reformed Church leaders became acquainted with new developments in the life of that church, they were impressed with its new church order and revision of the traditional liturgy. Its proposed new confessional statement was proving fruitful in helping that church to meet the new challenges before it. The new liturgy, church order, and confessional statement of the Netherlands Reformed Church had a strong eschatological theme running through them, with an emphasis upon the reign (kingdom) of God, on the "apostolate" (mission) of the church, and on the unity of the church in its calling in the world. [103]

## Living in Expectation of the Reign of God, I:
## A Revised Church Order

The Reformed Church in America adopted a radical revision of its constitution in 1967 in order that it might better fulfill "its call within the expectation of the reign of God as it participates in mission, in calling all persons to life in Christ, and in proclaiming God's promise and commands to all the world."[104] The first sentence of the preamble stated, "The purpose of the Reformed Church in America, together with all other churches of Christ, is to minister to the total life of all people by preaching, teaching, and proclamation of the gospel of Jesus Christ, the Son of God, and by all Christian good works."[105] With its focus on mission, the revised church order had become extroverted, focused

---

[103]  See Lester Kuyper, "The Netherlands Reformed Church: Her Faith and Life," *Reformed Review*, 13/4 (1959/60), 18-31.

[104]  "Preamble," *Book of Church Order*, 2; *Acts and Proceedings*, 1966, 200-201; 1967, 183, 185. For articles dealing with the theology of church order, see Isaac Rottenberg, "Is our Reformed Church Constitution Adequate?" *Church Herald*, September 20, 1957, 10-11; Eugene Heideman, "The Reformed Constitution—Here and Now," September 27, 1957, 10; and the series by Howard Hageman, "The Theology of the Urban Church" *Church Herald*, 7, 14, 21, November 28, 1958. For a full study of the Reformed Church in America's *Book of Church Order*, see Allan J. Janssen, *Constitutional Theology: Notes on the Book of Church Order of the Reformed Church in America*, Historical Series of the Reformed Church in America, no.33 (Grand Rapids: Eerdmans, 2000).

[105]  "Preamble," *Book of Church Order*, 1.

on the world outside, while not losing its historic role of meeting the pastoral needs of its members.

The revised church order developed out of the life of the church in the era following World War II. It codified much of what was already happening after the war. It opened the windows to experimentation with church life and order by making provision for union congregations with other denominations (1, I, 7), provided sanction for the ordination of ministers to be chaplains and enter other forms of ministry (1, II, 10, 4), required consistories to report on how they were faithfully witnessing to the gospel (1, II, 7, j),[106] and remained open to such additional changes as would emerge in the course of time.

Ordination of women to the offices of minister, elder, and deacon was one of the burning issues that remained open when the revised church order was adopted in 1967. The chair of the special committee on the ordination of women, Gerrit Vander Lugt, traced the history of the question in the Reformed Church. Overtures to permit ordination of women to one or more of the offices came to the General Synod seven times between 1918 and 1951. All of the overtures had come from classes in the eastern region. The issue became widespread in 1952, when six classes sent overtures that asked that women be permitted to be ordained, while seven classes sent overtures that opposed any change in the church order.[107] During the 1950s and 1960s most of the midwestern classes remained opposed to the ordination of women, while most of the eastern classes favored it.

Vander Lugt summarized the reasons given by classes in favor of ordination of women. Women should enjoy the same rights as are given to male members of the church; recognition of such rights would be "in accord with the action of our country in civil matters, and with the teachings of democracy, justice and equal opportunity by our Lord when on earth."[108] Reasons given by General Synods between 1918 and 1952 for not giving classes the right to vote on the matter included statements that such a vote would work injury by causing division in the church out of proportion to what would be gained or that the time is not ripe (1918, 1921, 1922, 1932) and that God created male and female with distinctive functions. If women were admitted to the offices, "The men would become content to let the women assume responsibilities which are properly theirs" (1932, same point made in 1951).[109]

---

[106]   All references to articles in the *Book of Church Order* are to its 2006 edition.
[107]   Gerrit T. Vander Lugt, "Ordination of Women in the Reformed Church," *Church Herald*, January 4, 1957, 10.
[108]   Ibid.
[109]   Ibid.

The committee reported to the General Synod in 1958 that it saw no theological reasons for continuing to refuse to permit the ordination of women, but it did recognize that there may continue to be strong sociological reasons for refusing to amend the church order. However, the synod voted to recommend that classes vote on the amendment that "the offices in the Reformed Church in America will be open to women and men alike beginning in 1962."[110] It was reported to the General Synod in 1969 that the proposed amendment was not yet permitted by the revised *Book of Church Order* in 1967.[111] The Church Order was finally revised in 1979 to permit the ordination of women.

## Living in Expectation of the Reign of God, II: The Christian Action Commission

The preamble's statement that "the church fulfills its call within the expectation of the reign of God as it participates in mission, in calling all persons to life in Christ, and in proclaiming God's promise and commands to all the world" meant that the church could not avoid making its witness known concerning issues of justice, peace,

---

[110] *Acts and Proceedings*, 1958, 328-30. The issue was explored on the pages of the *Church Herald* during 1957-1958. Members of the committee who wrote in favor of the amendment were Lambert Ponstein, "The Sociological Aspect of Ordaining Women," March 28, 1958, 10-11; Vernon Kooy, "Ordination of Women and the New Testament," January 18, 1957, 7, 21; Richard Oudersluys, "The Ordination of Women in the Teaching of the New Testament," March 15, 1957, 8-9. The most important articles opposing the amendment were by Jerome De Jong, "The Women in the Church," August 22, 1958, 10-11, and a series of articles by Elton Eenigenberg, "Does the Bible Permit Ordination of Women," August 29, 1958, 4, 15; September 12, 1958, 5, 15. Eenigenberg charged that the personnel on the committee were one sided. He maintained that "the Bible does not teach that men and women are created equal. It teaches a subordination of women in general to men in general." In the marriage relationship the wife is to be subordinate to the husband and therefore, particularly in regard to the marriage relationship, the church offices should be limited to men," August 29, 1958, 15. When the final vote on the issue was before the synod in 1979, Eenigenberg rose on the floor of the General Synod to say that he had changed his mind on the matter and urged that delegates vote in favor of the ordination of women. Some of those present remember that the remarks of the very respected member of the Western Seminary faculty played an important role in the action of the synod that opened the door to ordination of women; see *Acts and Proceedings*, 1979, 60-61.

[111] For a later statement, "The Role and Authority of Women in Ministry," see Cook, ed., *The Church Speaks*, Vol. 2, 165-66, 170-90.

and other matters of public concern. In 1955, the General Synod had created a Christian Action Commission to study, report, and make recommendations to the synod concerning public policy, social justice, war and peace, and similar matters.[112] After due consideration, the General Synod would pass recommendations for the guidance of members of the Reformed Church or as matters of Christian witness to the national government or other pertinent bodies.

The General Synod of 1959 received a statement entitled, "A Theological Basis for Christian Concern and Action," written by the chair of the Christian Action Commission, Jerome De Jong.[113] It begins with an affirmation of belief in the absolute sovereignty of God and God's love for creation in which God constantly operates by means of the Holy Spirit. It affirms fallen humankind as created in the image of God and the redemptive work of God in Jesus Christ. Human beings were created to live in community. The redeemed community, the church, lives with the paradox that its members must separate themselves from the world and yet fulfill their duty to witness in the world. Its "ultimate hope is the consummation of history by the divine act of God to bring in the new world of righteousness and truth."[114]

The role of the Christian Action Commission remained a matter of considerable controversy, with much of the reaction against it being centered in the Midwest. One objection to its role was that it marked a departure from a long tradition about the relation of the assemblies of the church to the civil authorities. Prior to the revision of 1967, Article 55 in the church order limited the range of matters that could be discussed legitimately in ecclesiastical assemblies. Article 55 read, "Ecclesiastical matters only shall be considered and transacted in ecclesiastical assemblies."[115] In *Notes on the Constitution*, William

[112] The name, "The Committee on Social Welfare, (Public Morals)" was changed to "Christian Action Commission"; see *Acts and Proceedings*, 1955, 189-90.

[113] Jerome De Jong, "A Theological Basis for Christian Concern and Action," *Church Herald*, January 9, 1959, 21.

[114] Ibid. In view of the suspicion of some people regarding the role and bias of the Christian Action Commission, the statement provided a solid basis for the right of the church to make statements and promote Christian action on public issues as well as on matters of personal morality.

[115] Quoted in William H.S. Demarest, *Notes on the Constitution of the Reformed Church in America* (New Brunswick.: Printed at Thatcher-Anderson Co., 1928, rev. 1946), 87. The Rev. Dr. William H.S. Demarest (1863-1956) taught at New Brunswick Theological Seminary, 1901-1906 and 1925-1935. He was president of Rutgers College from 1906-1924. His *Notes on*

H.S. Demarest observed that it was a wise provision, although it was difficult to determine its boundary regarding specific matters.[116] The General Synod had always assumed that it had a responsibility to take positions on matters of personal and public morals such as the use of alcoholic beverages and prohibition, sexual practice, and Sabbath observance, as well as slavery and loyalty to the Union during the Civil War. More controversial was whether the synod had the right to make pronouncements on matters of labor relations, world peace, and women's suffrage. Some feared that removal of Article 55 would lead to a situation in which the agenda of ecclesiastical assemblies would be clogged with items calling upon the church to support every special interest group and humanitarian campaign in the community and nation.

In an editorial entitled, "The Church's Business," Louis Benes attempted to draw a line to distinguish between the responsibility of the church and the responsibilities of individual Christians. He began by objecting to a comment by a regional director of the United Steel Workers of America, who rebuked the church for doing very little about three major areas of concern in American life: automation, poverty, and civil rights.[117] Benes said that he was tired of hearing the critics telling the church what it ought to be doing. Christ did not institute the church to be busy about everybody else's business, such as supporting the Red Cross, the Community Chest, Safe Driving Week, and Health Week, valuable as those are.

> Christ instituted His Church to preach the Gospel, to teach His Word, and to carry out His will among men. His Church is something other than a social-service organization, an arm of the state, or an organization for community welfare. St. Paul was already doing something about poverty 2,000 years ago when he took up collections for the poor Christians in Jerusalem, but he never suggested that the Church should be busy with social and economic programs or that she should take on "action programs" in these areas.[118]

---

the *Constitution* was regarded generally as the authoritative exposition of the constitution from the time it was published until the revised *Book of Church Order* was adopted.

[116] Ibid., 88.
[117] Louis Benes, "The Church's Business," *Church Herald*, April 17, 1964, 6.
[118] Ibid.

Benes held that *individual Christians* should be doing more in the areas of poverty, automation, and civil rights.[119] Individual Christians should become personally involved in fighting poverty, unemployment, lack of education, and other social ills. But "all of this, and more, is the responsibility of the individual Christian, involved in society and its organizations, but not of the Church *as Church*."[120] Benes opposed the deletion of Article 55 from the church order. He wrote:

> The provision protects our Synods and Classes from the temptation and the mistake of speaking out on all sorts of secular matters, on which they may have little knowledge, for which they have no responsibility, concerning which they have no right to speak for their constituency, and which would inevitably distract and divert their attention from the main business of the Church.[121]

Benes wrote that he did not oppose the responsibility of the church to speak to its own members about matters pertaining to its life and mission and existence in the world, such as freedom of religion, the separation of church and state, and the sanctity of marriage and the home. As an example of what he opposed, he pointed to the Woman's Division of Christian Service and of the Board of Missions of the Methodist Church, who urged women's organizations to take action on support for the United Nations, revision of the McCarran-Walter immigration act, limitation of the Senate's rule on debate, opposition to the Bricker amendment, limitation of nuclear tests and disarmament, and compulsory military training.[122] Involvement in such a broad range of causes only tends to divert attention of the church from its main business.

The differences about the role of the church in public policy became especially sharp in the pages of the *Church Herald* with regard to

[119]  Benes was a persistent advocate of civil rights and opposed to discrimination against black Americans. He supported desegregation of restaurants, theaters, hotels, and churches. He supported the right of blacks to vote, *Church Herald*, June 14, 1963, 6. He supported the proposed civil rights law, April 24, 1964, 6; commended the stand taken by black ministers about the church bombings in the South, February 1, 1957, 6-7; and was pleased with the General Synod's "Credo on Race Relations," July 5, 1957, 4-5. He printed articles regularly by other writers who opposed discrimination and had positive suggestions for overcoming racial injustice.
[120]  Benes, "The Church's Business," April 17, 1964, 6.
[121]  Benes, "The Business of the Church?" *Church Herald*, July 25, 1958, 6.
[122]  Ibid.

racial policy and civil disobedience in the 1960s. In a 1964 article, the Reverend John H. Muller, pastor of the Hope Community [Reformed] Church in Orlando, Florida, opposed the church and Christians using civil disobedience, picketing, courting arrest, and flouting of the law in support of civil rights. He agreed that churches and individuals should oppose racial discrimination and that all races should be treated equally by Christians. However, "Jesus Christ was not a reformer or a revolutionary. He was a redeemer. He came to give liberty to the captives, to set men free from the guilt and the power of sin. He did not interfere in civil affairs."[123] He went on to contend, "But race relations are seldom bettered by legislation or by demonstrations. Christian race relations are a matter of the heart. Without a work of regeneration man's relations with man are at best tenuous."[124]

A number of readers objected to the lines Muller drew regarding "the business of the church." The Reverend Donald Blackie claimed that the apostles' statement in Acts 5, "We must obey God rather than men," did encourage civil disobedience. He defended Martin Luther King's call for the bus boycott in Montgomery and civil disobedience in Birmingham, Alabama. Civil disobedience was his only recourse to gain justice there. To say, as Muller did, that "public demonstrations and picket lines do not change the hearts or attitudes of people" is simply to shut one's eyes to modern history.[125]

The Reverend Dr. John W. Beardslee, III, professor of church history at New Brunswick Seminary, accused Muller of holding to an Anabaptist rather than a Reformed view of the world. He asked, "Do we believe that the world is simply unredeemed (or evil) or do we, with Calvin, believe that it also is to be led to show forth the glory of God, its Creator?"[126] The Reverend Donald De Young wrote from the Elmendorf Reformed Church in Harlem, New York City, to express his deep disappointment with the article that reeks "of the 'status-quo stagnation' which holds so much of our denomination in captivity."[127] The Reverend Bert Van Soest, pastor of the Mountain View Reformed Church in Denver, Colorado, charged, "You seem to be making a dualism. The impression is that the Church should speak but not act.

[123] John H. Muller, "Is it the Church's Business?" *Church Herald*, October 23, 1964, 14.

[124] Ibid.

[125] Donald K. Blackie, "Letters to the Editor," *Church Herald*, November 13, 1964, 16.

[126] "Letters to the Editor," *Church Herald*, November 13, 1964, 16.

[127] "Letters to the Editor," *Church Herald*, November 13, 1964, 16.

This is contrary to the teachings of Jesus Christ. The Church is people, people who believe in Jesus Christ, witnessing in word and deed for Jesus Christ. When Christ's people are united in belief, they should be united in action."[128]

The Christian Action Commission had been formed specifically to help the churches deal with the controversial issues of the day. Therefore, the annual reports of the Christian Action Commission were often the center of a storm at the meetings of the General Synod. Although individuals consistently objected to the time given by the synod to discussion of the annual reports, there was no move to abolish the commission. The members of the Reformed Church in America, East and Midwest, did want the church to be free to speak and act for the sake of justice and peace in the world, even though they had deep disagreements about the issues at hand. There was agreement in the church on the point made in the concluding two sentences of "A Theological Basis for Christian Action and Concern":

> The church in following the instruction of this Scripture will critically, yet sympathetically, study the social and moral problems of her age and locality and seek to apply the Word of God to her day. It is equally the task of the church in repentance to exercise continuous self-discipline so that the witness of the church may be genuine and sincere.[129]

## Living in Expectation of the Reign of God, III: The Revised Liturgy

The General Synod appointed a committee to revise the Liturgy in 1950.[130] The Reformed Church was sometimes known as a "semi-liturgical" church because its Church Order required that certain liturgical forms be used on particular occasions, most notably in the administration of baptism and the Lord's Supper. It allowed more

---

[128] "Letters to the Editor, *Church Herald*, August 21, 1964, 18-19.
[129] "A Theological Basis for Christian Concern and Action," *Church Herald*, January 9, 1959, 21. "This Scripture" refers to the verses quoted at various points throughout the document.
[130] For the history of the revision of the liturgy in the Reformed Church in America, see Daniel J. Meeter, *Meeting Each Other in Doctrine, Liturgy, & Government*, Historical Series of the Reformed Church in America, no. 24 (Grand Rapids: Eerdmans, 1993), 149-58; Howard Hageman, "Our Liturgical History," *Church Herald*, May 4, 1951, 12.

freedom with regard to prayers, scripture reading, music, and forms of worship.

The new 1966 Order for the Sacrament of the Lord's Supper offered the most radical mandatory shift from the liturgy adopted in 1906.[131] A change in tone reflected a shift in the practice of piety throughout the Reformed Church between 1906 and 1966. The tone of the 1966 order was joyful, in contrast to the somber tone of the 1906 order, which placed heavy emphasis upon the depth of our sin and the sacrifice and atonement of Christ on the cross. The 1906 liturgy was heavily didactic in nature. It required the reading of a long exposition of the meaning of the Lord's Supper. It was followed by the admonition to "humble ourselves before God and with true faith implore His grace." The admonition was followed by the prayer that by the power of the Holy Ghost, we may be "fed and comforted with His [Christ's] true body and blood."[132]

In the 1966 order, the meaning of the sacrament was presented in a personal rather than a didactic form. The meaning is summed up in three short paragraphs that begin respectively with, "We come in remembrance...;" "We come to have communion...;" and "We come in hope...;" plus a summary paragraph. The last two paragraphs read:

> We come in hope, believing that this bread and this cup are a pledge and foretaste of the feast of love of which we shall partake when his kingdom has fully come, when with unveiled face we shall behold him, made like unto him in his glory.
>
> Since by his death, resurrection, and ascension he has obtained for us the life-giving spirit who unites us all in one body, so are we to receive this Supper in true brotherly love, mindful of the communion of Saints.[133]

---

[131] Christopher Dorn, *The Lord's Supper in the Reformed Church in America* (New York: Peter Lang, 2007) is a meticulous study of the process of revisions from the order of the sixteenth-century church of the Palatinate through the Synod of Dort and the colonial era in America. It is a careful study of the nineteenth- and twentieth-century revisions that were the forerunners of the 1966 liturgy. His thesis is that the 1966 liturgy is a radical revision from the Reformed position that was adopted in the Palatinate and the Synod of Dort.

[132] *The Liturgy of the Reformed Church in America Together with Prayers for Various Occasions* (New York : The Board of Publication, 1951), 34-35.

[133] *Liturgy*, 1968, 65. In what follows, either the 1966 date of adoption by the General Synod or the 1968 date of publication will be used, depending on the context.

The 1968 Order for the Administration of Baptism represented less of a change from the 1906 order than did that of the Order for the Sacrament of the Lord's Supper. Nevertheless, it brought to the surface theological questions that had remained dormant in previous decades. One question was what it means to say that the sacraments of baptism and the Lord's Supper are "means of grace" and "visible signs and seals of an inward and invisible action, whereby God works in us through the power of the Holy Spirit."[134] A second question was what was intended when, according to a new paragraph in the 1968 Liturgy, the minister declared that "this child is now received into the visible membership of the Holy Catholic Church, and *is* engaged to confess the faith of Christ crucified, and to be his faithful servant unto *his/her* life's end."[135] The third question was how baptism is related to the need for conversion. Each of these questions will now be considered in turn.

First, a number of midwestern ministers maintained that it was important to guard against any idea that the sacraments work "as magic, possessing some occult power of their own."[136] The Reverend Dr. Garret Wilterdink wrote that "the sacraments are the reminder and proclamation of our salvation, not the means of it."[137] Rather than speaking of a sacrament as a "means of grace," he contended that the grace of God is not bound up with the sacrament as a rite. "The sacrament is a means of stimulating and reminding the believer of that grace that has already been received and of encouraging the believer to seek it anew."[138] Louis Benes wrote an editorial that took the same position when he wrote that the sacraments are "signs and seals of grace rather than purveyors of grace."[139]

James Eelman and Howard Hageman reacted sharply against Wilterdink's contention that a sacrament is "a reminder and proclamation of our salvation, not the means of it." They pointed out that the distinction between reminder and means ignores the role of

---

[134]  Belgic Confession, 33; see also Heidelberg Catechism, Q. 65-68.
[135]  *Liturgy*, 1968, 31.
[136]  Louis Benes, "Some Thoughts on the Proposed Liturgy," *Church Herald*, March 6, 1964, 7.
[137]  "Some Comments on the Proposed Revised Liturgy," *Church Herald*, February 14, 1964, 10. Garret Wilterdink (1927-1990) was pastor of the Reformed Church in Midland, Michigan, at the time he wrote the article. He served as a professor at Western Theological Seminary from 1967-1986.
[138]  Ibid.
[139]  Benes, "Some Thoughts on the Proposed Liturgy."

the Holy Spirit and misunderstands the nature of grace. Hageman responded to Benes. He wrote:

> What is still more distressing, however, is the implication of your position that grace is a thing. This is a medievalism upon which every Reformer turned his back. Grace is nothing more than the gracious and saving presence of God in Jesus Christ. Certainly we believe in that presence in the preaching of the Word. Is the gracious and saving presence of God in Jesus Christ present to the believer in baptism? In the Holy Supper? If not, then why do we perform such dumb shows at all....Either Jesus Christ is present in the act which He Himself commanded us to do or he is not.[140]

The distinction Hageman drew between grace as a thing and grace as the saving presence of Christ is crucial for the Reformed doctrine of the sacraments. There was a tendency in midwestern Reformed thought to think of grace as a regenerating seed implanted in the believer. The seed once implanted then would enable the believer to grow spiritually. If grace is a commodity that is "purveyed" or catered as a gift from God, then the bread and the wine in the Lord's Supper are reminders of Christ's death and resurrection for us, but Christ's presence is not related intrinsically to the bread and the wine. Hageman charged that Benes's formulation of the issue fell in line with the error of the Anabaptists that was abhorred by the Reformed fathers because the sacraments became "naked and bare signs" that have no place in Reformed theology.[141]

Eelman and Hageman emphasized that grace is not a thing but a relationship that God has decided to have with those who are united in Christ by the Holy Spirit.[142] Thus the water of baptism and the bread and wine of the Lord's Supper become means by which God encounters us in Christ. It is the Holy Spirit, the giver of faith, "who makes the communion efficacious in the participants at the Lord's Table."[143] It is the promise that Christ will "be with you always, to the close of the age" in the relationship of grace that is conveyed to the one baptized. Grace is a living relationship in union with Christ that is sustained in

[140] Howard Hageman, "Letters to the Editor," *Church Herald*, April 3, 1964, 16.
[141] Ibid.
[142] Lester Kuyper at Western Theological Seminary also taught that "grace" is a word indicating a relationship of fidelity or steadfast love on the part of a superior to an inferior, such as a lord to a vassal, rather than some*thing* bestowed; "Grace and Truth" *Reformed Review*, 16/1 (1962), 2-3.
[143] James Eelman, "Letters to the Editor," *Church Herald*, March 13, 1964, 22.

the celebration of the sacraments. Unbelief that denies the relationship is what can render them naked and bare signs, or "dumb shows," to use Hageman's term.

The second question or objection to the proposed 1968 Order for the Administration of Baptism was the insertion of the declaration by the minister that "N.N.... is now received into the visible membership of the Holy Catholic Church." Critics said that Reformed theology has always taught that children of believing parents were by virtue of the convenantal relationship already incorporated into the church as the body of Christ. Therefore, argued Gordon Girod, the proposed new liturgy is in contradiction to the 1906 Liturgy statement that parents "shall acknowledge that the child is a member of the church, and therefore, ought to be baptized."[144]

Justin Vander Kolk put Girod's argument to rest by reminding him that the phrase in the declaration was based on Article 34 of the Belgic Confession, which refers to baptism as a "sacrament by which we are *received* into the Church of God, and separated from all other people and strange religions."[145] Vander Kolk argued further that "while one readily agrees that there is a sense in which 'a child is born a member of the church,' if this is not qualified or explained, it might suggest that the Christian life is simply a matter of natural heritage."[146] He went on to comment, "To the present writer it appears that the counter proposal that we are by birth members of the church offends by obscuring the central doctrine of the Reformed Faith that our Christian life so far from inhering in nature rests purely on divine grace."[147]

The third question that surfaced with regard to the proposed Form for the Administration of Baptism was the relation of baptism to conversion and "full membership" in the church. Three ministers from the North Grand Rapids Classis wrote an article for the *Church Herald* in which they made two complaints about the proposed new form. The first was that the new form did not contain an adequate insistence on acknowledging original sin; it did not state that by nature we are sinful and guilty before God and are heartily sorry for our sins.[148] The proposed liturgy stated:

---

[144] "Straining at a Gnat," *Church Herald*, April 20, 1956, 10.

[145] "Letters to the Editor," *Church Herald*, May 18, 1956, 17. The Rev. Dr. Justin Vander Kolk was professor of theology at New Brunswick Theological Seminary.

[146] Ibid.

[147] Ibid., 23.

[148] Bert Van Soest, Morris Folkert, Arthur Johnson, "Shall We Approve the Revised Liturgy," *Church Herald*, March 2, 1956, 11.

In the celebration of Christian Baptism we confess that we with our children are sinful by nature and under the judgment of God. We cannot enter into God's kingdom unless we are born again and seek our cleansing and salvation in him alone.

The parents then were asked,

Do you acknowledge that *this child* with us is sinful by nature and under the judgment of God, but is received by grace, sanctified in Christ, and numbered among his people, of which Baptism is the sign and seal?[149]

The real issue was not that the words of the questions were clear enough about the fallen nature of the child. The real objection was that the new Form for the Administration of Baptism did not address adequately the importance of conversion and the need to instruct children in the faith before young people would be admitted into "full membership in the Church."[150] The critics went on to write that "candidates coming for admission into full membership of the Church must come *not only to confirm* the Christian faith, *but also to tell of conversion.*"[151]

The concern that those seeking "admission into full membership of the church" "tell of conversion" reflected the pervasive influence of the revival tradition of American evangelical Christianity in the midwestern Reformed Church. In that tradition, it is the conversion experience that is crucial, and the matter of salvation always remains in some doubt. Therefore one is not a "full member of the church" until one can testify to the church about one's conversion and personal acceptance of Jesus Christ as Savior and Lord. In response to the critics, it must be noted that the issue of personal faith is not in doubt when attention is paid to the words in the liturgical form. The Order for Admission to the Lord's Table of Those Baptized in Infancy affirms that at the time of admission to the Lord's Supper[152] it is important to

---

[149] Ibid.
[150] Van Soest, et. al., "Shall We Approve...."
[151] Ibid.
[152] In the practice of the Reformed Church in America at that time, only those baptized persons who had been admitted to the Lord's Table by the elders were permitted to partake of the elements of bread and wine. In the new liturgy, they were admitted according to The Order for Admission to the Lord's Table following their affirmative answers to four questions: "Do you accept Jesus Christ as your Lord and Savior? Do you rely on him and

confess personally that Jesus Christ is Lord and Savior, that one relies on him alone for salvation, and that one accepts the scriptures as the only rule of faith and practice in the church.

However, the demand that those coming tell specifically about their conversions went beyond what was asked in the old as well as the new liturgical forms. The tradition of nurturing children in the faith through the influence of the Christian home and teaching the Heidelberg Catechism assumed that the children were not "heathen" in need of a conversion experience, but were covenant children within the family of God so long as they did not deny the faith and the Christian way of life. Moreover, the practice of admitting formally those who had been baptized as infants to full communion in their teens did not mean that membership was a two-step process. Children were members of the church visible by virtue of their position in the covenant and their baptism. With admission to the Lord's Table, they were expected to fulfill responsibilities that young children were not yet able to understand or ready to assume.[153]

## Living in Expectation of the Reign of God, IV: Church Architecture

It remains to mention in brief the important theological development in the understanding of church architecture during the period 1945-1966. During the 1950s many congregations were renovating their sanctuaries and building new buildings that favored neo-Gothic architectural styles "that had little more to offer Protestantism than the warmed-over medievalisms of the Anglo-

---

him alone for your salvation? Do you accept the Scriptures of the Old and New Testament as the only rule of faith and practice in the Church? Will you confess Christ publicly before men, and by God's grace seek to work worthily of your Christian calling?" *Liturgy*, 1968, 54.

[153] There was no minimum age for admission to the Lord's Table. Like many other matters in the Reformed Church in America, the time or age of admission was left to the discretion of the elders. Beginning in 1977, the General Synod was called upon to decide whether young children could be admitted to the Lord's Table without having been received into "full communion" and without having followed the procedures prescribed or having formally answered the questions in The Form for Admission to the Lord's Table. The first report on this controversial question is in *Acts and Proceedings*, 1977, 293-306. The matter came up for review again in 1984, 1985, and 1988, when the General Synod agreed that baptized children could partake of Holy Communion according to several procedures outlined by the General Synod, *Acts and Proceedings*, 1988, 383-85.

Catholic ecclesiologists of a century before."[154] The need for church buildings that gave full expression to Reformed worship began to be accepted by congregations in the 1950s. A report adopted by the Particular Synod of Chicago for guidance of Reformed churches was printed in the *Church Herald* in its June 10, 1955, issue. It called attention to the importance of the pulpit and Communion table as symbols of God's coming to men and women, and to the doctrine of the priesthood of believers.

Between 1955 and 1964, the *Church Herald* published a number of articles that called attention to the importance of Reformed theological emphases in the planning of church buildings.[155] With the appearance in 1965 of the influential book by Donald J. Bruggink and Carl H. Droppers, *Christ and Architecture*, a new era began for dealing seriously with the theological dimensions of church architecture. Its basic thrust ran parallel to the central themes of the revised liturgy.

Bruggink and Droppers were influenced by new approaches to Reformed church architecture in Europe when many new church buildings had to be erected after the devastation of World War II. They placed many photographs in their book to show how Word and sacrament were communicated in the very architecture of the building. They wrote:

> How does Christ communicate with his people? The answer of the Church of Jesus Christ reformed according to the Word of God is that Christ communicates himself to his Church through Word and Sacrament....One must never forget that Christ comes to us not only in his Word, but also in his Sacraments! The Sacraments must receive an emphasis fully commensurate with their God-given importance. They should in no way be neglected, as has all too frequently happened within the Reformed tradition.[156]

---

[154] Bruggink and Droppers, *Christ and Architecture*, 19.

[155] Among these were James Hastings Nichols, "Architecture for Reformed Worship," January 11, 1957, 4-5; the series by Carl Droppers, "An Architecture for our Church," January 10, 1958, 12-13, 22; January 17, 1958, 11; January 31, 1958, 10; Richard C. Oudersluys, "Reformed Theology and Church Architecture," May 22, 1964, 10-12.

[156] Bruggink and Droppers, *Christ and Architecture*, 58. In the last sentence quoted they are objecting to the practice in most midwestern churches and many American Protestant churches of placing the pulpit in the center of a raised platform while the Communion table is on the floor below in front of the pulpit. The table then was used as a place to put a bouquet of flowers and the offering plates on Sundays when the Lord's Supper was not being

They emphasized that architecture must reflect the role of the Holy Spirit in relation to Word and sacrament. They wrote:

> The foundation of Christian faith is that we have life and light in Christ, that in him we have salvation, newness of life, and life beyond death, even to the resurrection of the dead. This is to be had in Christ, and the biblical, the Reformed, doctrine of Word and Sacrament is that as the Holy Spirit of God works in each, we are joined to Christ.[157]

The theological and practical considerations, together with photographs, led to great changes in the way Reformed congregations thought about the pulpit, Communion table, and baptismal font in the architecture of the church. The Communion table became larger, more visible, and easily accessible,[158] with nothing other than Communion vessels and perhaps a small reading stand designed to hold the liturgy book on it. It was not to be based below the pulpit or against the back wall, but in a prominent place in the midst of the congregation, or in front of it where it would be easily seen. Baptismal fonts became permanent and sometimes large, perhaps sculptured, and weighing several hundred pounds.[159]

## Living in Expectation of the Reign of God: V: Living with a Sure Hope

The year 1966 marks the end of the century that began with the first graduating class of Hope College and the founding of the midwestern religious paper, *De Hope*, in 1866. It also marks the approximate midpoint in the decade in which the midwestern Reformed Church in America went through its own change of climate. Television sets entered almost every home. Those who had always opposed movies and dancing now discovered that they enjoyed watching those activities in their own homes. They bought Sunday newspapers and watched football on Sunday afternoons. Reformed Church women entered the American work force in large numbers. Children went off to college and

---

administered. A small baptismal bowl was placed in the church somewhere near the pulpit only on Sundays when there was a baptism.

[157] Ibid., 69. Bruggink and Droppers were influenced by the book by Howard G. Hageman, *Pulpit and Table*, which is quoted at a crucial point on page 77 in *Christ and Architecture*.

[158] Ibid., 221-22.

[159] Ibid., 168-71.

moved away. The last family members who knew the Dutch language died.

The Dutch enclaves eroded in the cities as people of African American, Asian, and Latin American heritage entered their neighborhoods. The major problems of urban America became local issues. New issues took center stage in communities where issues about Sunday observance, the use of alcoholic beverages, dancing, and matters of personal morality had long been at the top of the agenda. Congregations were called upon to make moral decisions about care for the homeless, whether and how to fight against racial prejudice and discrimination, and how to respond to young men who burned their draft cards rather than go to Vietnam. Other issues were on the horizon and would become increasingly divisive. Equal rights amendments, abortion, and homosexuality were just three such issues. New divisions arose over the issue of ordination of women to the offices of minister, elder, and deacon.

In 1966 the Reformed Church in America was approaching a fork in the road. It reached the fork at the General Synod meeting in 1969, when a succession of controversial issues reached the floor day after day. Delegates were confronted by emotions of anger and bitterness, especially on the part of eastern delegates, when it was announced that the proposed union with the (Southern) Presbyterian Church in the United States had been defeated. A young man appeared before the synod to request that the General Synod take custody of his draft registration card and support him pastorally in his conscientious objection to the war in Vietnam. A Black movement had taken over the Reformed Church offices in New York City. Its leader appeared before the synod to demand reparations for a century and more of injustice. Decisions were called for about the permissibility of ordaining women.[160]

Delegates went home wondering whether the Reformed Church in America could continue to exist as a united denomination. The great efforts to devise a new church order and new liturgical forms and to enter into new forms of Christian action were in jeopardy. However, by the grace of God, by the time delegates arrived at the meeting of the General Synod in 1970, it was clear that the members of the Reformed Church in America did not wish to break their union with each other.[161]

[160] Lynn Japinga, "The Synod of 1969: An Overview," *Reformed Review*, 58/3 (2005), on line, n.p.
[161] The General Synod committee of eighteen, appointed by the General Synod in 1969 with a mandate to "explore every possibility for understanding and

Instead, the General Synod decided that it was time to celebrate by holding three denomination-wide festivals, a Festival of Evangelism, a Festival of Mission, and a Family Festival. In those festivals, members of the Reformed Church in America from across the United States and Canada learned once again how much they enjoyed studying the Word of God together, singing together, praying together, and acting together. At the end of each festival, they enjoyed celebrating Holy Communion together.[162]

By 1970, the Reformed Church in America—East, Midwest, Far West, and Canada—had left an old era behind as it encountered the newer forms of moral, spiritual, and cultural issues. During the decades after World War II, it had laid a foundation in liturgy and church order for living obediently under God within the framework of the climate of a new age. In 1970, there remained the unfinished business of writing a new confessional statement that would supplement the confessions that had been adopted by the Synod of Dort in 1618-1619. After the turmoil at the General Synod in 1969, people were left wondering whether it was possible to find any way to agree on a new confession of faith.

There had been calls in the Reformed Church in America for a new confessional statement ever since World War II. In the decades of worldwide anxiety following World War II, a number of other churches in America and Europe felt also the need for a confessional statement that spoke in contemporary language and provided a clear message for hope in a world threatened by radical social changes and secularism. The Netherlands Reformed Church was considering a confessional statement with the title, "Foundations and Perspectives of Confession" [English translation of title]. The matter came to the official attention of the General Synod in 1958. The Theological Commission began work on a draft in 1964. In 1965 a provisional document was distributed to the classes for comment. In 1967 the Theological Commission reported to the General Synod that it believed it to be unwise to proceed further in the matter. The issue did not go away, however, with the result that a new beginning was made in 1970. In 1974 a draft statement

---

commitment." It published "A Day of Commitment," a litany to be read in every congregation on May 17, 1970 (printed in *Church Herald*, April 17, 1970, 24).

[162] The *Church Herald* devoted its issue of April 14, 1970, to a report on the Festival of Evangelism held in Cobo Hall in Detroit, April 1-4, 1970. A full report on Mission Festival '71 is in the November 5 issue, 4-14. A report on the Family Festival is to be found in the August 25, 1972, issue, 5-9.

was approved for use in the churches for a trial period of four years. Ultimately, in 1978 the General Synod approved without major debate the text of "Our Song of Hope" as "a statement of the Church's faith for use in ministry, teaching, and worship."

"Our Song of Hope" is an expression of Christian faith that "invites a broken world to renew its hope in God and to live according to the will of Jesus Christ."[163] It is the fruit of the denomination's careful consideration of its church order and liturgy, search for justice in society, and its theological understanding of the relation of church architecture to preaching the Word and celebrating the sacraments. "Our Song of Hope" gave expression to the ways in which the Reformed Church in America anticipated living under the reign of God in the remaining decades of the twentieth century and into the new millennium.

In the year that this is written, 2008, the Reformed Church in the Midwest has not reached the end of the road. It will undoubtedly continue to meet more forks in the road of faith, but at each fork we can anticipate that it will remain faithful to its decision to move forward with the denomination with which it united in 1850. In its history, it rejected the slogan, "In isolation is our strength," in favor of the Dutch language motto of the Reformed Church in America, "*Eendracht Maakt Macht*" (In unity there is strength). It moves forward with hope, at one with the ecumenical spirit of the concluding prayer in "Our Song of Hope," accepted by Reformed Church in America in 1978,

Come, Lord Jesus:
We are open to your Spirit.
We await your full presence.
Our world finds rest in you alone.[164]

---

[163] *Our Song of Hope, Acts and Proceedings*, 1974, 170-73.
[164] *Acts and Proceedings*, 1978, 37. "Our Prayer" follows stanza 21 of *Our Song of Hope*. The General Synod adopted *Our Song of Hope* as "a statement of the Church's faith for use in witness, teaching and worship."

# Name Index

189-91
Hoedemaker, Ph. J., 192-93
Hoeksema, Herman, 101
Hofstede de Groot, Petros, 55
Holtzmann, Otto, 171
Hoover, Herbert, 159
Hospers, Gerrit H., 198
Hospers, Henry, 6
House, Renee, 16
Hudson, Winthrop, 67-68
Hulst, Lambert J., 61, 99-100, 105, 129
Hutchinson, William R., 177-78

Inge, Dean, 234
Ironside, Harry Emerson, 202

Janssen, Allan, 245
Japinga, Lynn, 80-81, 261
Jefferson, Thomas, 57
Jenkins, Jerry B., 202
Jeschke, Canning Renwick, 21
Johnson, Arthur, 256

Kansfield, Mary, 15
Kansfield, Norman, 136
Karsten, John H., 5, 47, 71-72, 75, 77,
    110, 115, 122, 132, 147, 176
Kee, Howard Clark, 170
Kennedy, Cornelia B., 42
Kennedy, E. William, 36
Kennedy, James S., 10
Kennedy, John F., 159
King William I, 20-21, 55
Kollen, G.J., 147
Kolyn, Matthew, 7-8, 119-20
Kooy, Vernon, 245
Kremer, John, 147
Kromminga, John, 55, 61, 122
Kropveld, E., 207
Kruithof, Bastian, 46, 100
Kuiper, Henry J., 61, 158
Kuizenga, John E., 32, 88, 93, 143-46,
    157, 184, 188
Kuyper, Abraham, 23, 64, 75, 107,
    139-46, 158, 192, 203, 255
Kuyper, Lester, 79, 229, 238-42, 245

Labadie, Jean, 48

La Haye, Timothy, 202
Lewis, Edwin, 234
Longfield, Bradley, 187
Lucas, Henry S. 4-5
Luidens, Donald, 211-12
Luther, Martin, 36, 85, 113

Machen, John Gresham, 189
Marsden, George, 128, 158-59, 178,
    189, 211, 218, 221
Mast, Gregg, 77
McGowan, A.T.B., 101
McKee, Elsie, xi
McKinley, William, 159
Meeter, Daniel J., 30, 54, 65, 136, 252
Mennenga, George, 229
Merle d'Aubigne, 12
Moerdyk, Peter, 28-29, 48-49, 71-72,
    75, 77, 133, 147
Moerdyk, William, 122, 127, 132
Moody, Dwight L., 112, 179
Mulder, Bernard J., 46
Mulder, John R. 28, 88, 99-100, 102,
    107, 111-12, 115, 123-26, 130,
    144, 147, 157, 182, 186, 234-35
Muller, John H., 251
Muller, Richard A., 22, 100
Murch, James de Forest, 71

Nemeth, Roger, 211-12
Nettinga, Siebe, 19, 105, 155-56, 180,
    234
Nevin, John, 71-72, 175-76
Nichols, James H., 176, 259
Niebuhr, Reinhold, 234

O'Brien, John A., 213
Oggel, Engelbert Christian, 28
Oggel, Pieter J., 12
Oman, John, 234
Opzoomer, Cornelis Willem, 141
Osterhaven, M. Eugene, 19, 87, 91,
    99, 107-08, 145, 149, 227-29, 231,
    234-36
Oudersluys, Richard C., 229, 231-33,
    237, 259

Piet, John, 222-24, 229-30, 237

# Subject Index

Pantheism, 182
Patriotism, 20, 119ff.
Perfectionism, 115-16, 147-48
Pietism, x-xi, 18, 42, 45, 87, 205,
    228-29
Piety, xii, 4, 7, 14, 16n, 25ff.
Postmillenialism, 198
Post-World War II anxiety, 213-15
Prayer, 48, 217
Preaching the way of salvation, 108-17
Preaching the Word, 27-33
Predestination, 26, 74, 86, 90, 96-99,
    105, 236-37
Premillenialism, 197-205, 207-08
Presbyterian Alliance, 70, 78
Presbyterian churches, 69, 77-78
Presbyterian Church in the United
    States, 80, 176-79, 188, 261
Presbyterian Church in United States
    of America, 72
Presumptive regeneration, 107
Princeton Theological Seminary, 88,
    179, 181
Principles (Beginselen), 137, 139, 140-
    46, 154, 156, 159, 199, 204
Professorial certificate, 17
Progress, 179, 187
Prohibition, 131-33, 154
Prophecy, 167-69, 171
Protestant principle, 175-77
Providence, 26, 42, 49-50, 91-94, 182,
    226, 231
Psalms, 4, 33-34, 40-47
Public schools, 10, 19

Racial justice, 149, 159, 181, 221, 250,
    261
Rationalism, 164-65, 177
Reason, 164, 180
Redemption, 91-92, 146, 182
Reformed Church in America, ix, 6,
    53-57, 78, 211-12, 261
Reformed Church in the United
    States (German), 58, 62, 67-78, 176
Reformed orthodoxy, 17
Reformed Review, 212
Regeneration, 82, 86,113-15,140-46,
    178
Remonstrants, 73

Repentance, 87, 114
Reprobation, 74, 75, 98-99, 111
Republican Party, 158-60
Resurrection, 81
Revelation, 167-70, 234
Revivals, 112, 114, 148, 215-22
Richard Baxter, 36
Roman Catholicisim, 33, 34, 36-37,
    70, 134, 143, 176, 215-17, 223

Sabbath, 4, 7, 26, 123, 130, 133-
    36,153, 207, 240, 249, 260
Sacramental Presence of Christ, 35-41
Salvation, social/individual, 148-51
Sanctification, 87, 113-17, 238
Scholasticism, 22, 87
Schools, Christian, 4, 10, 136-39, 141
Schools, Dutch, 4, 137
Schools, parochial, 215
Schools, public, 136-39, 216
Science, 145
Scientists, 145
Scofield Reference Bible, 199-209
Secession of 1834 (Afgescheidene), 1,
    6, 21, 54, 64, 67, 104, 160, 163
Second coming, 82, 199-205
"Second Reformation" (Nadere Refor-
    matie), 42, 86
Sermons, 17
Sexuality, 123-26, 217
Sin, 97-99, 148
Social gospel, 81, 139, 146-54, 158
Socialism, 153, 154-57, 158, 160
Society (Maatrschappij), 48-51
Spanish-American War, 159
Sphere sovereignty, 51, 138, 142-46
Spirituality, xi
Standards of Unity, 20, 54, 224, 244
State, 51, 142
Subscription, 20-21, 66, 164
Sunday School Guide, 46, 133
Supreme Court, 139
Synod of Dort, x, 20, 27, 29, 40, 67,
    74, 86, 226, 244, 251, 262
Systematic theology, 88, 190-91

T.U.L.I.P., 99, 100, 111
Ten Commandments, 19, 32, 117,
    133-34, 154

P, 169  in  l. of